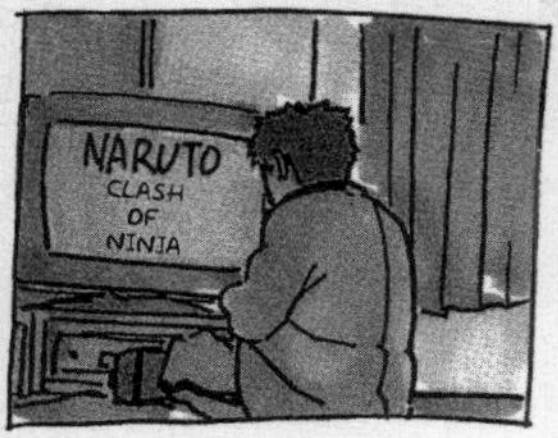
NARUTO
CLASH
OF
NINJA

岸本斉史

My cover image for this volume was inspired by the Nine-Tailed Fox Naruto that appears in the GameCube game, *Clash of Ninja*. They did such an awesome job with the presentation that I couldn't resist imitating it.

—*Masashi Kishimoto, 2005*

Author/artist Masashi Kishimoto was born in 1974 in rural Okayama Prefecture, Japan. After spending time in art college, he won the Hop Step Award for new manga artists with his manga **Karakuri** (Mechanism). Kishimoto decided to base his next story on traditional Japanese culture. His first version of **Naruto**, drawn in 1997, was a one-shot story about fox spirits; his final version, which debuted in **Weekly Shonen Jump** in 1999, quickly became the most popular ninja manga in Japan.

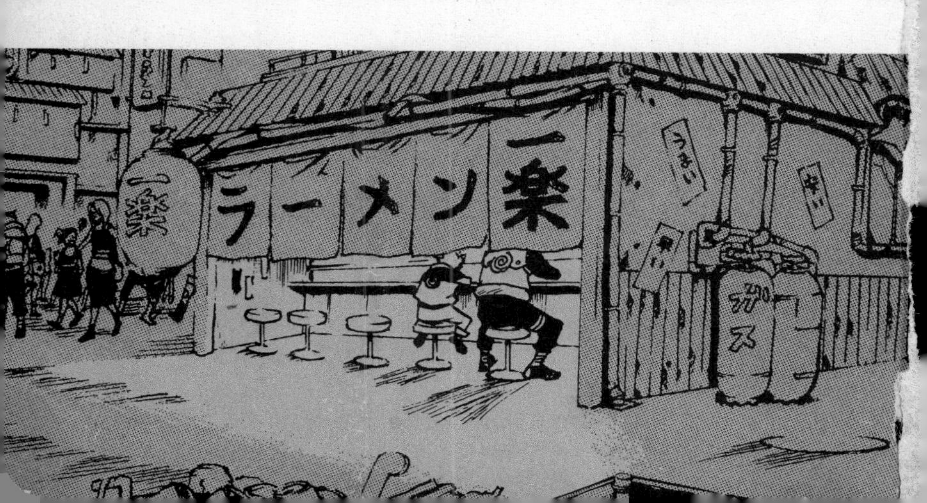
一楽
ラーメン一楽
うまい

NARUTO VOL. 26
SHONEN JUMP Manga Edition

STORY AND ART BY MASASHI KISHIMOTO

Translation & English Adaptation/Naomi Kokubo, Eric-Jon Rössel Waugh
Touch-up Art & Lettering/Gia Cam Luc
Design/Yvonne Cai
Editor/Joel Enos

Printed in the U.S.A.

Published by VIZ Media, LLC
P.O. Box 77010
San Francisco, CA 94107

10 9 8 7 6 5
First printing, December 2007
Fifth printing, September 2013

www.viz.com

THE WORLD'S
MOST POPULAR MANGA
www.shonenjump.com

はたけカカシ
Kakashi
綱手
Tsunade
シズネ
Shizune
テマリ
Temari
シカマル
Shikamaru
パックン
Pakkun

The Story So Far...

Twelve years ago a destructive nine-tailed fox spirit attacked the ninja village of Konohagakure. The Hokage, or village champion, defeated the fox by sealing its soul into the body of a baby boy. That boy is Naruto, once the bane of the Konohagakure Ninja Academy.

Despite the rough start, he and his friends, Sasuke and Sakura, successfully join the ranks of the ninja. During the Chûnin Ninja Selection Exam, they are attacked by Orochimaru, who vanishes only after he places a curse mark on Sasuke. Halfway through the third exam, however, Orochimaru and his henchmen launch *Operation Destroy Konoha.* The attack is thwarted when the Third Hokage sacrifices his life. After the deadly battle, Tsunade steps up to become the Fifth Hokage.

Charmed by the power of Orochimaru, Sasuke departs Konoha in the company of the Sound Ninja. In pursuit of Sasuke, Shikamaru and his team weather desperate battles. As Naruto finally closes in on his friend, Sasuke's mind is struck by vivid memories of his brother, Itachi.

CONTENTS

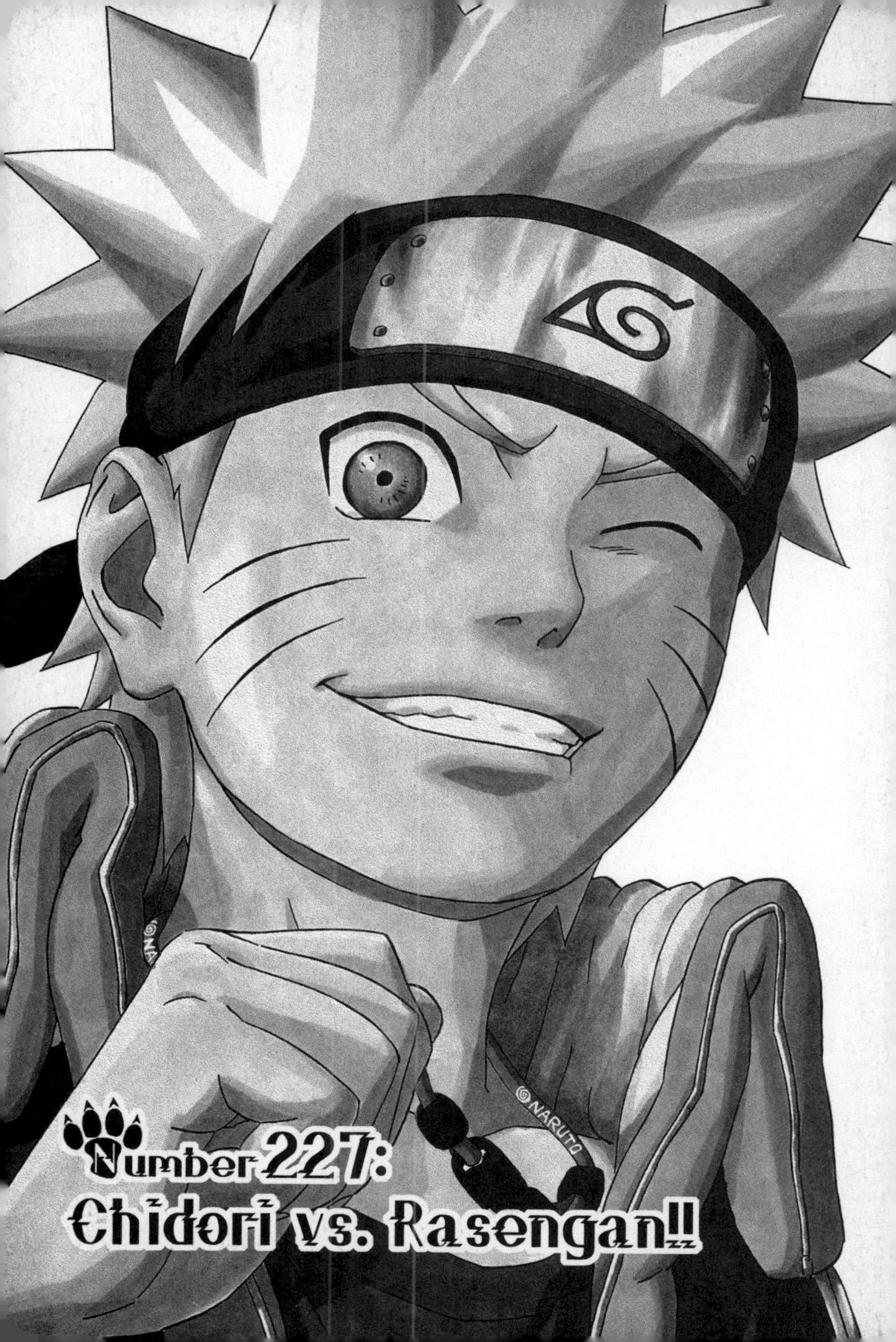
NARUTO

Number 227: Chidori vs. Rasengan!!

NARUTO

KICK SASUKE'S BUTT!!

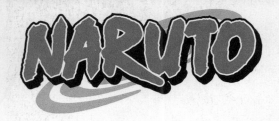

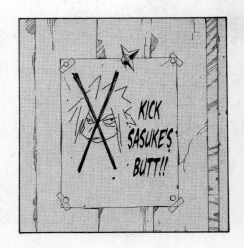

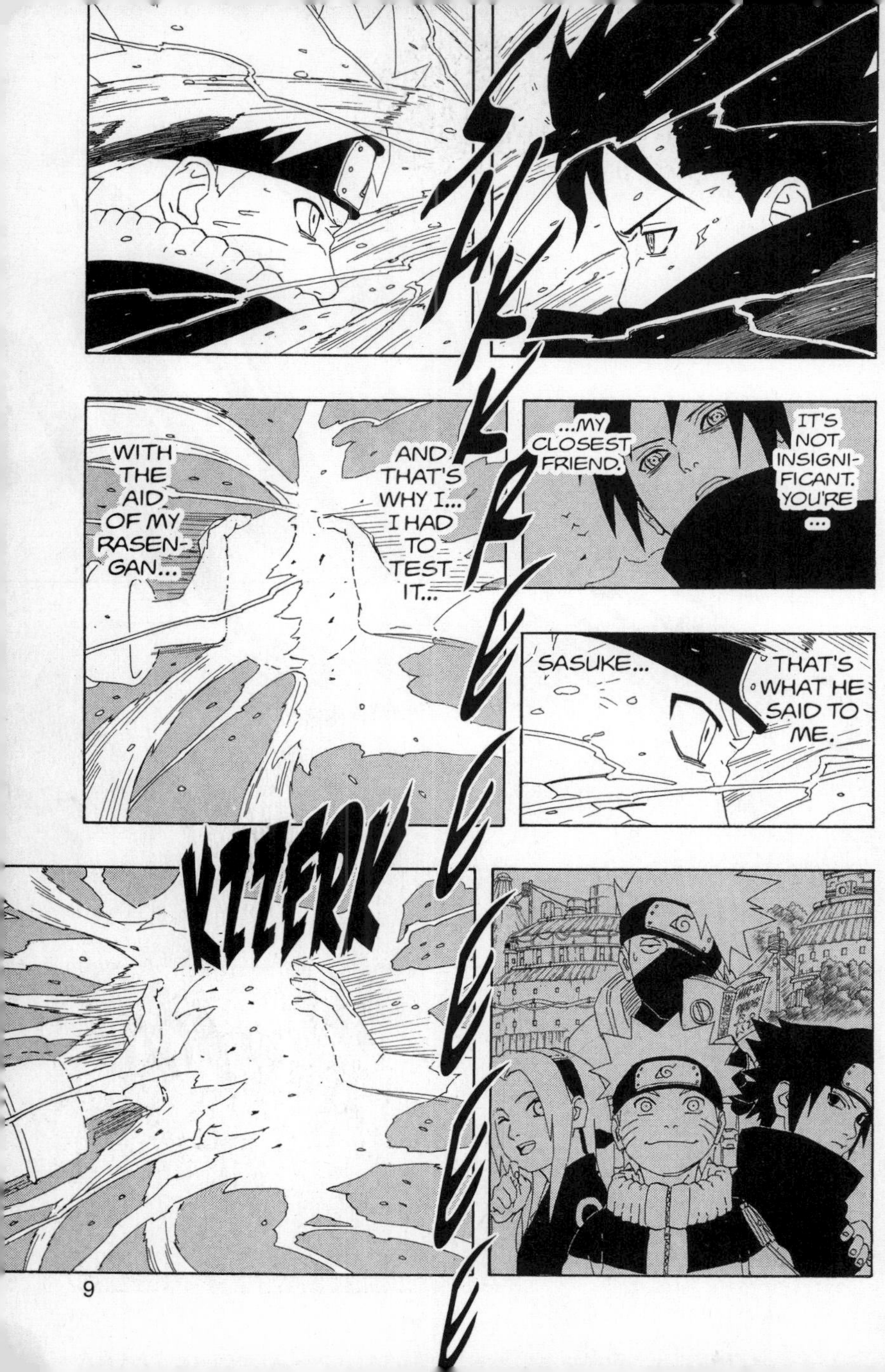
IT'S NOT INSIGNIFICANT. YOU'RE ...
...MY CLOSEST FRIEND.
THAT'S WHAT HE SAID TO ME.
SASUKE...
AND THAT'S WHY I... I HAD TO TEST IT...
WITH THE AID OF MY RASEN-GAN...
KZZERK

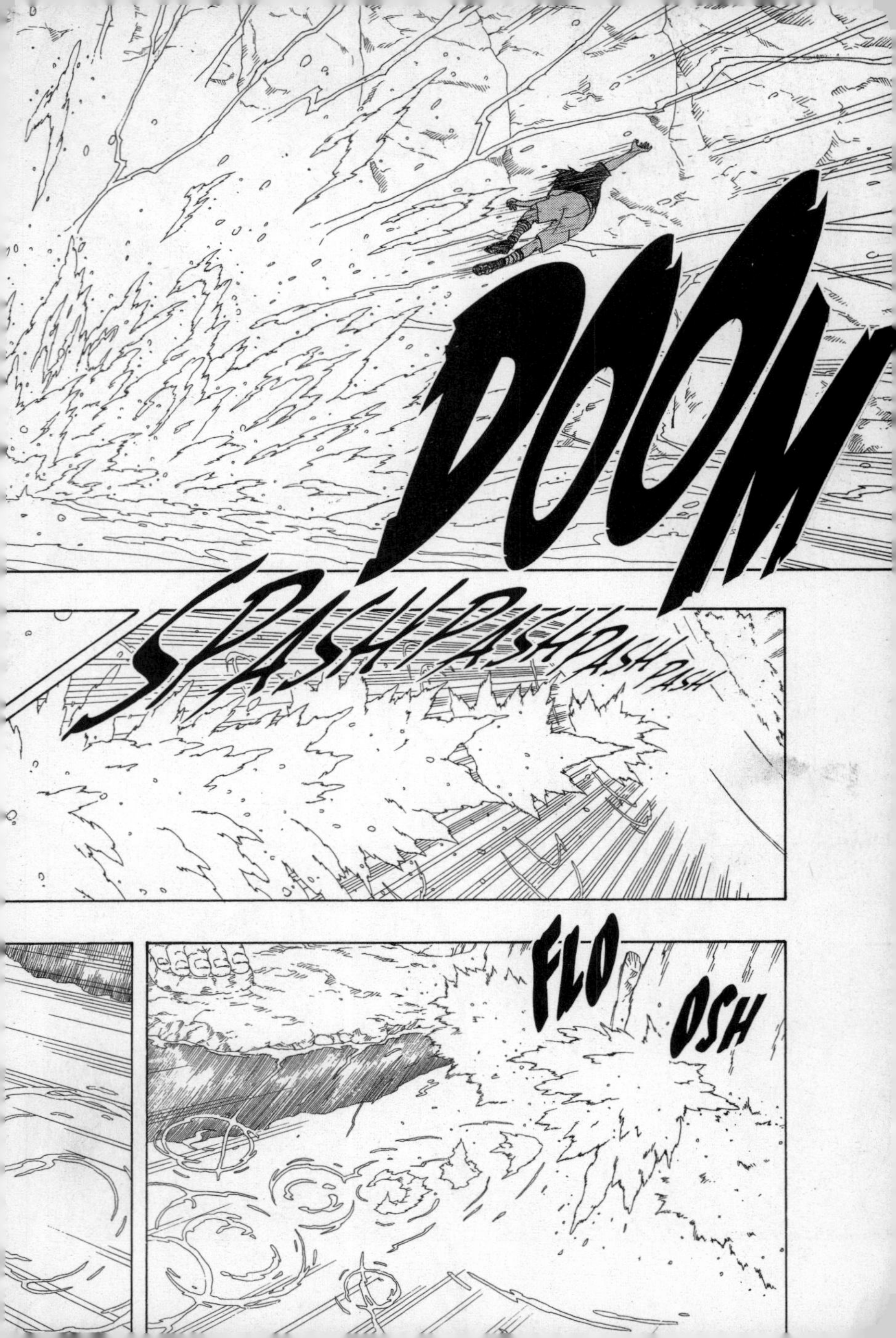
DOOM
SPASH PASH PASH PASH
FLO
OSH

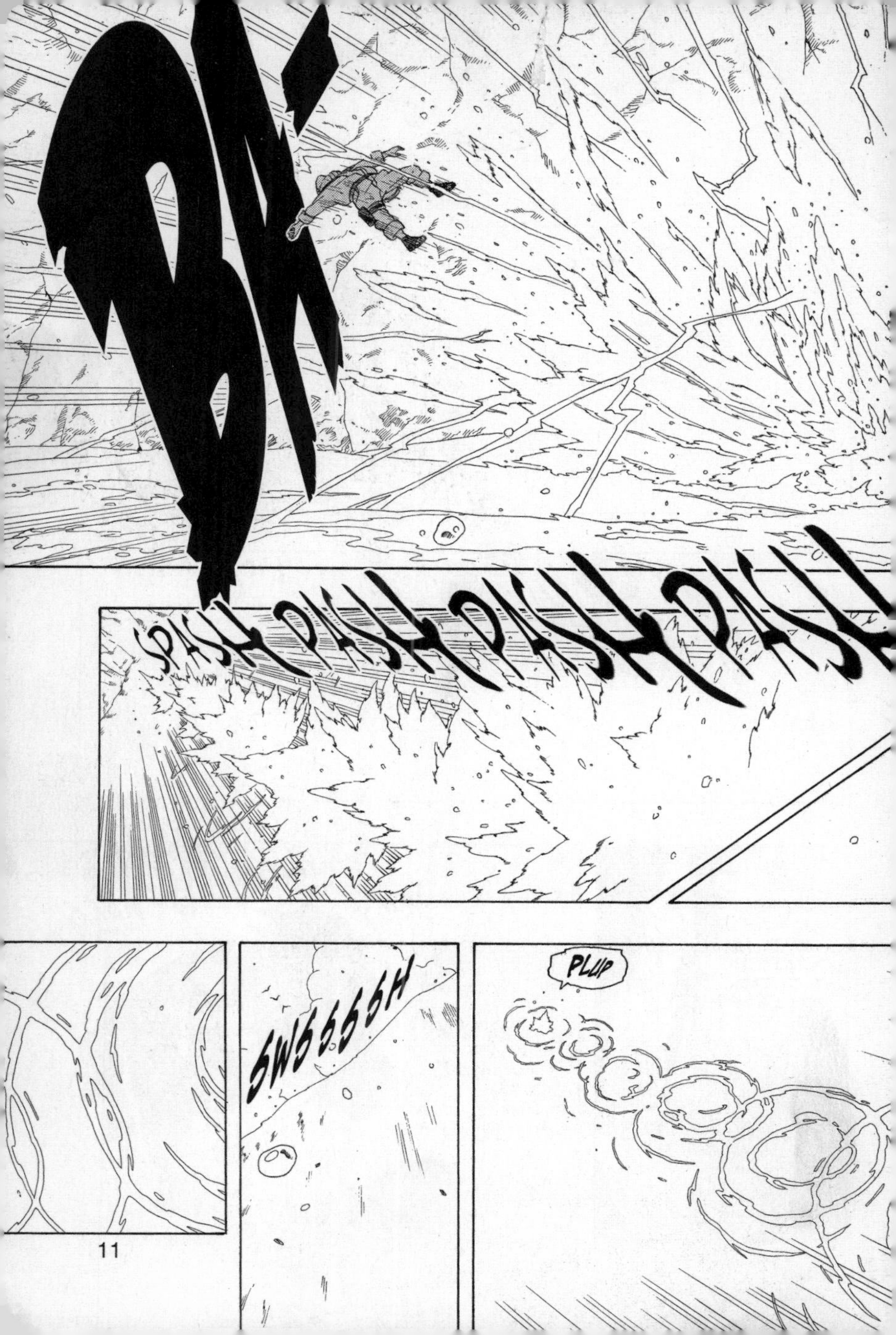
BA
SPASH PASH PASH PASH
PLUP
SWSSSH

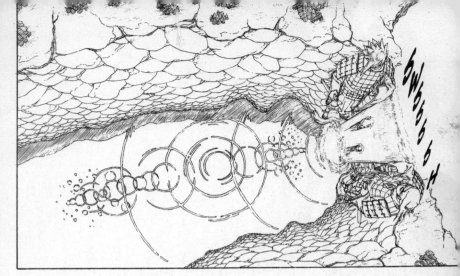

SPOOSH!

SWURP

ARGH! AND I WAS AT FULL POWER, WHEN HE COUNTERED MY CHIDORI... AND HIS JUTSU...

HUF

HUF

SPAASS!

READ THIS WAY

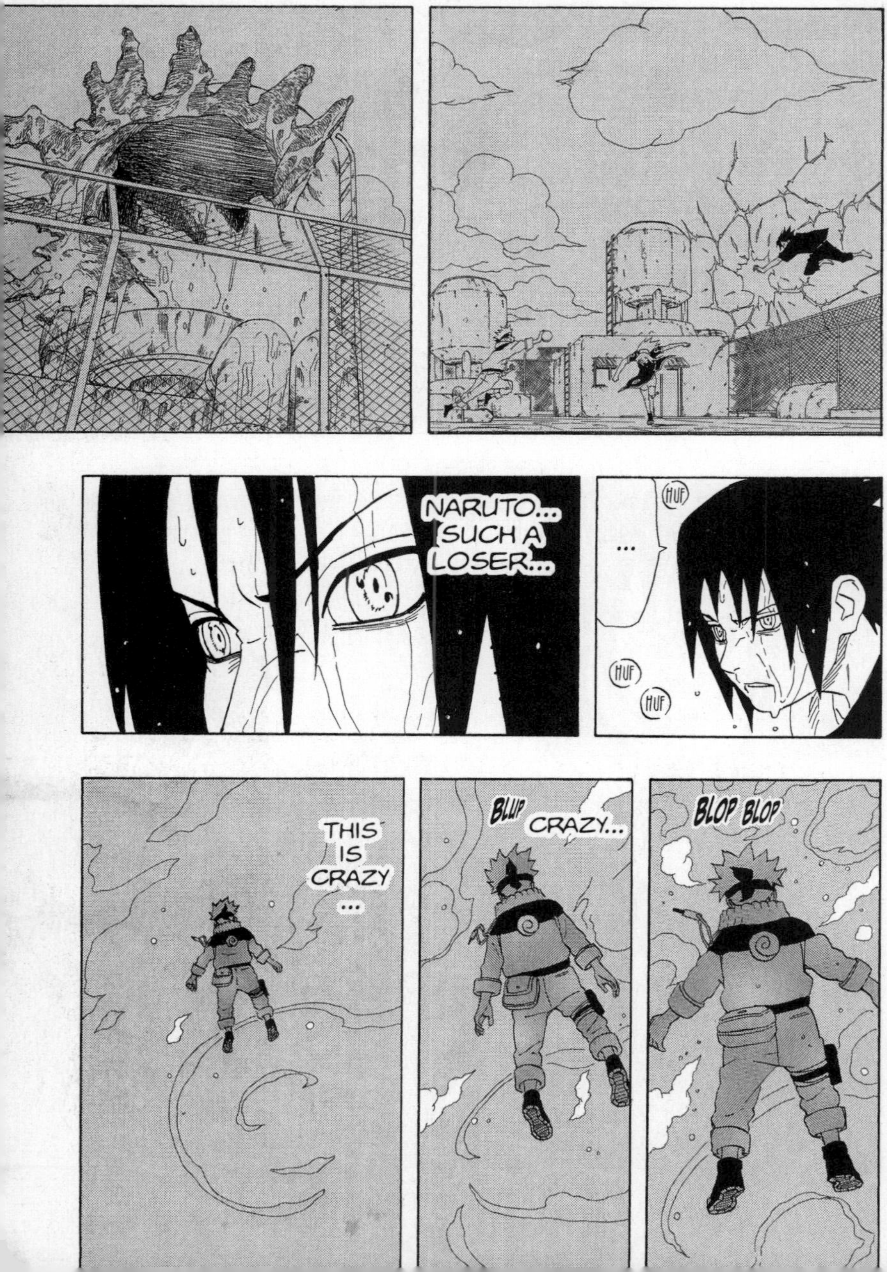
HUF
...
HUF
HUF
NARUTO... SUCH A LOSER...
BLOP BLOP
BLUP
CRAZY...
THIS IS CRAZY ...

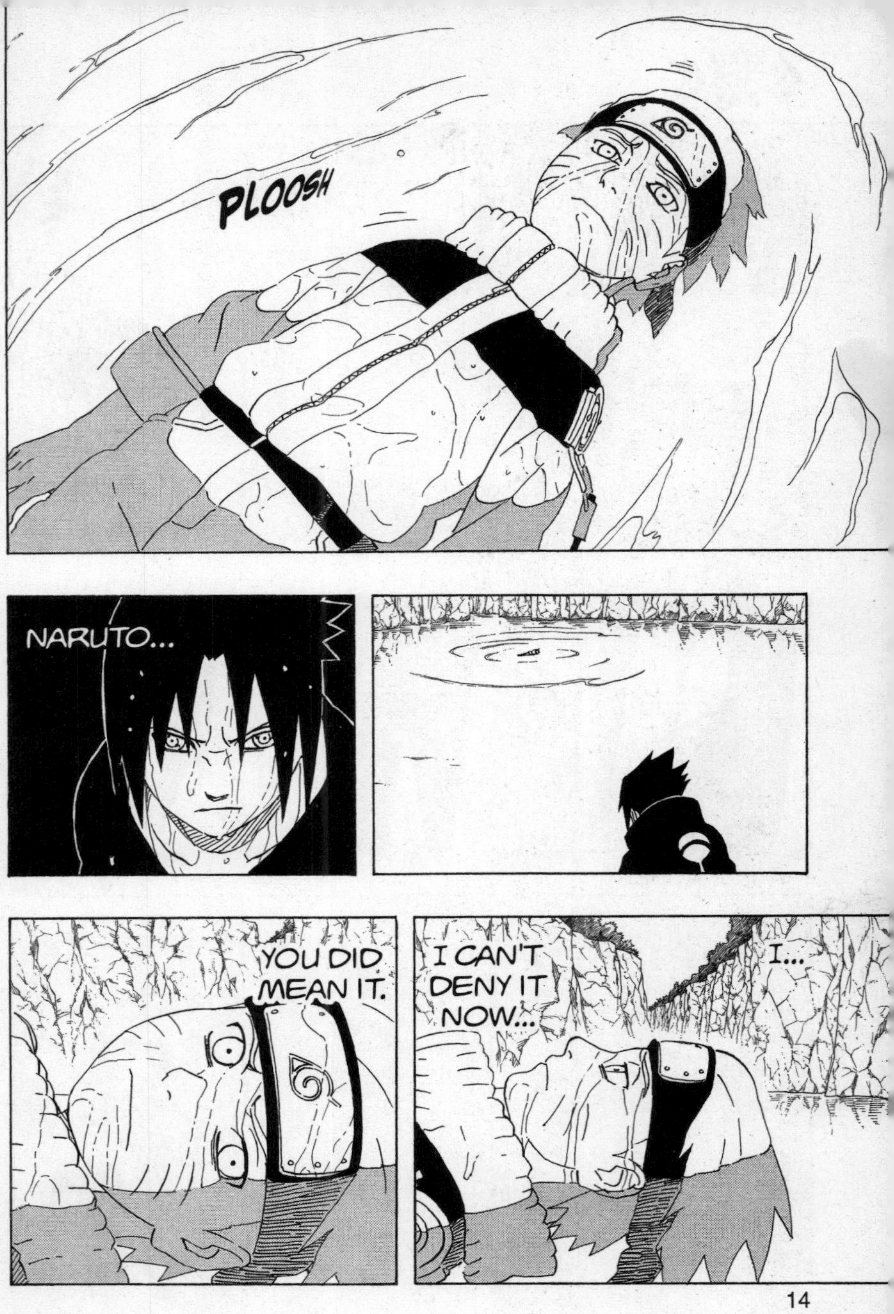
PLOOSH
NARUTO...
I...
I CAN'T DENY IT NOW...
YOU DID MEAN IT.

READ THIS WAY

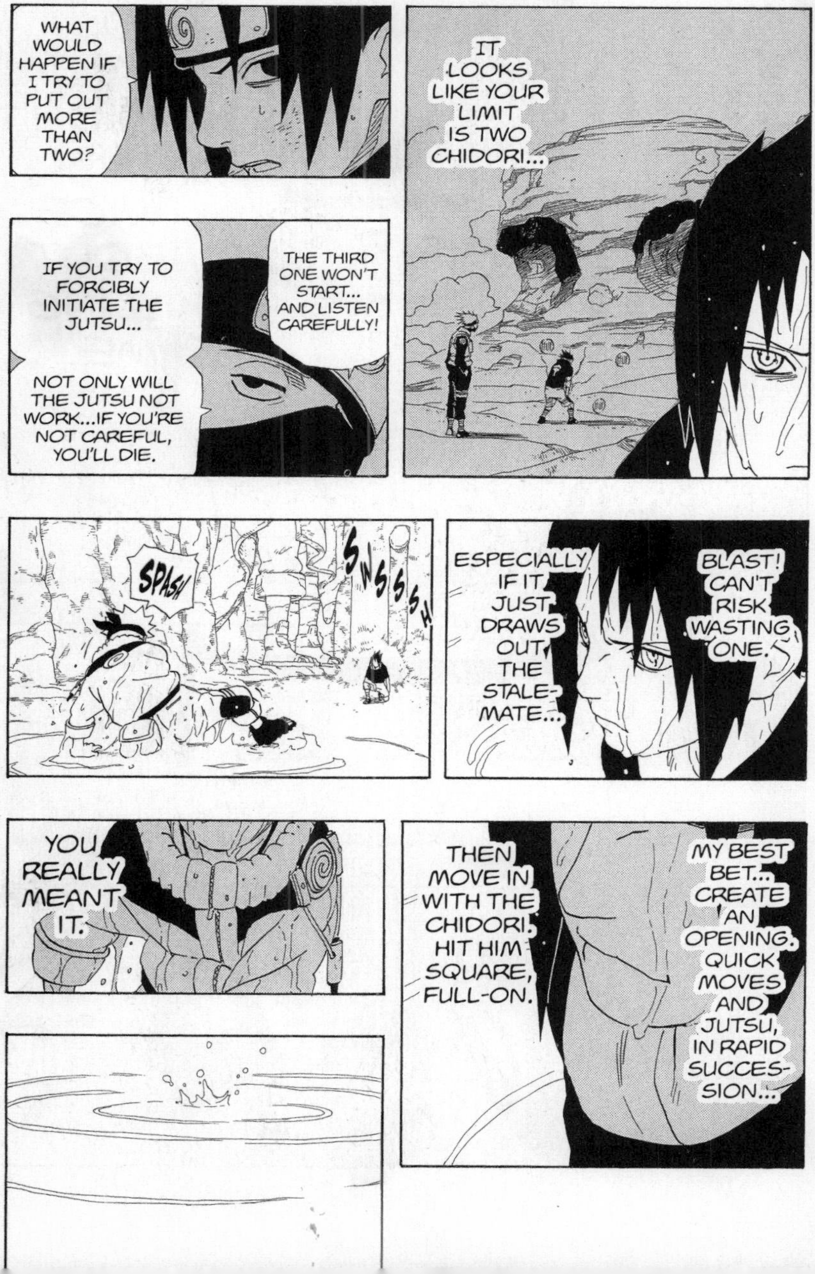
IT LOOKS LIKE YOUR LIMIT IS TWO CHIDORI...
WHAT WOULD HAPPEN IF I TRY TO PUT OUT MORE THAN TWO?
THE THIRD ONE WON'T START... AND LISTEN CAREFULLY!
IF YOU TRY TO FORCIBLY INITIATE THE JUTSU...
NOT ONLY WILL THE JUTSU NOT WORK...IF YOU'RE NOT CAREFUL, YOU'LL DIE.
BLAST! CAN'T RISK WASTING ONE.
ESPECIALLY IF IT JUST DRAWS OUT THE STALEMATE...
SWSSSH
SPASH
MY BEST BET... CREATE AN OPENING. QUICK MOVES AND JUTSU, IN RAPID SUCCESSION...
THEN MOVE IN WITH THE CHIDORI. HIT HIM SQUARE, FULL-ON.
YOU REALLY MEANT IT.

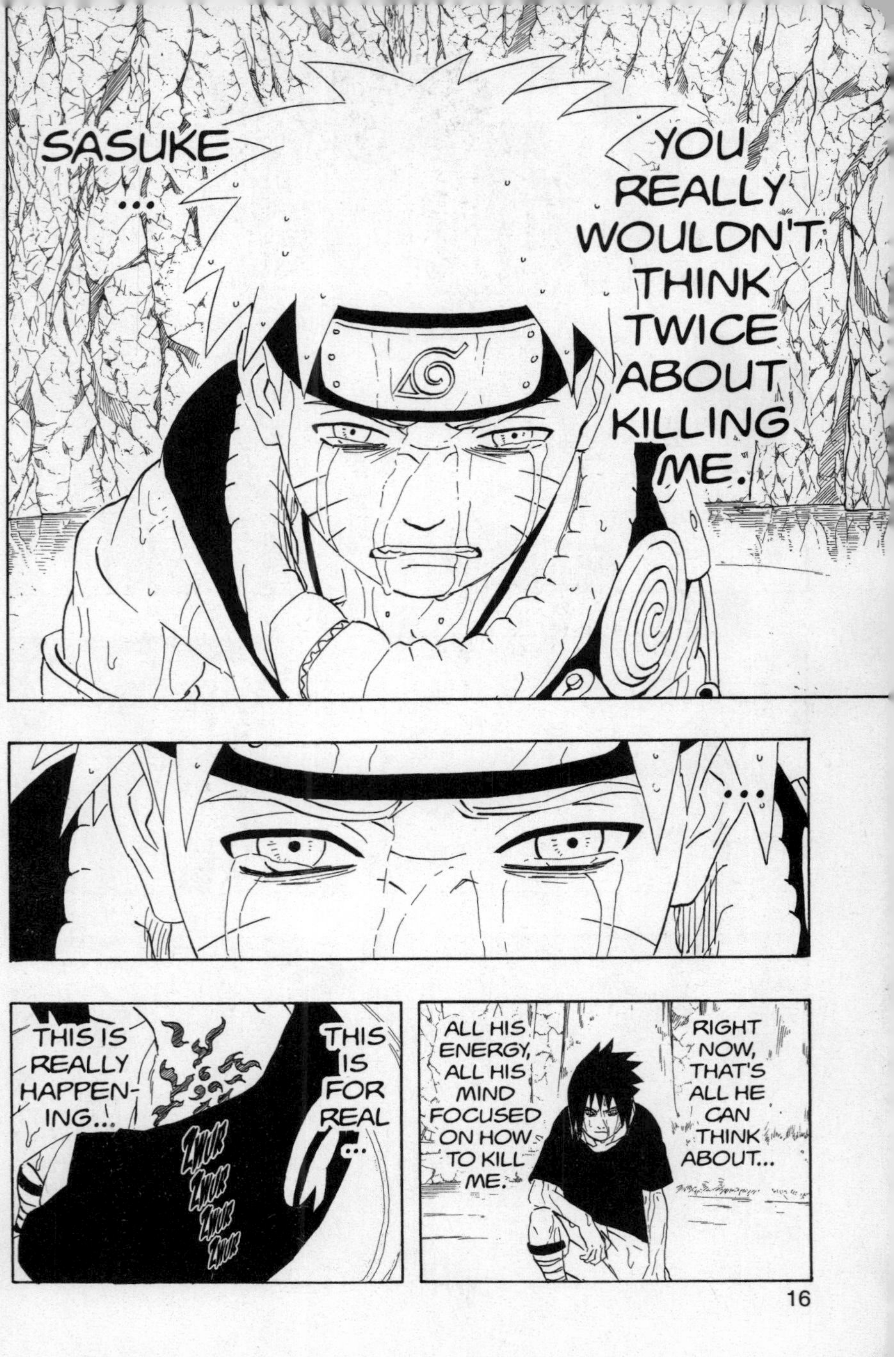
YOU REALLY WOULDN'T THINK TWICE ABOUT KILLING ME.
SASUKE ...
...
RIGHT NOW, THAT'S ALL HE CAN THINK ABOUT...
ALL HIS ENERGY, ALL HIS MIND FOCUSED ON HOW TO KILL ME.
THIS IS FOR REAL ...
THIS IS REALLY HAPPEN-ING...

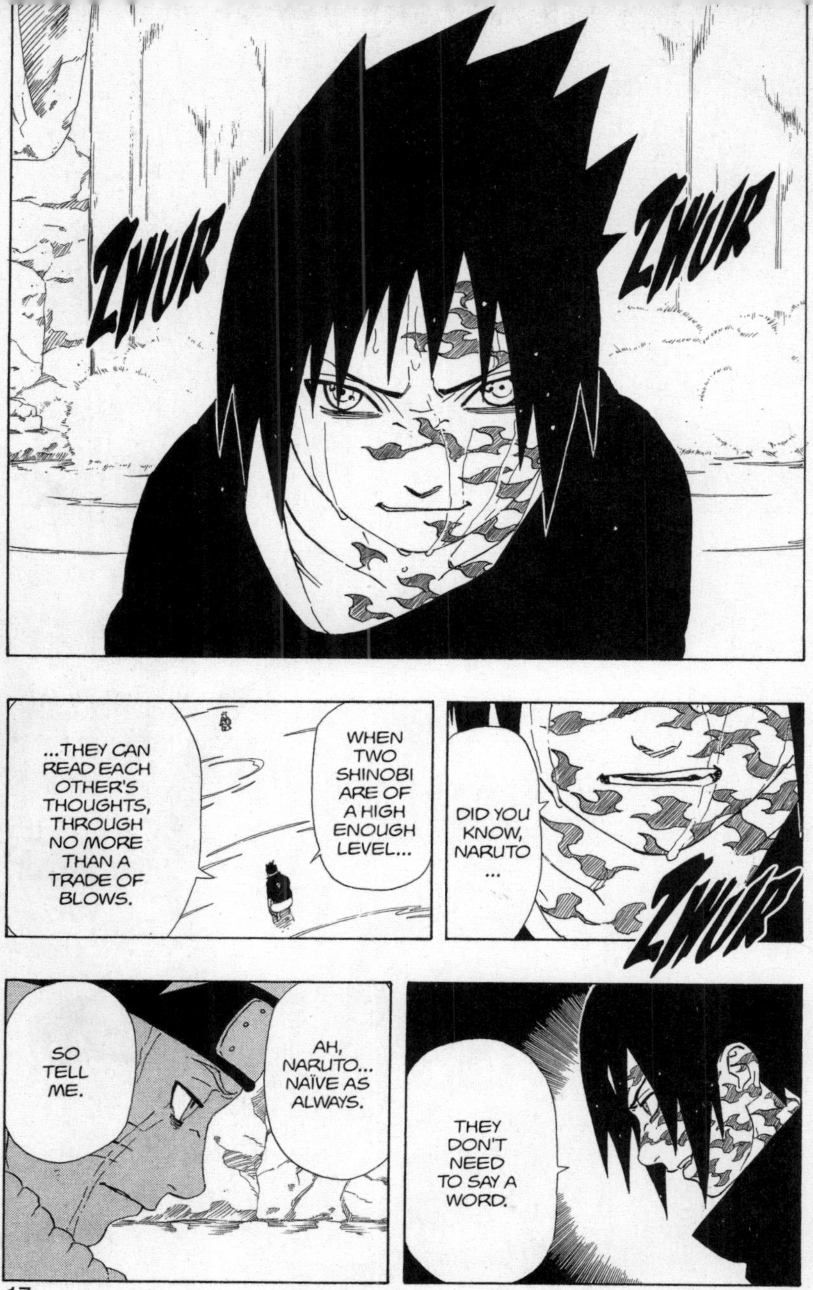
ZWUR
ZWUR
DID YOU KNOW, NARUTO ...
ZWUR
WHEN TWO SHINOBI ARE OF A HIGH ENOUGH LEVEL...
...THEY CAN READ EACH OTHER'S THOUGHTS, THROUGH NO MORE THAN A TRADE OF BLOWS.
THEY DON'T NEED TO SAY A WORD.
AH, NARUTO... NAÏVE AS ALWAYS.
SO TELL ME.

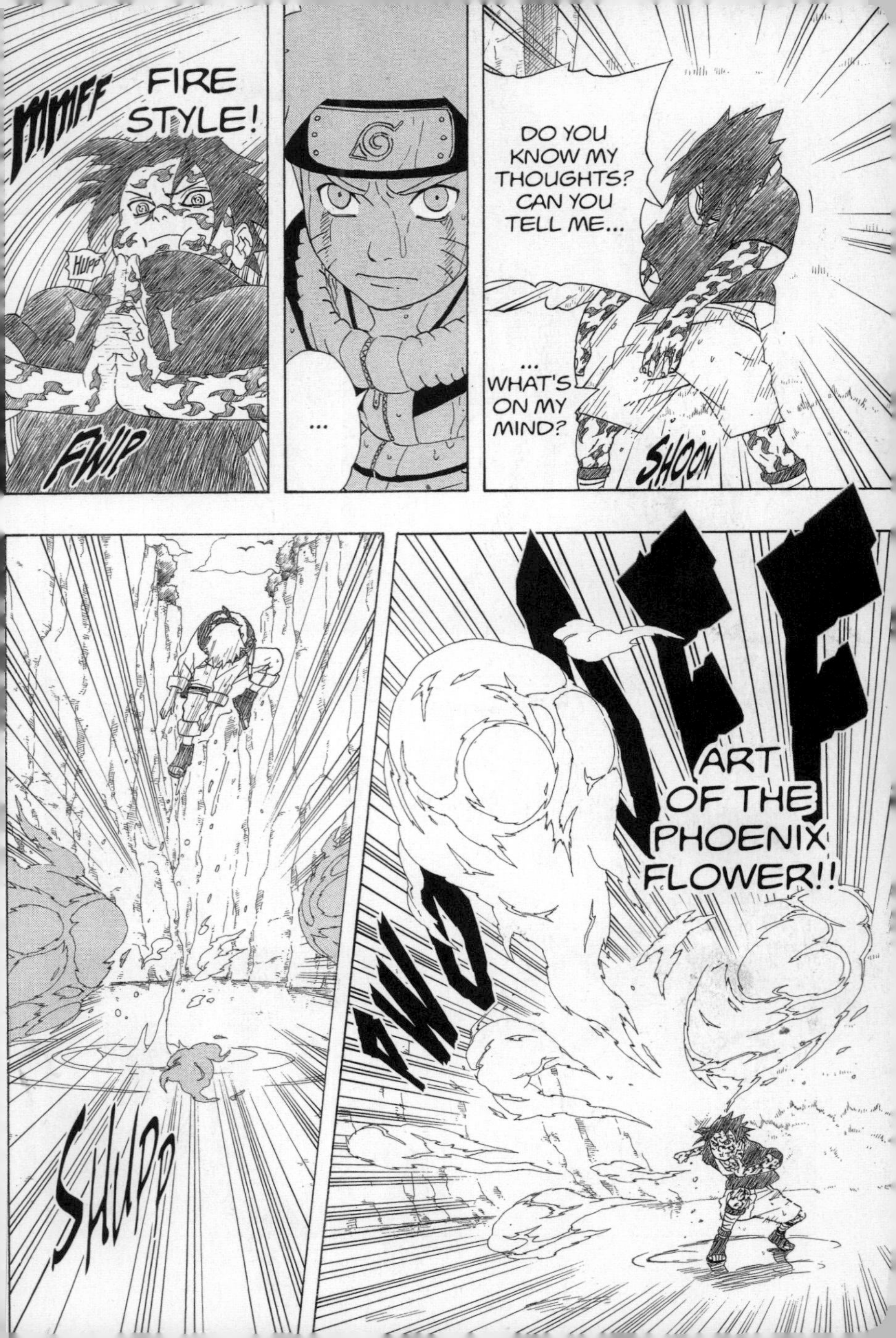
DO YOU KNOW MY THOUGHTS? CAN YOU TELL ME...
... WHAT'S ON MY MIND?
SHOOM
...
MMFF
FIRE STYLE!
HUPP
FWIP
ART OF THE PHOENIX FLOWER!!
SHUPP

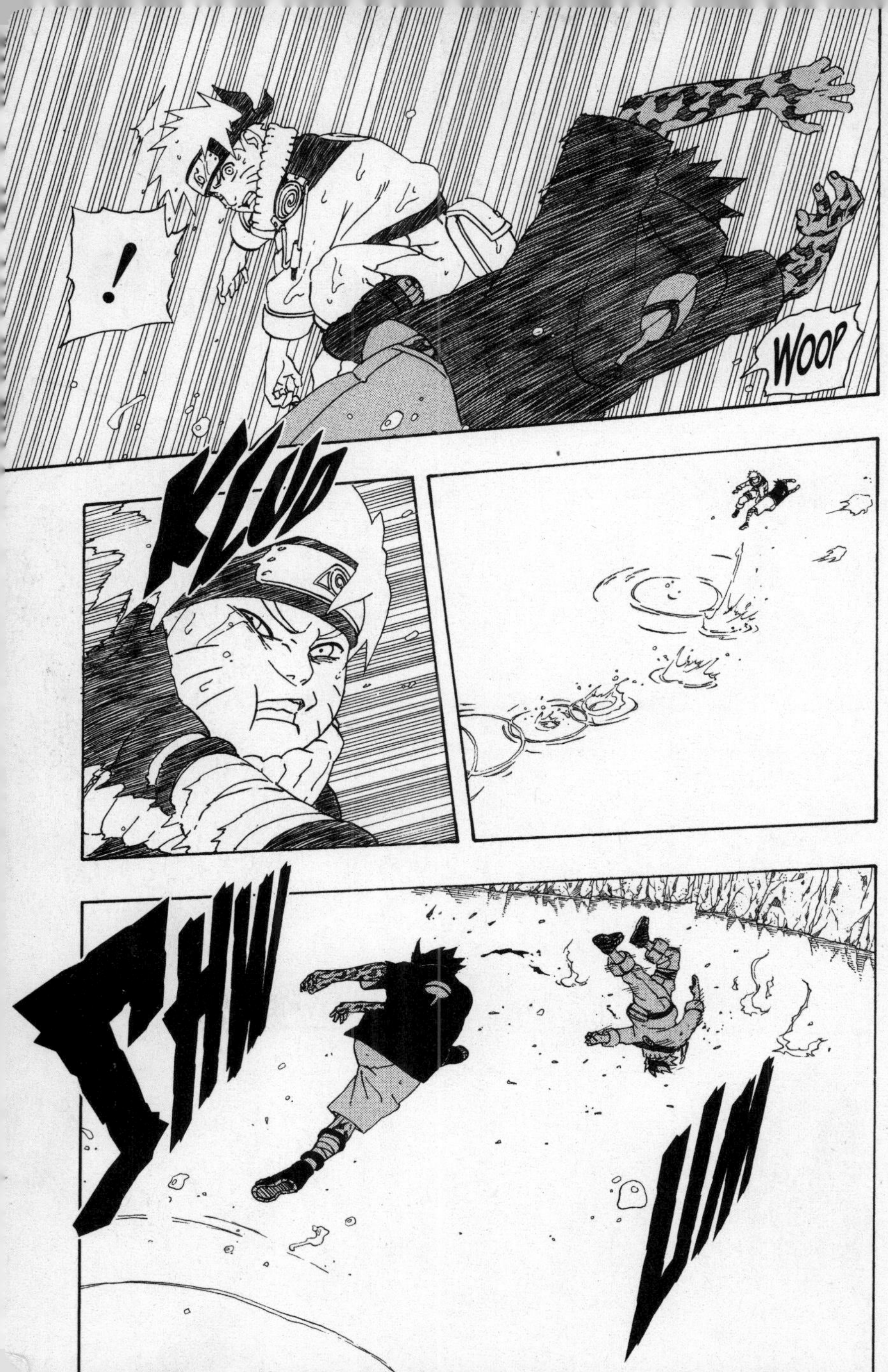
!
WOOP
KLUD
SHW
UM

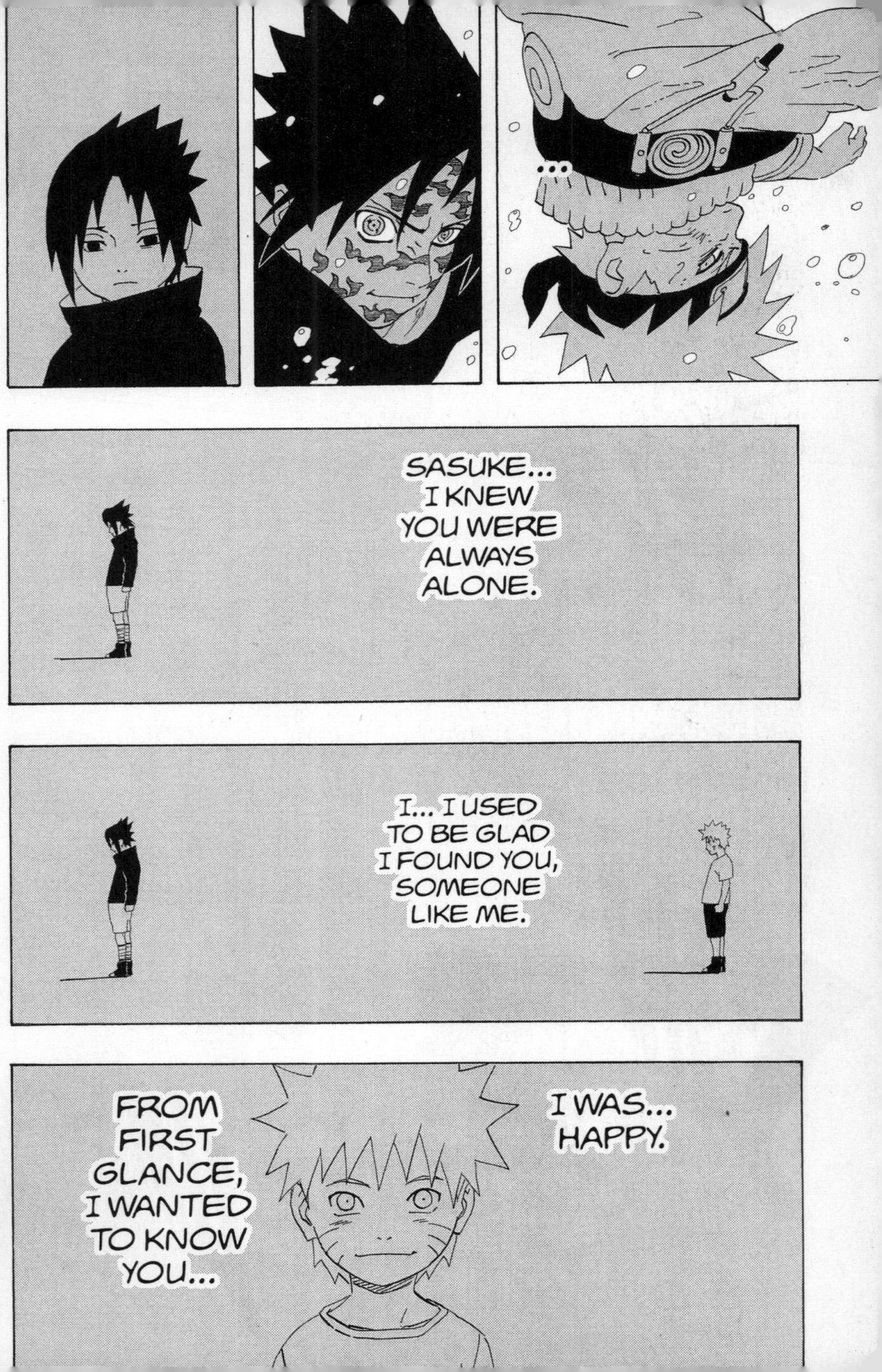
...
SASUKE... I KNEW YOU WERE ALWAYS ALONE.
I... I USED TO BE GLAD I FOUND YOU, SOMEONE LIKE ME.
I WAS... HAPPY.
FROM FIRST GLANCE, I WANTED TO KNOW YOU...

READ THIS WAY

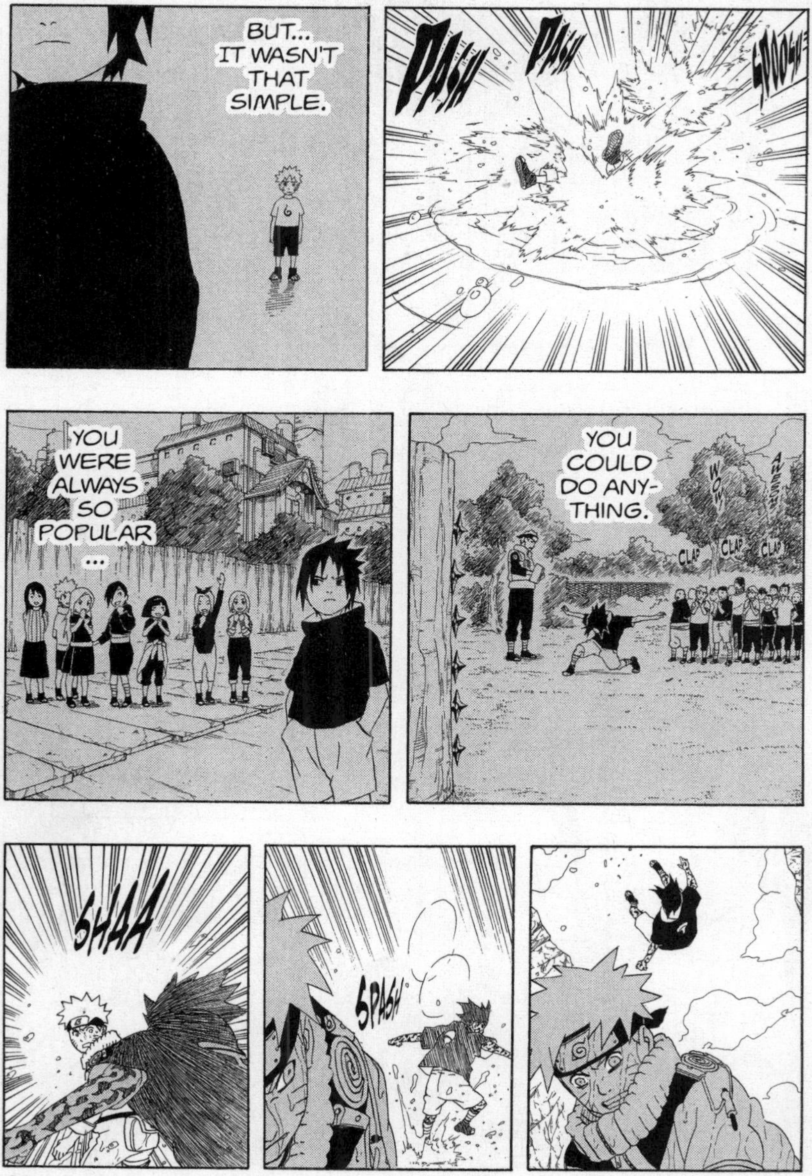
PASH
PASH
SPOOSH
BUT... IT WASN'T THAT SIMPLE.
YOU COULD DO ANY-THING.
AWESOME
WOW!
CLAP
CLAP
CLAP
YOU WERE ALWAYS SO POPULAR ...
SPASH
SHAA

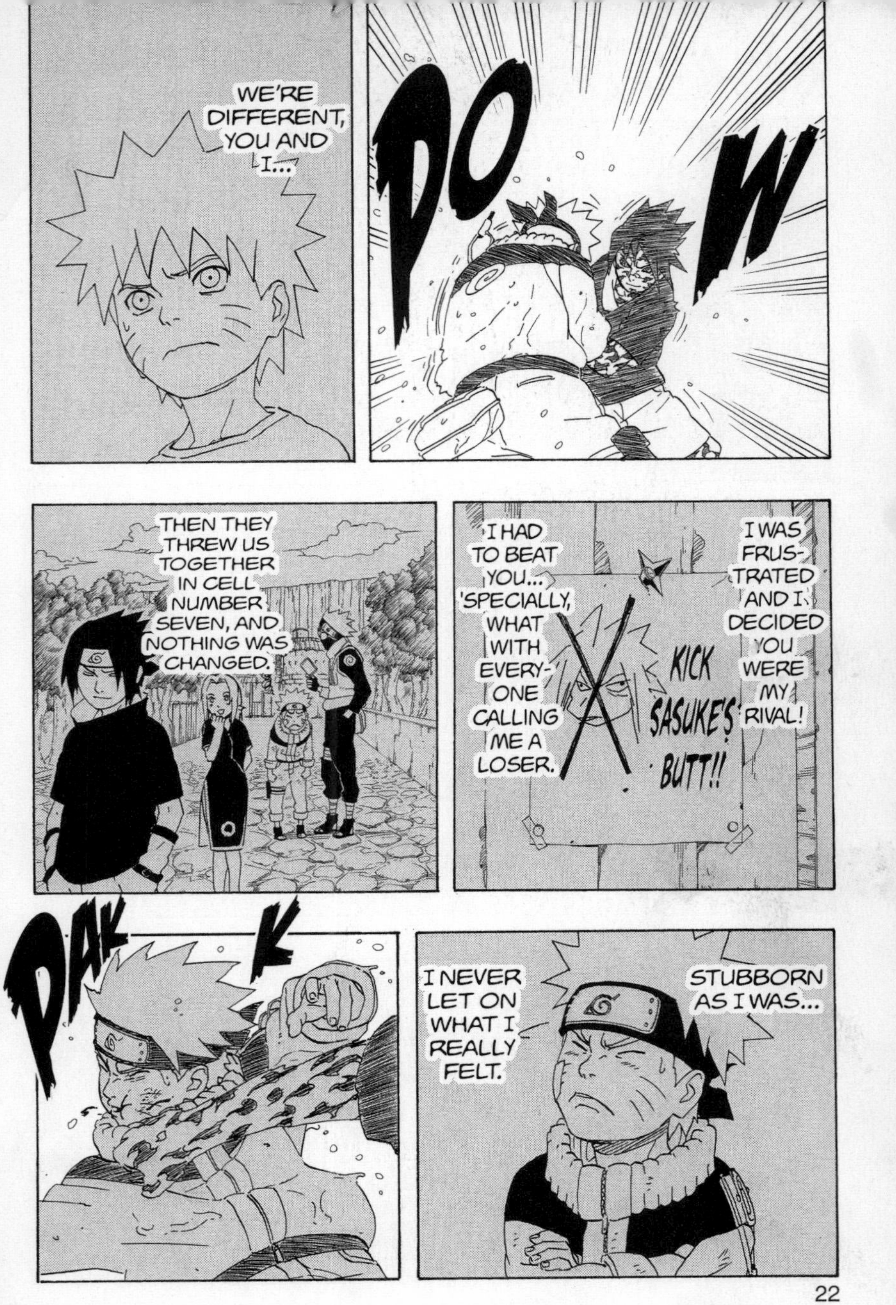
POW
WE'RE DIFFERENT, YOU AND I...
I WAS FRUS-TRATED AND I DECIDED YOU WERE MY RIVAL!
KICK SASUKE'S BUTT!!
I HAD TO BEAT YOU... 'SPECIALLY, WHAT WITH EVERY-ONE CALLING ME A LOSER.
THEN THEY THREW US TOGETHER IN CELL NUMBER SEVEN, AND NOTHING WAS CHANGED.
STUBBORN AS I WAS...
I NEVER LET ON WHAT I REALLY FELT.
PAKK

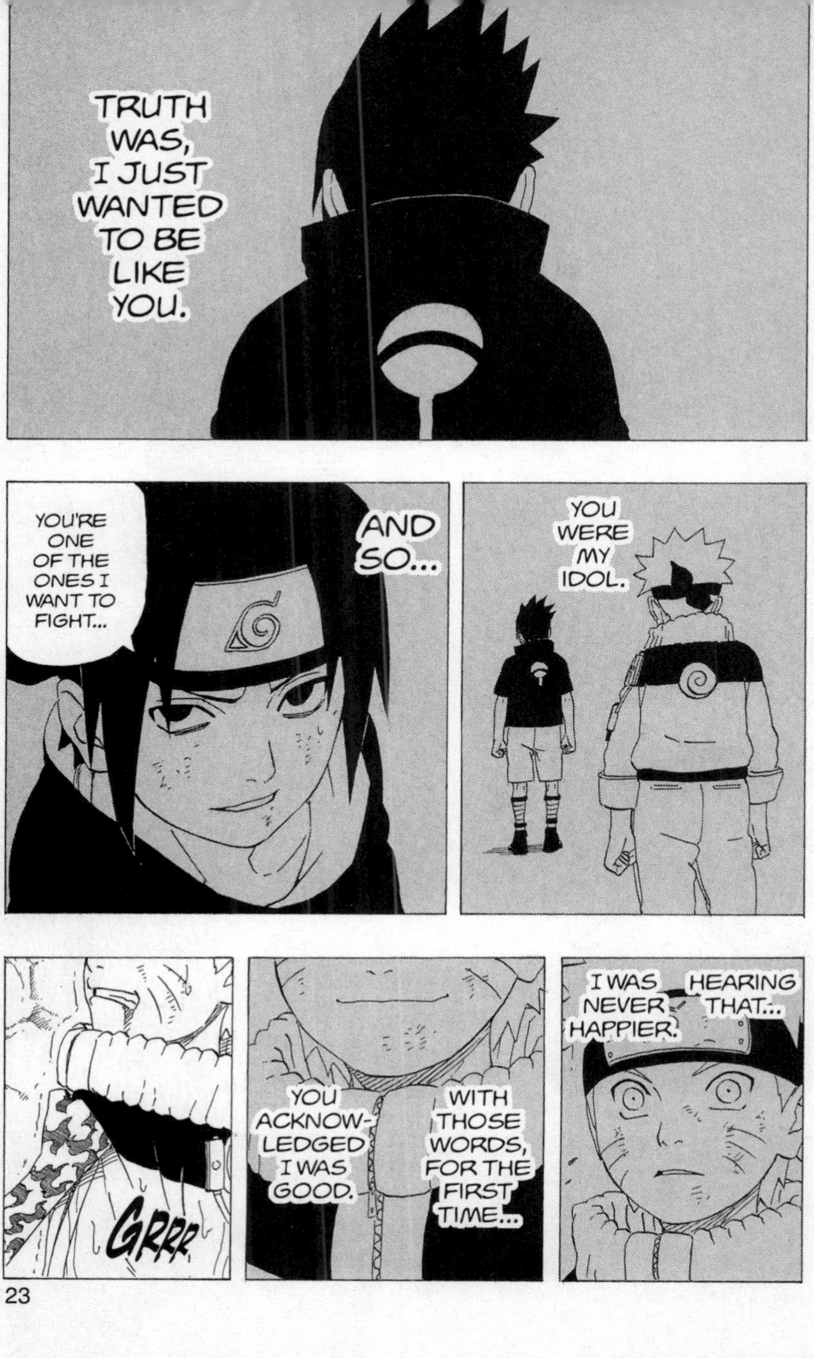
TRUTH WAS, I JUST WANTED TO BE LIKE YOU.
YOU WERE MY IDOL.
AND SO...
YOU'RE ONE OF THE ONES I WANT TO FIGHT...
HEARING THAT...
I WAS NEVER HAPPIER.
WITH THOSE WORDS, FOR THE FIRST TIME...
YOU ACKNOW-LEDGED I WAS GOOD.
GRRR

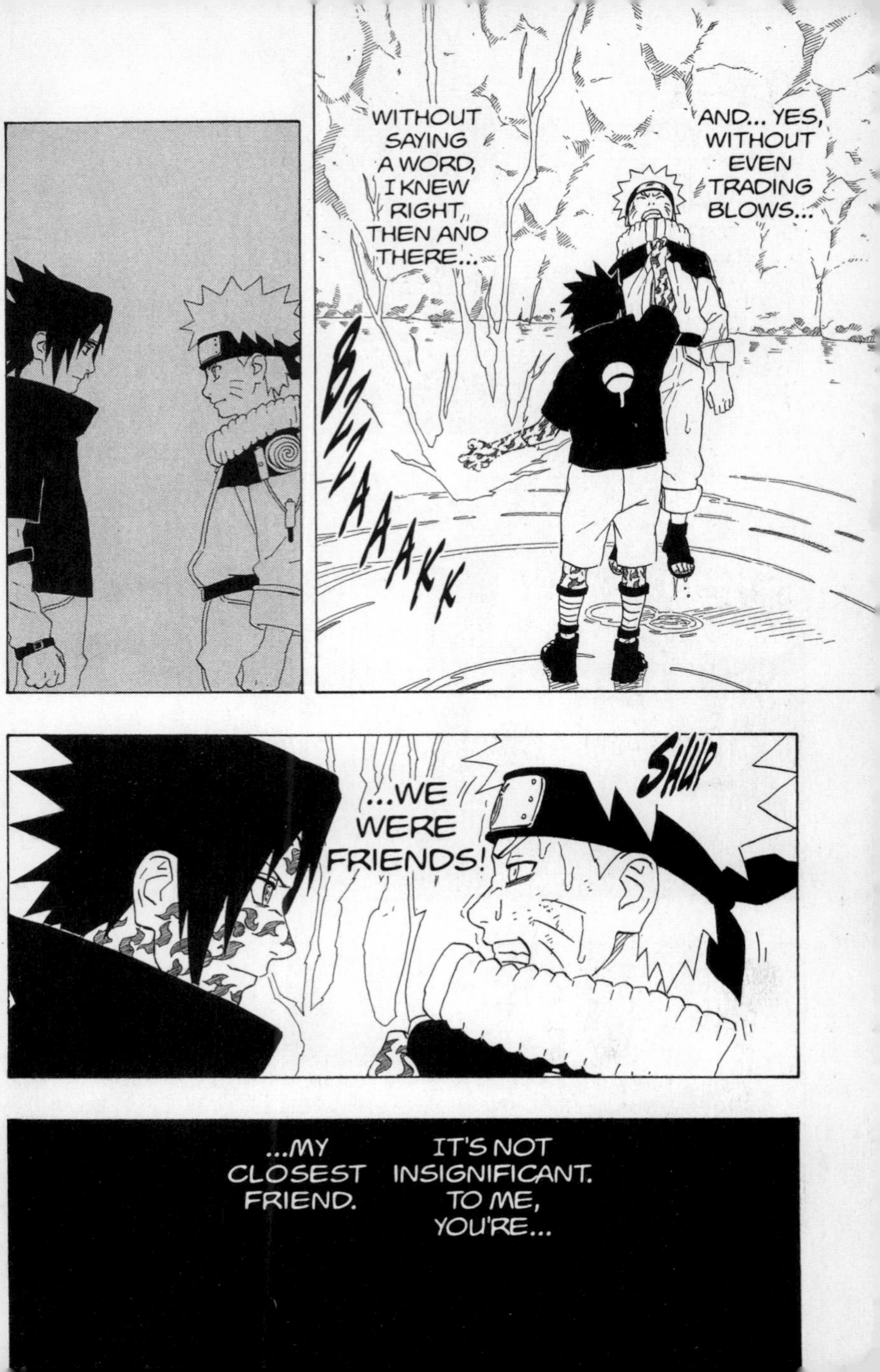
AND... YES, WITHOUT EVEN TRADING BLOWS...
WITHOUT SAYING A WORD, I KNEW RIGHT, THEN AND THERE...
BWAAAAKK
SHUP
...WE WERE FRIENDS!
IT'S NOT INSIGNIFICANT. TO ME, YOU'RE...
...MY CLOSEST FRIEND.

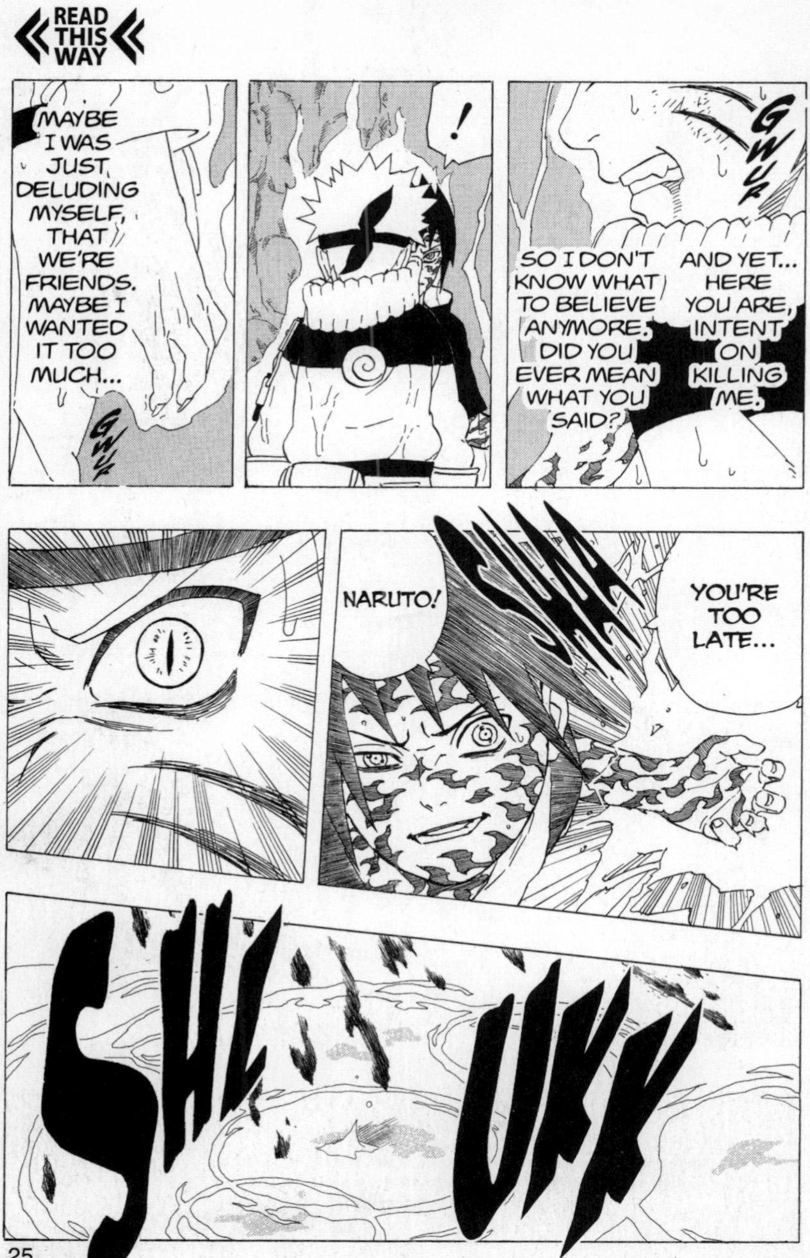
READ THIS WAY
GWUR
AND YET... HERE YOU ARE, INTENT ON KILLING ME.
SO I DON'T KNOW WHAT TO BELIEVE ANYMORE. DID YOU EVER MEAN WHAT YOU SAID?
!
MAYBE I WAS JUST DELUDING MYSELF, THAT WE'RE FRIENDS. MAYBE I WANTED IT TOO MUCH...
GWUR
YOU'RE TOO LATE...
SHAA
NARUTO!
SHLUNK

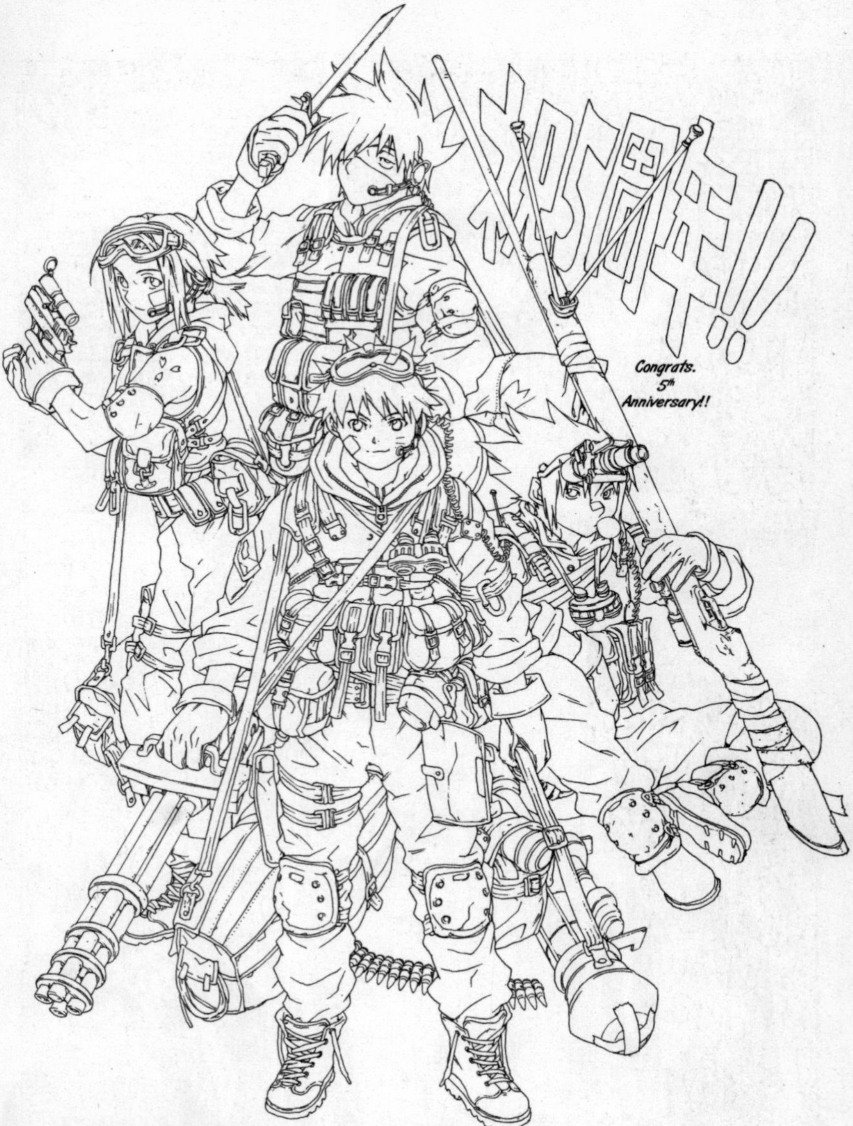
祝5周年!!
Congrats. 5th Anniversary!!

There's nothing wrong with a bit of depression. It just shows you're human.
That said, I'm fond of Naruto and Mr. Kishimoto: characters unburdened by doubt,
who always try to bring out their best.

2004.11.8 タカハシカズヒロ
Kazuhiro Takahashi

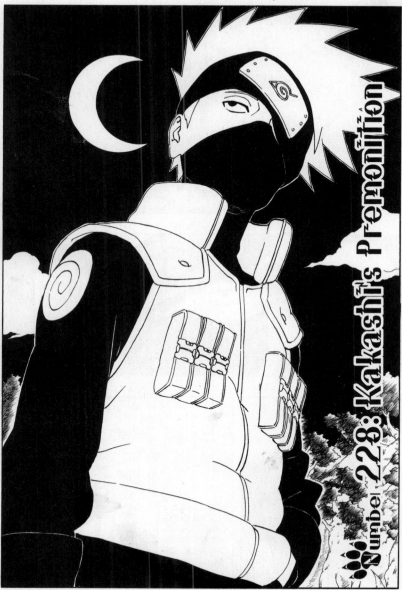

Number 228: Kakashi's Premonition

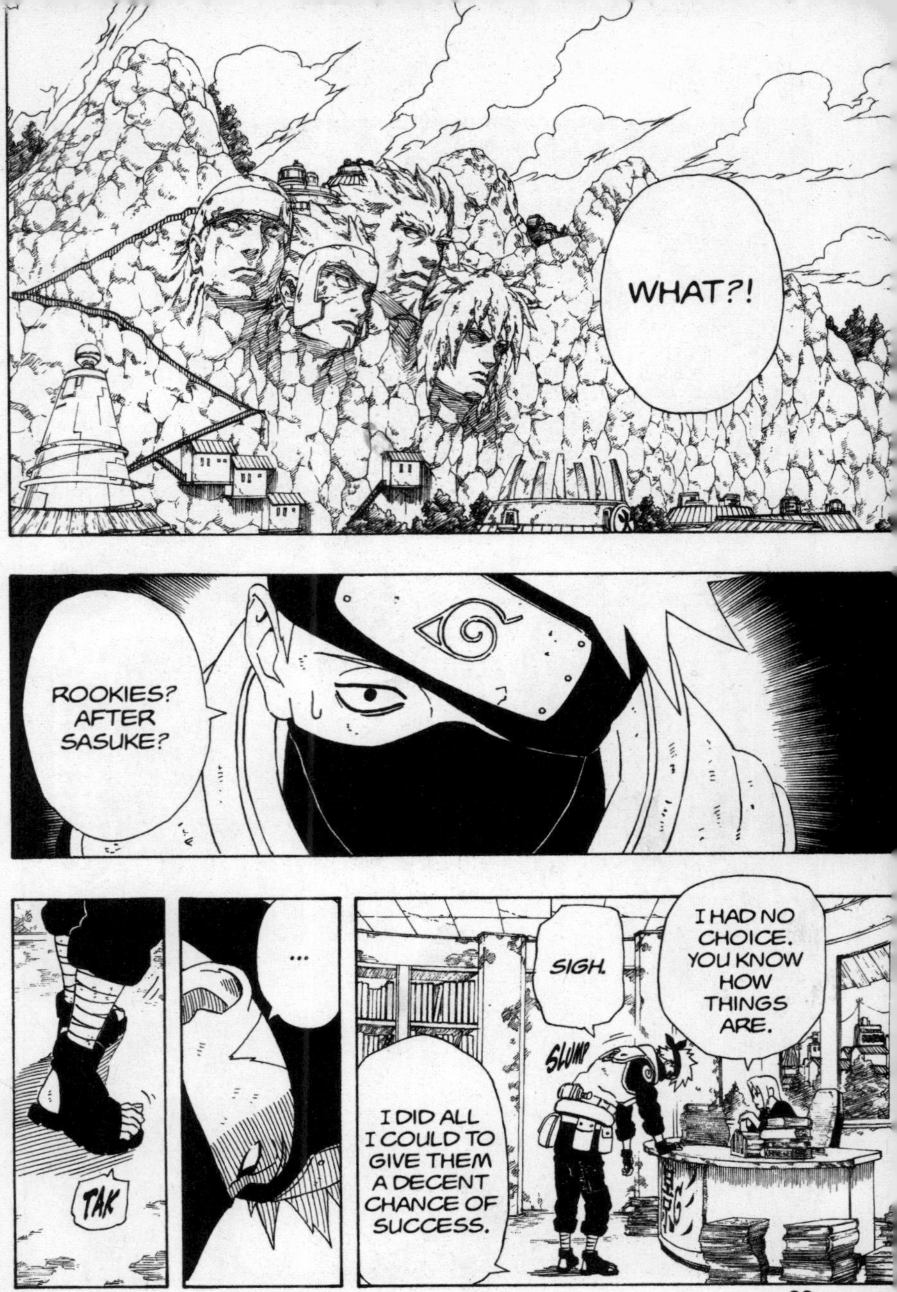
WHAT?!
ROOKIES? AFTER SASUKE?
I HAD NO CHOICE. YOU KNOW HOW THINGS ARE.
SIGH.
SLUMP
I DID ALL I COULD TO GIVE THEM A DECENT CHANCE OF SUCCESS.
...
TAK

READ THIS WAY

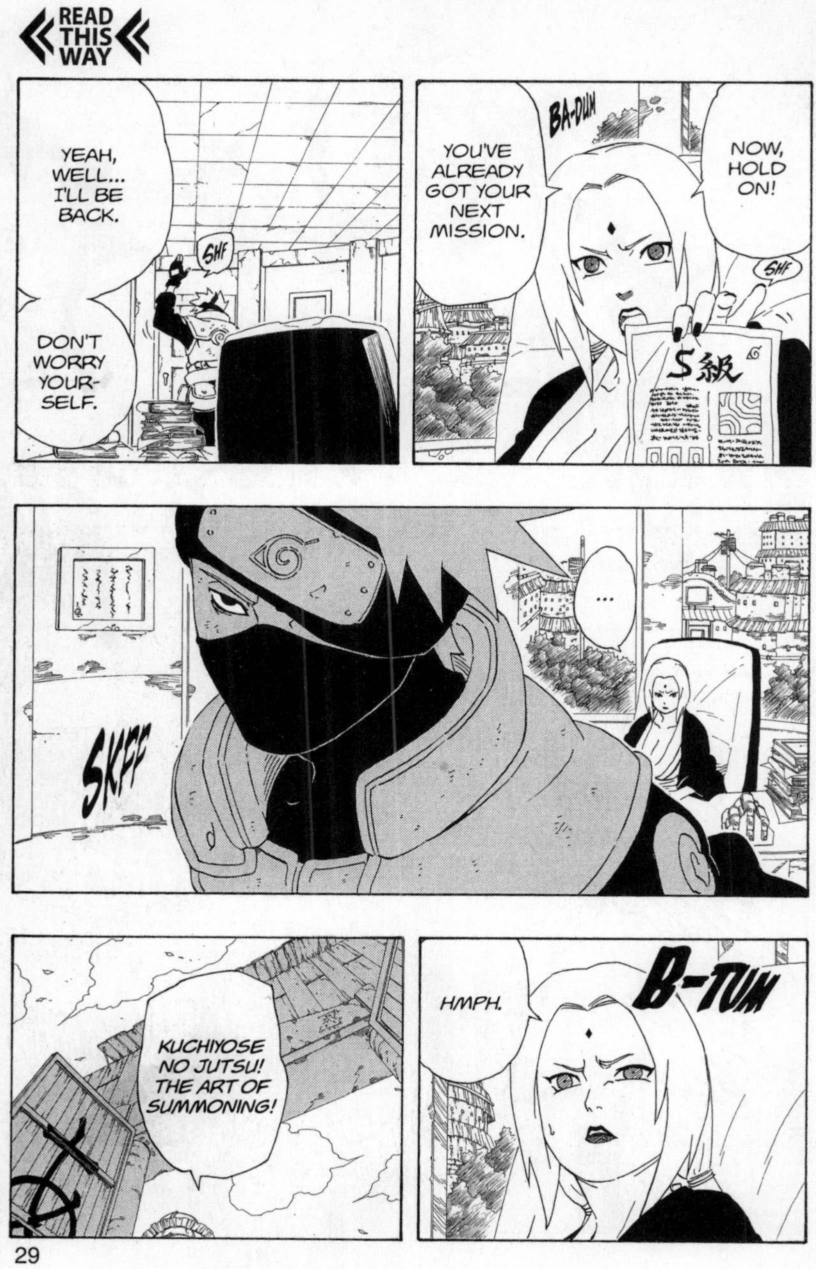
NOW, HOLD ON!
BA-DUM
YOU'VE ALREADY GOT YOUR NEXT MISSION.
SHF
S級
YEAH, WELL... I'LL BE BACK.
SHF
DON'T WORRY YOURSELF.
...
SKFF
B-TUM
HMPH.
KUCHIYOSE NO JUTSU! THE ART OF SUMMONING!

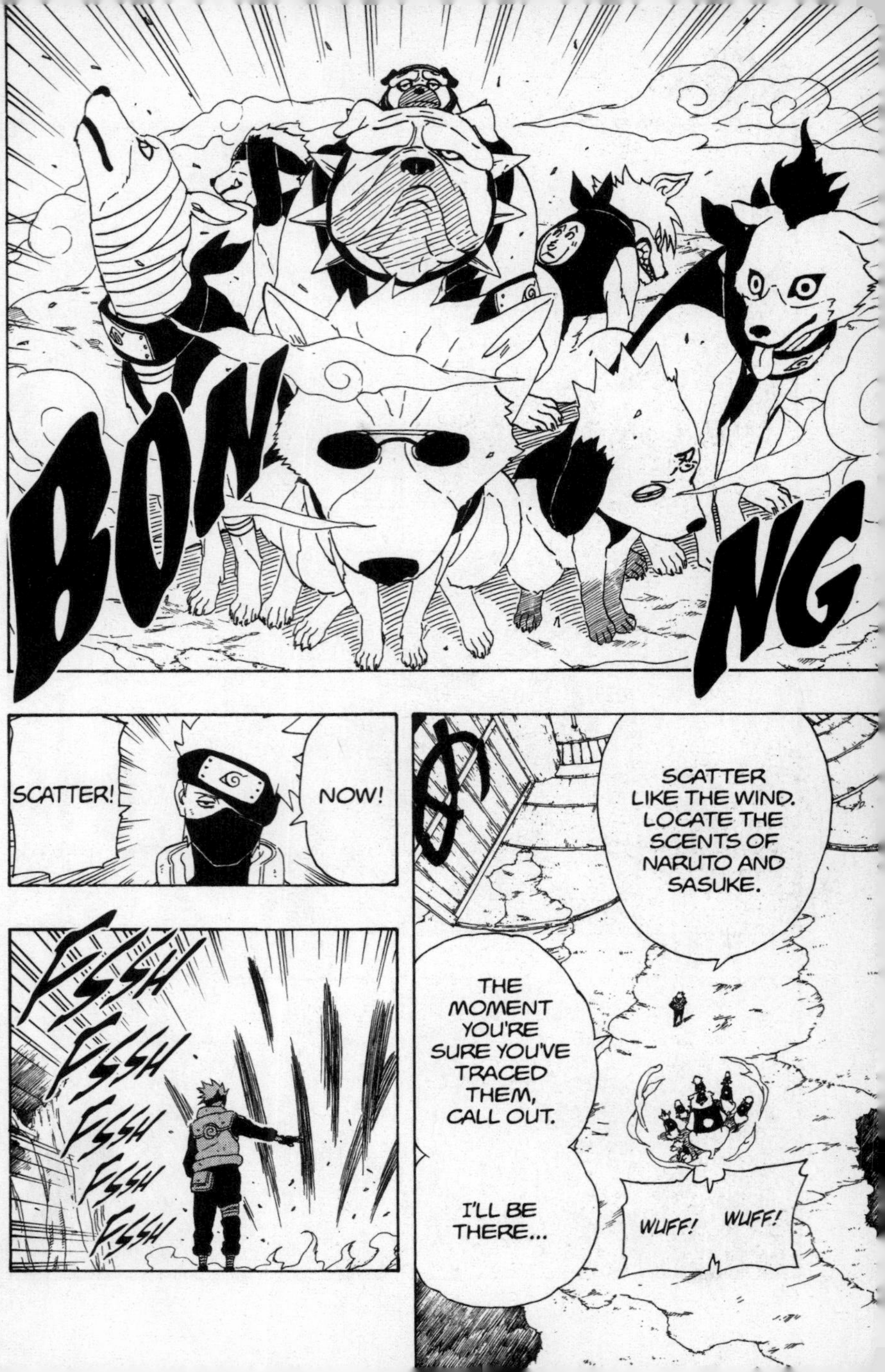
BONNG
SCATTER LIKE THE WIND. LOCATE THE SCENTS OF NARUTO AND SASUKE.
THE MOMENT YOU'RE SURE YOU'VE TRACED THEM, CALL OUT.
I'LL BE THERE...
WUFF! WUFF!
NOW!
SCATTER!
FSSH FSSH FSSH FSSH FSSH

READ THIS WAY

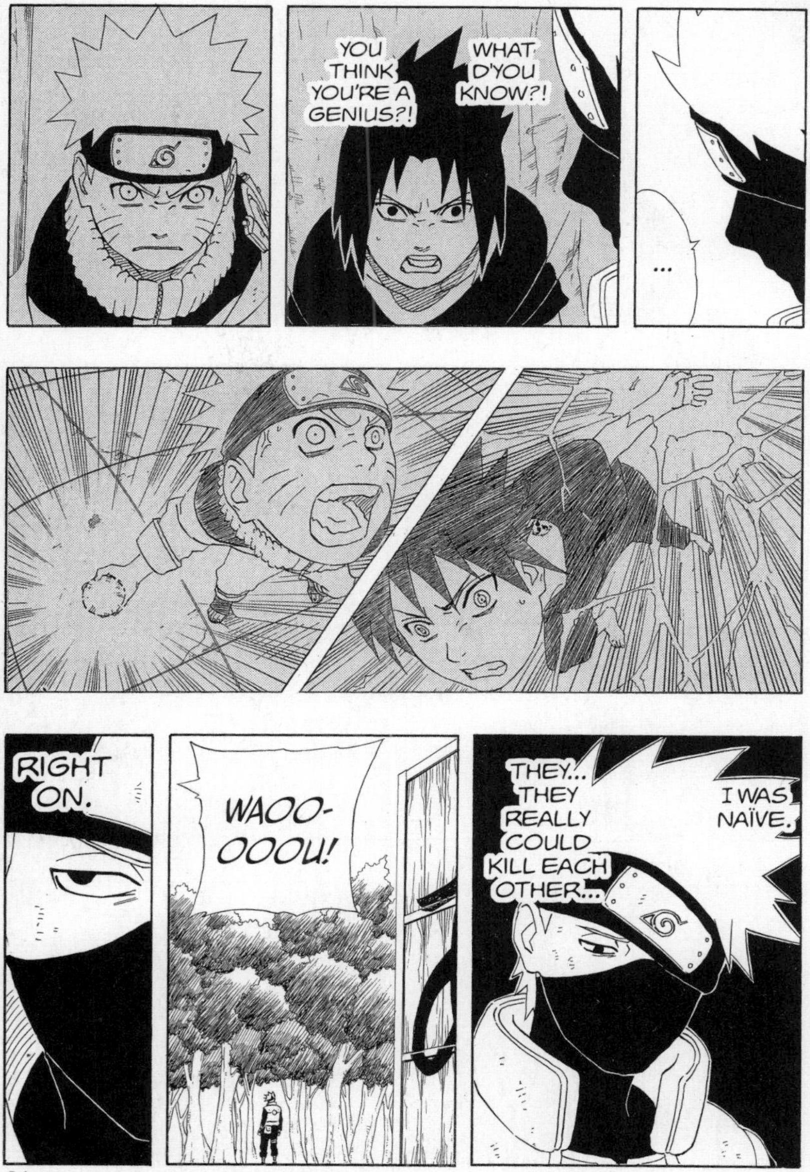
...
WHAT D'YOU KNOW?!
YOU THINK YOU'RE A GENIUS?!
I WAS NAÏVE.
THEY... THEY REALLY COULD KILL EACH OTHER...
WAOO-OOOU!
RIGHT ON.

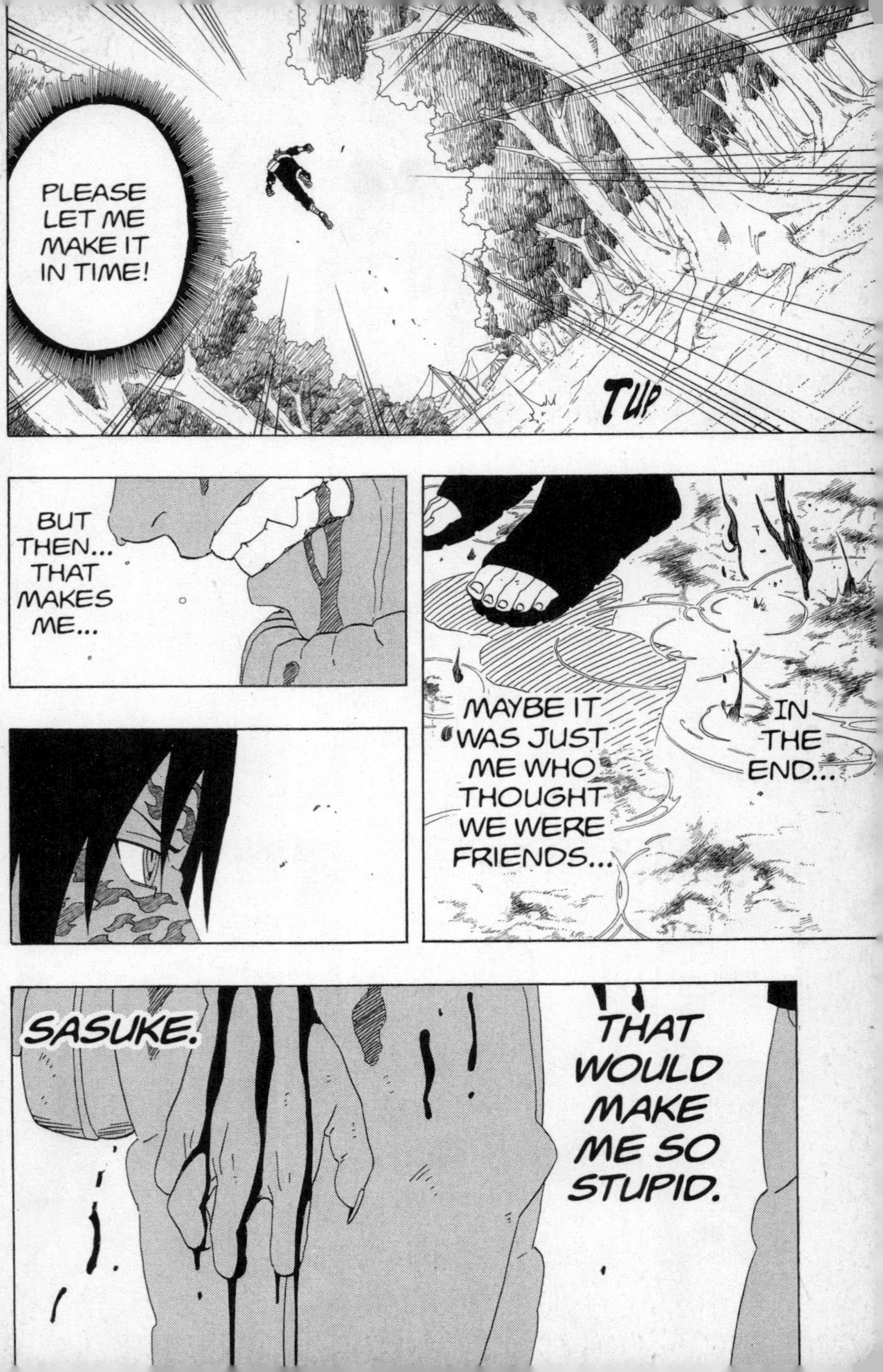
PLEASE LET ME MAKE IT IN TIME!
TUP
IN THE END...
MAYBE IT WAS JUST ME WHO THOUGHT WE WERE FRIENDS...
BUT THEN... THAT MAKES ME...
THAT WOULD MAKE ME SO STUPID.
SASUKE.

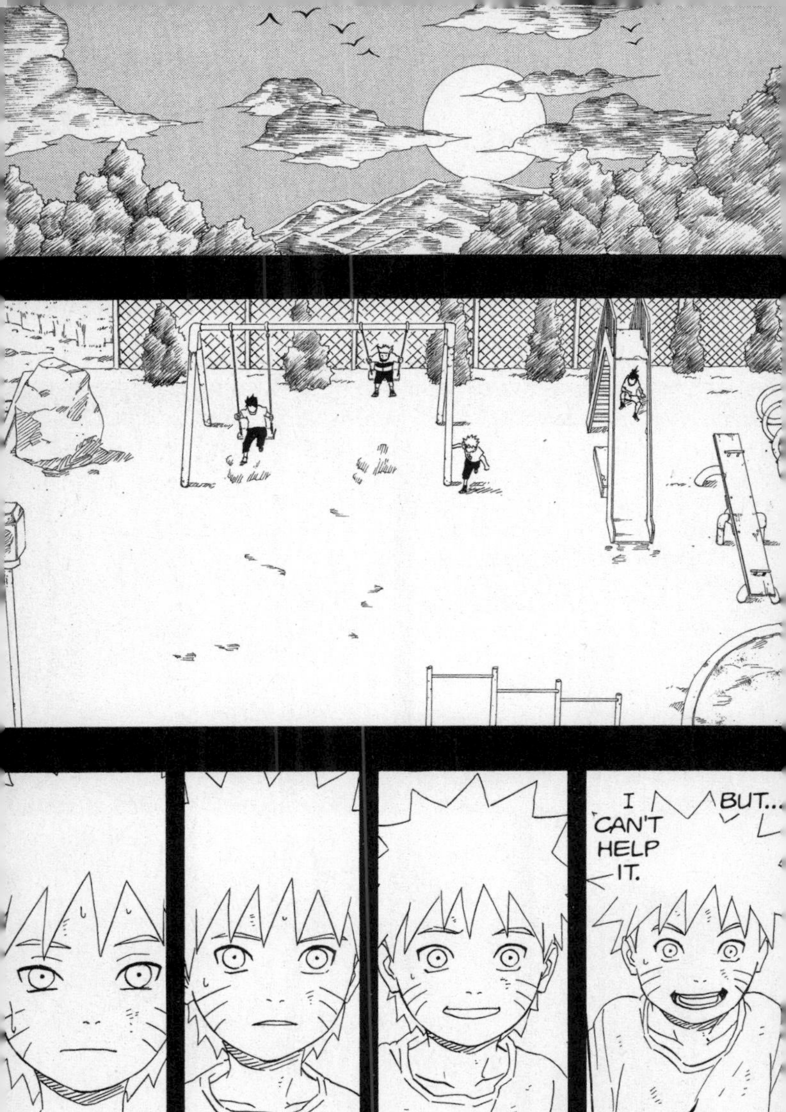
BUT...
I CAN'T HELP IT.

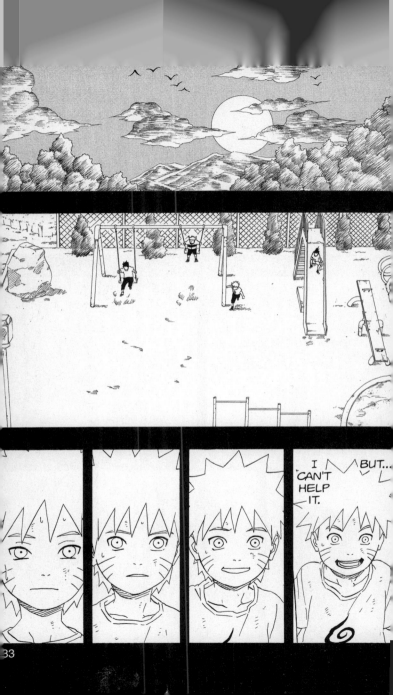

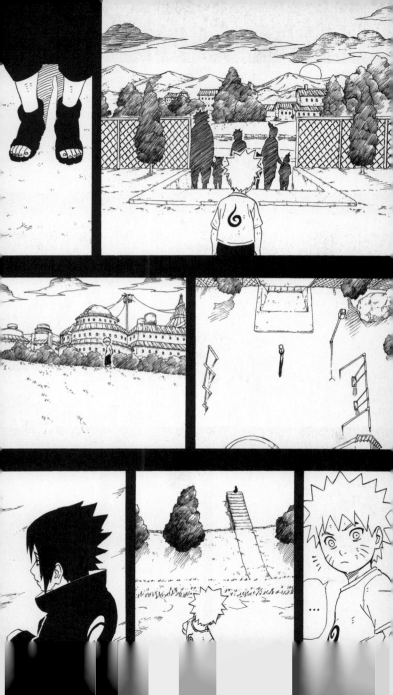

...

READ THIS WAY

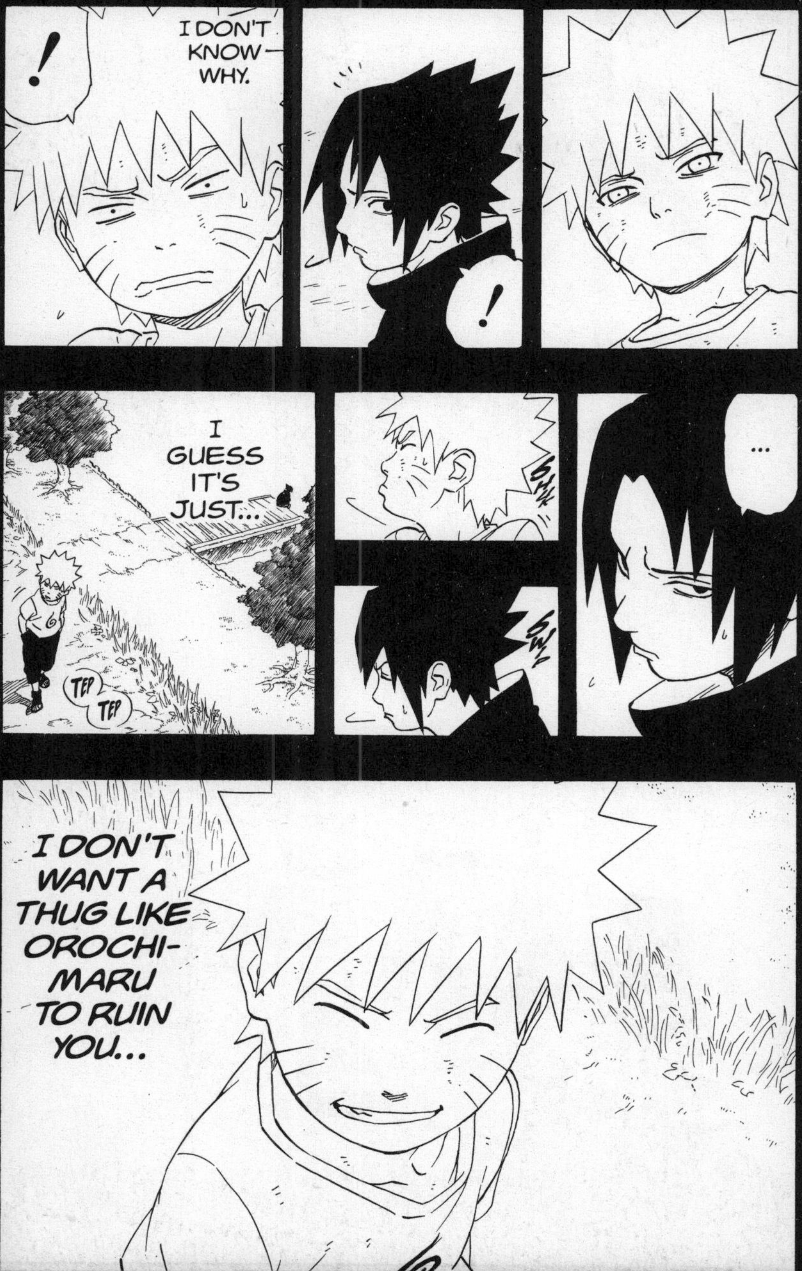
!
I DON'T KNOW WHY.
!
...
I GUESS IT'S JUST...
TEP
TEP
I DON'T WANT A THUG LIKE OROCHI-MARU TO RUIN YOU...

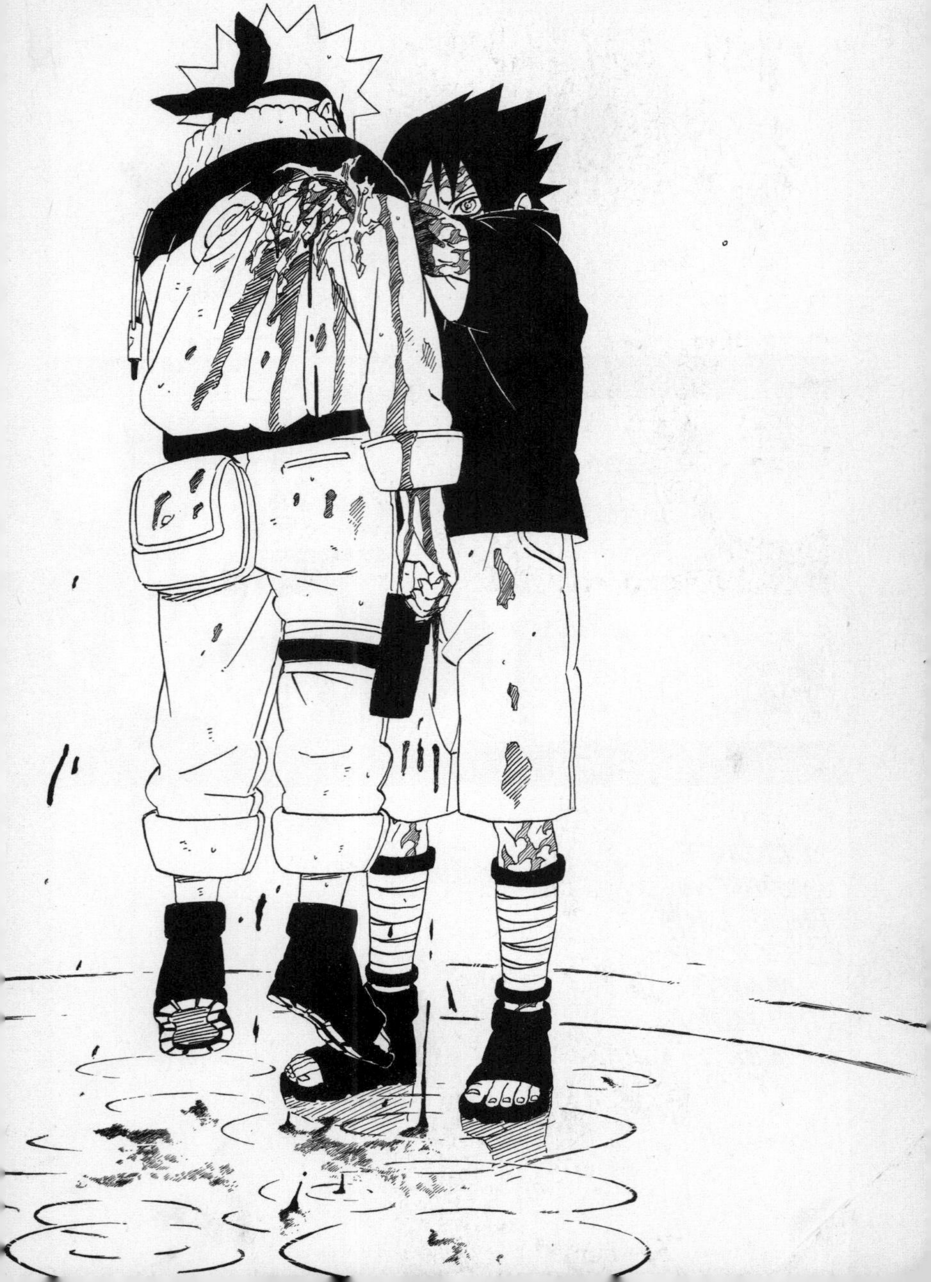

READ THIS WAY

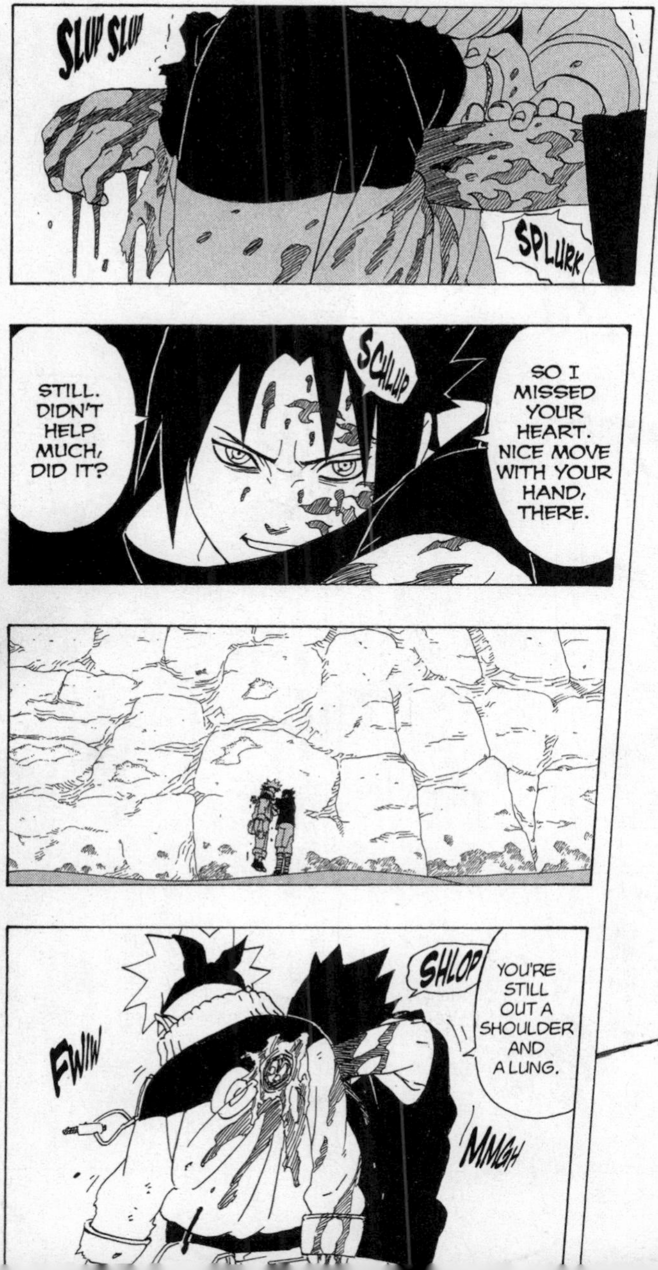
SLUP SLUP
SPLURK
SO I MISSED YOUR HEART. NICE MOVE WITH YOUR HAND, THERE.
SCHLUP
STILL. DIDN'T HELP MUCH, DID IT?
SHLOP
YOU'RE STILL OUT A SHOULDER AND A LUNG.
FWIW
MMGH

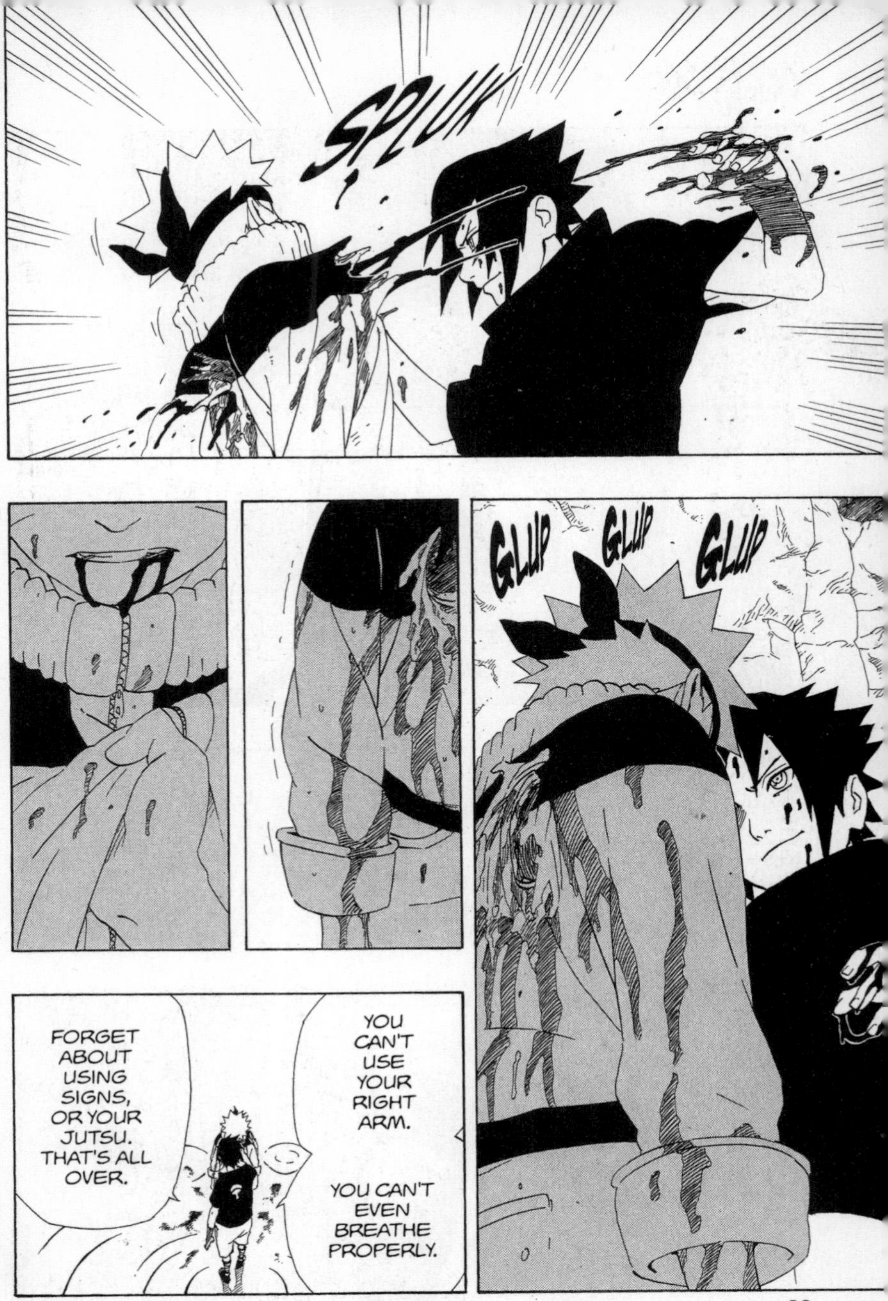
SPLUK
GLUP
GLUP
GLUP
YOU CAN'T USE YOUR RIGHT ARM.
YOU CAN'T EVEN BREATHE PROPERLY.
FORGET ABOUT USING SIGNS, OR YOUR JUTSU. THAT'S ALL OVER.

READ THIS WAY

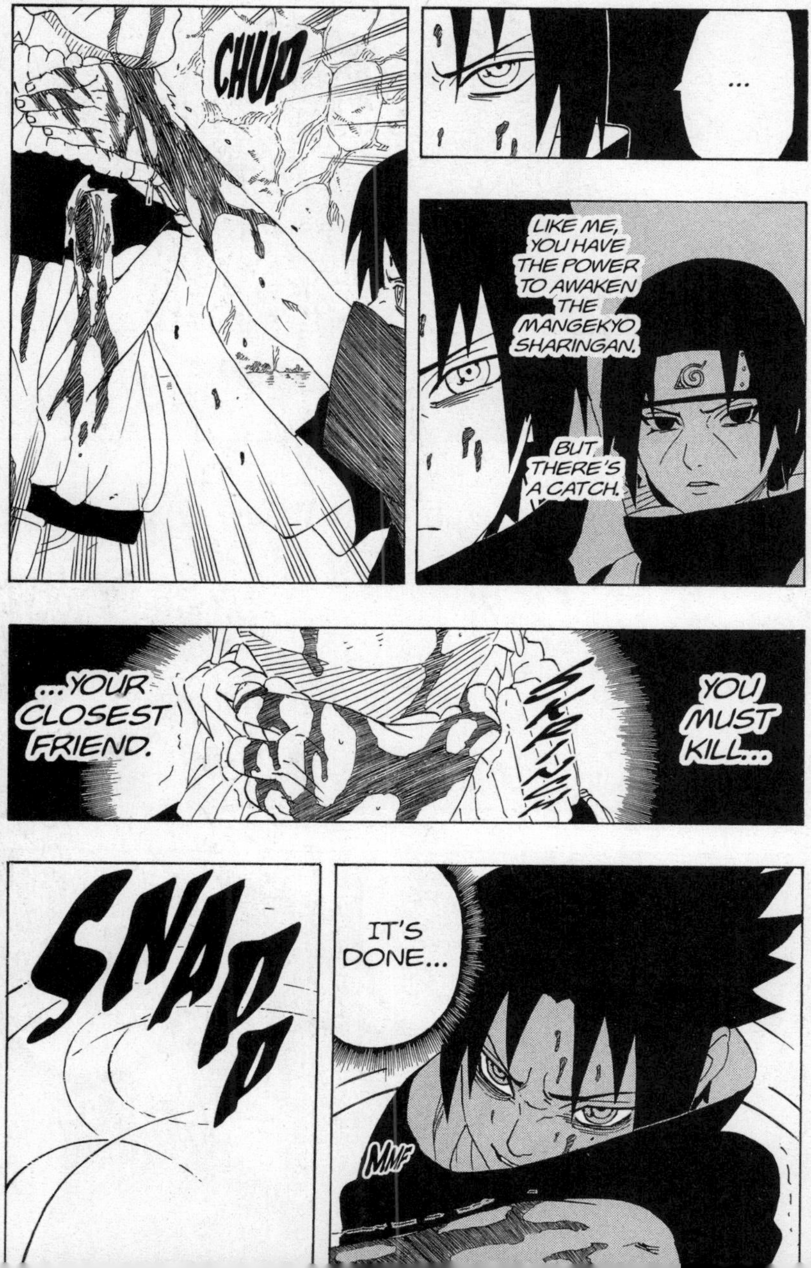
...
LIKE ME, YOU HAVE THE POWER TO AWAKEN THE MANGEKYO SHARINGAN.
BUT THERE'S A CATCH.
CHUP
YOU MUST KILL...
...YOUR CLOSEST FRIEND.
IT'S DONE...
MMF
SNAP

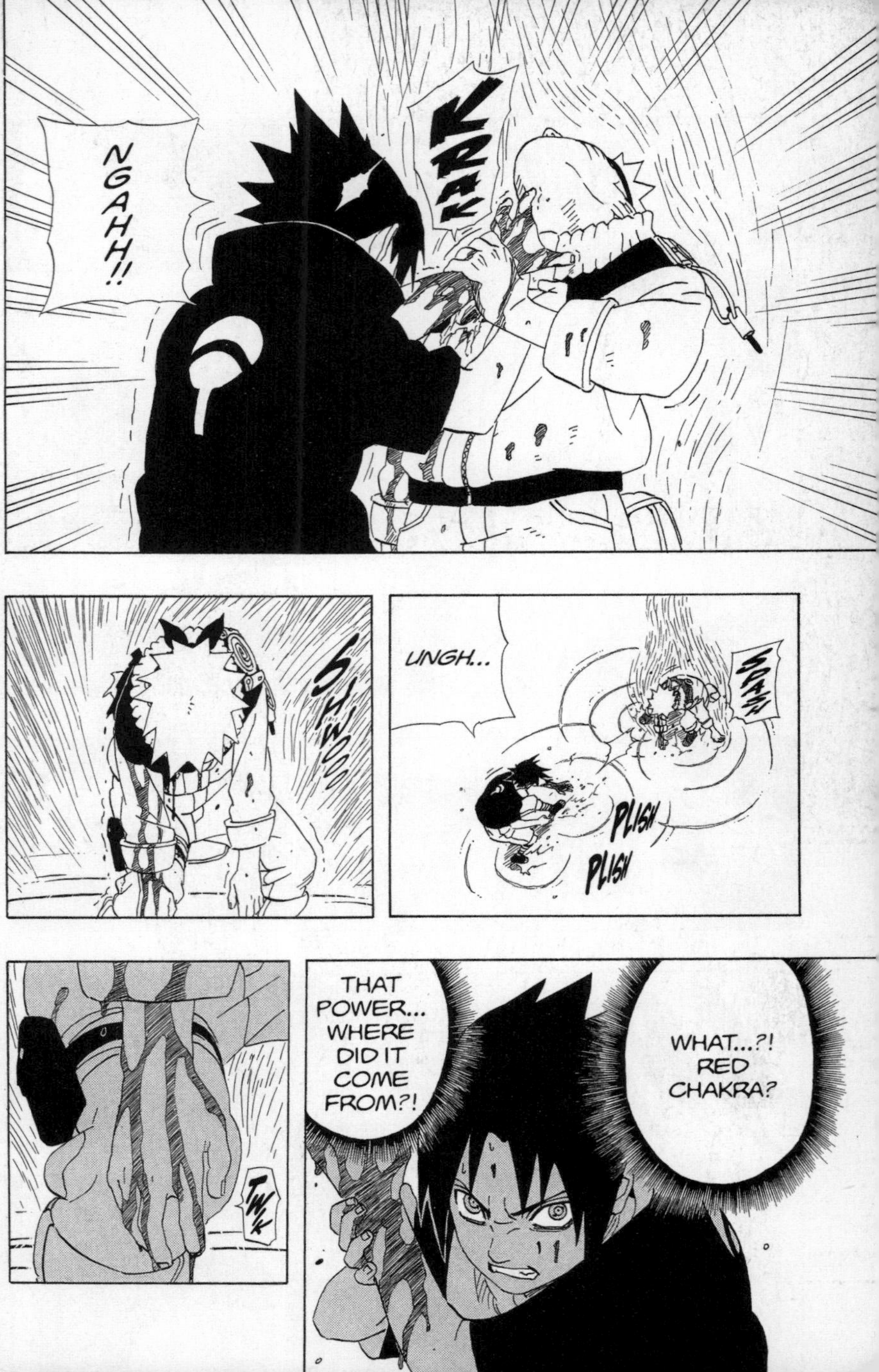
KRAK
NGAHH!!
UNGH...
SPASH
PLISH
PLISH
SHWOOO
WHAT...?! RED CHAKRA?
THAT POWER... WHERE DID IT COME FROM?!
TWIK

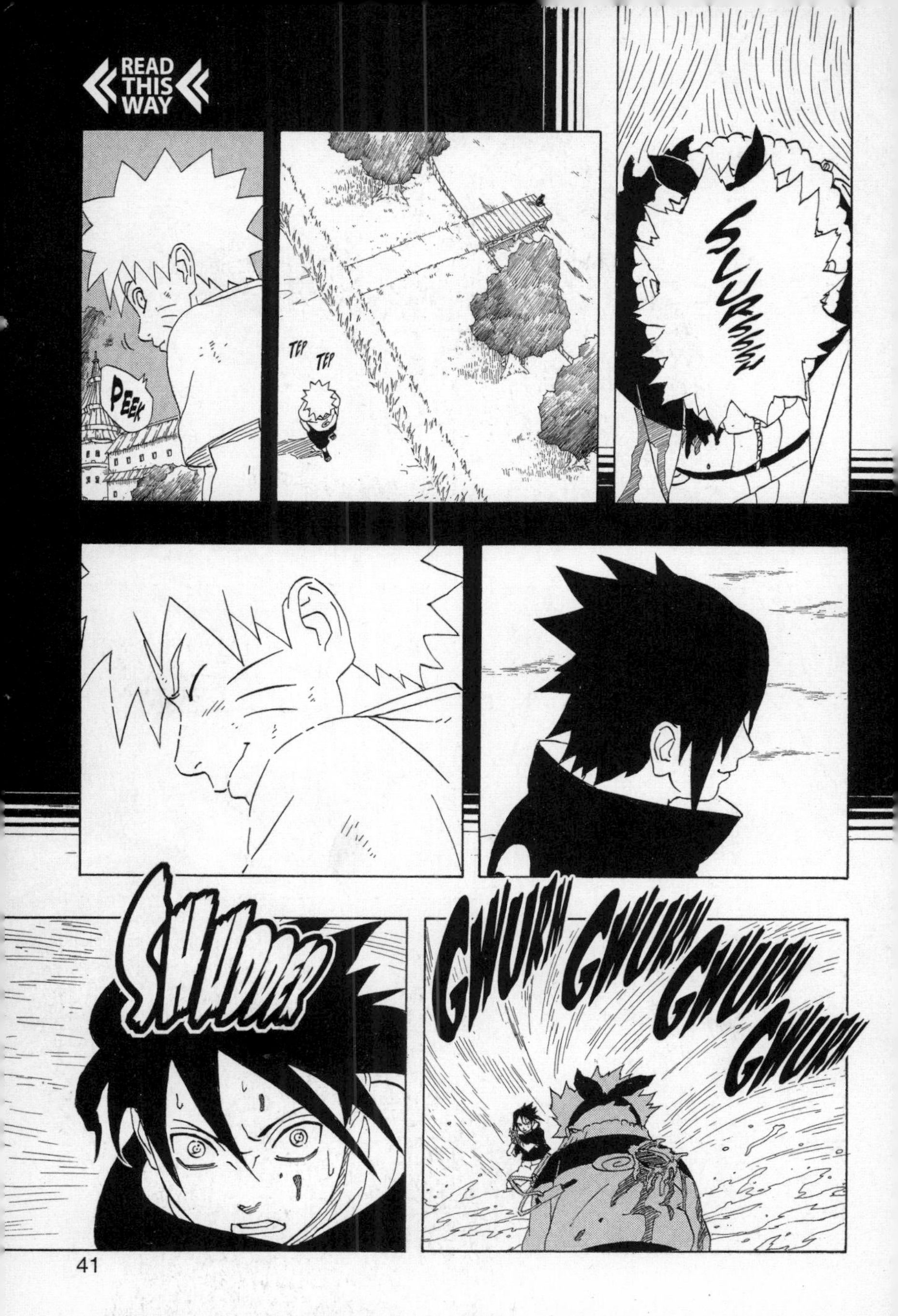
READ THIS WAY
SLURRRRRP
TEP TEP
PEEK
SHUDDER
GHURK GHURK GHURK GHURK

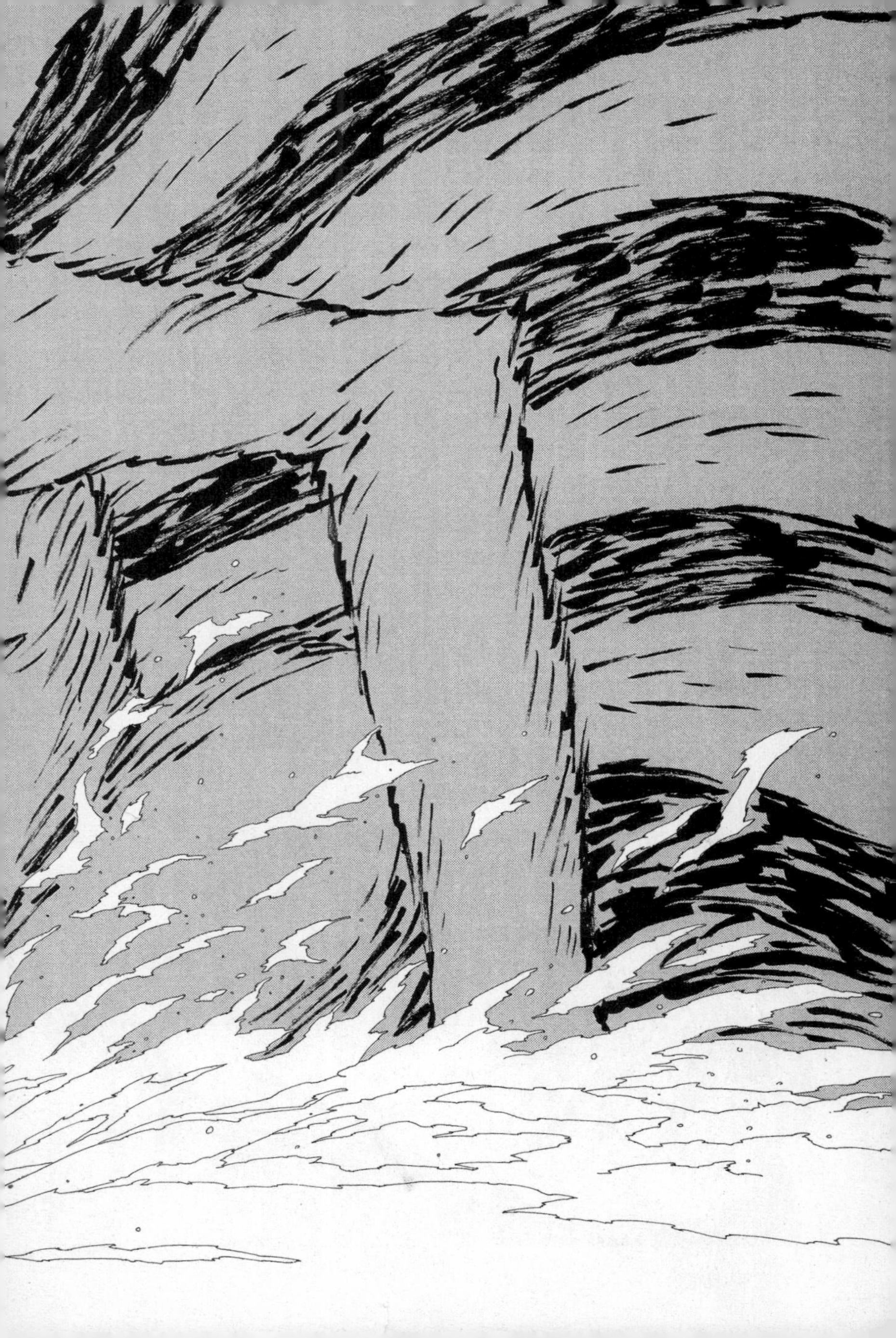

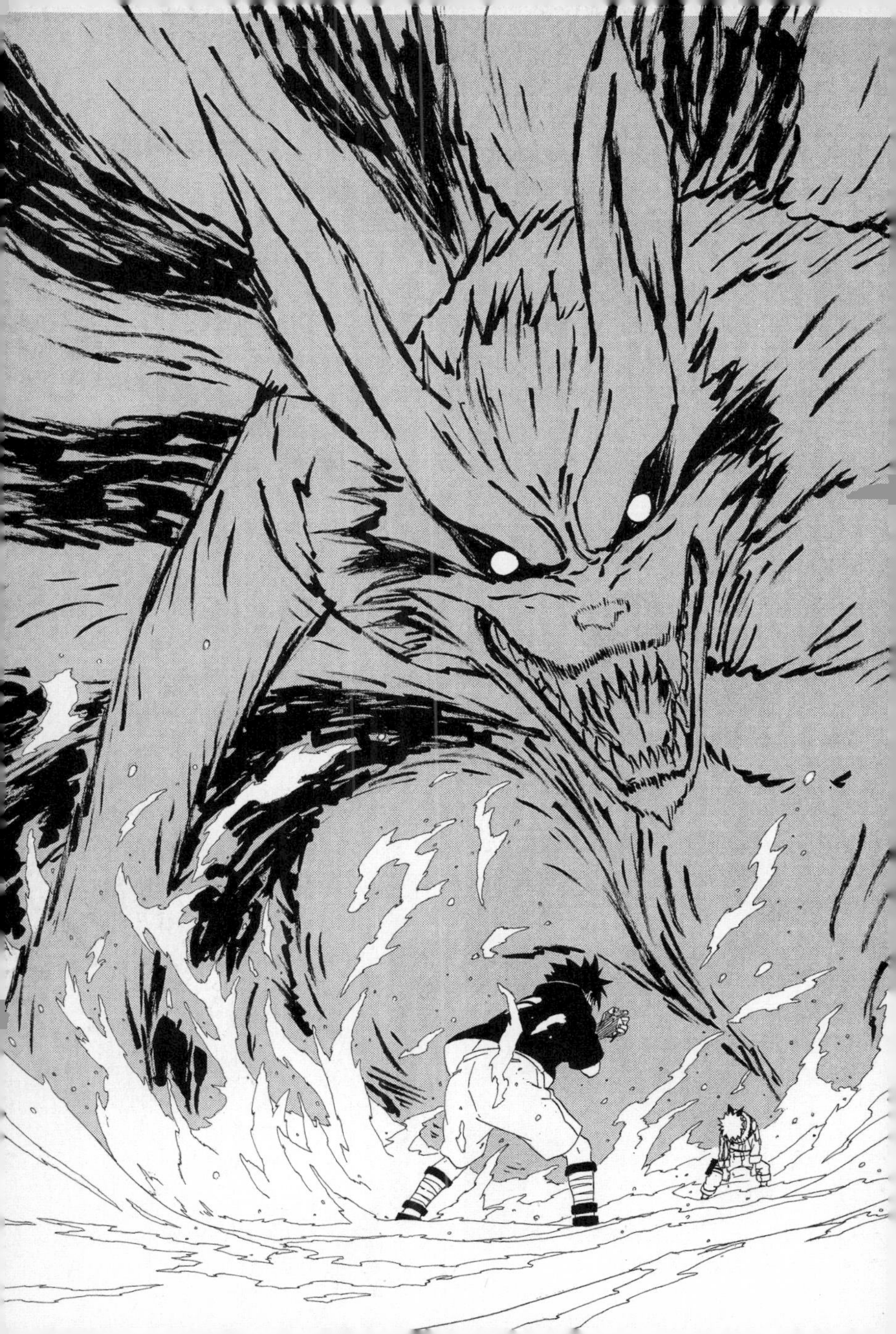

WHA...
WHAT
IN...
?!!

SLURSSS

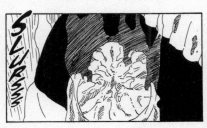

SLURSSS

SSSH

READ THIS WAY

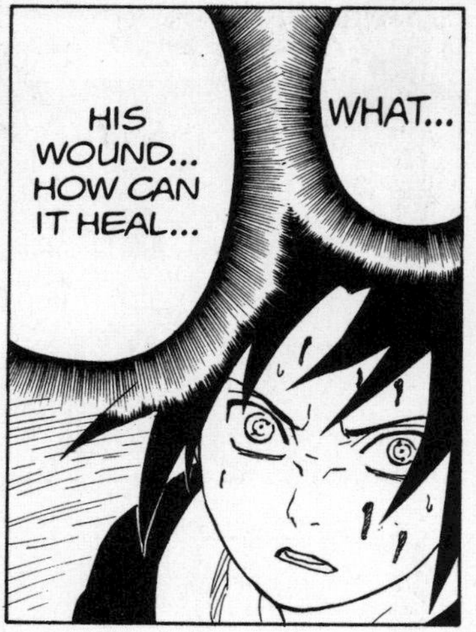
WHAT...
HIS WOUND... HOW CAN IT HEAL...

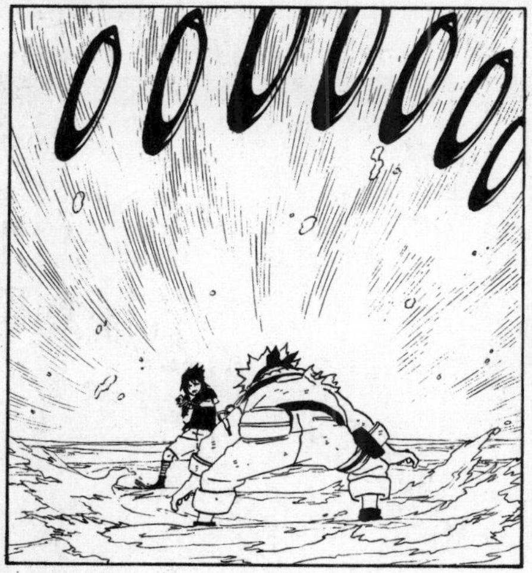

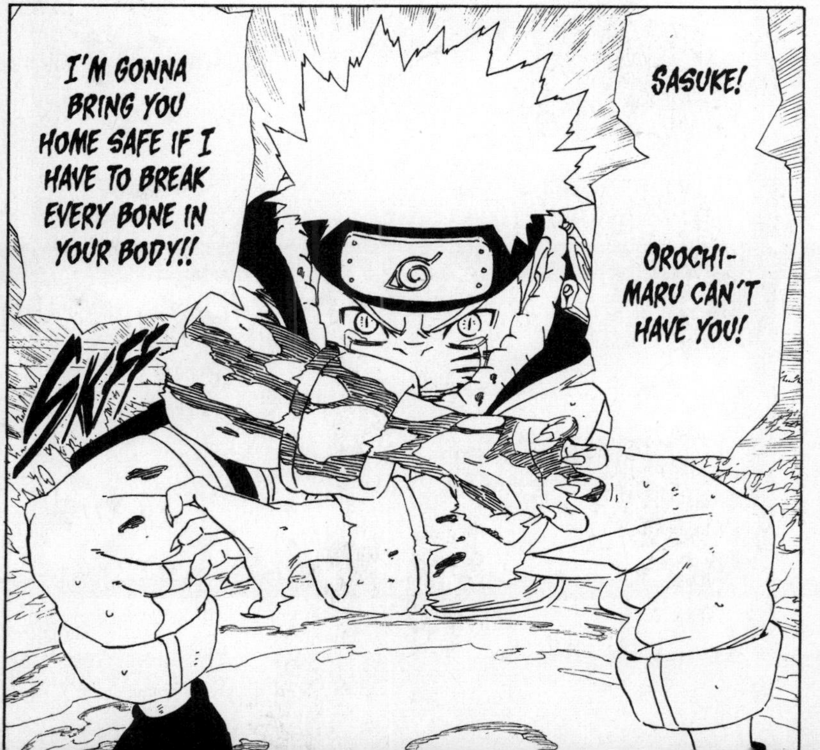
SASUKE!
OROCHI-MARU CAN'T HAVE YOU!
I'M GONNA BRING YOU HOME SAFE IF I HAVE TO BREAK EVERY BONE IN YOUR BODY!!
SKFF

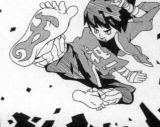

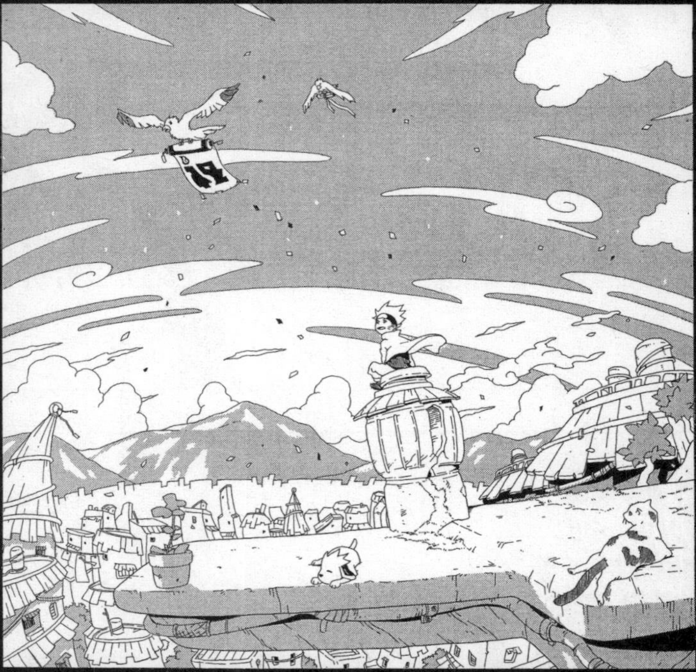
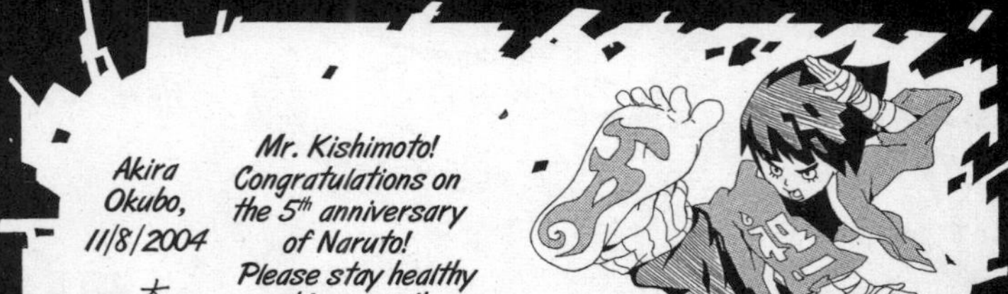
Mr. Kishimoto! Congratulations on the 5th anniversary of Naruto! Please stay healthy and keep up the good work!
Akira Okubo, 11/8/2004
大久保彰

Number 229: The Bond...!!

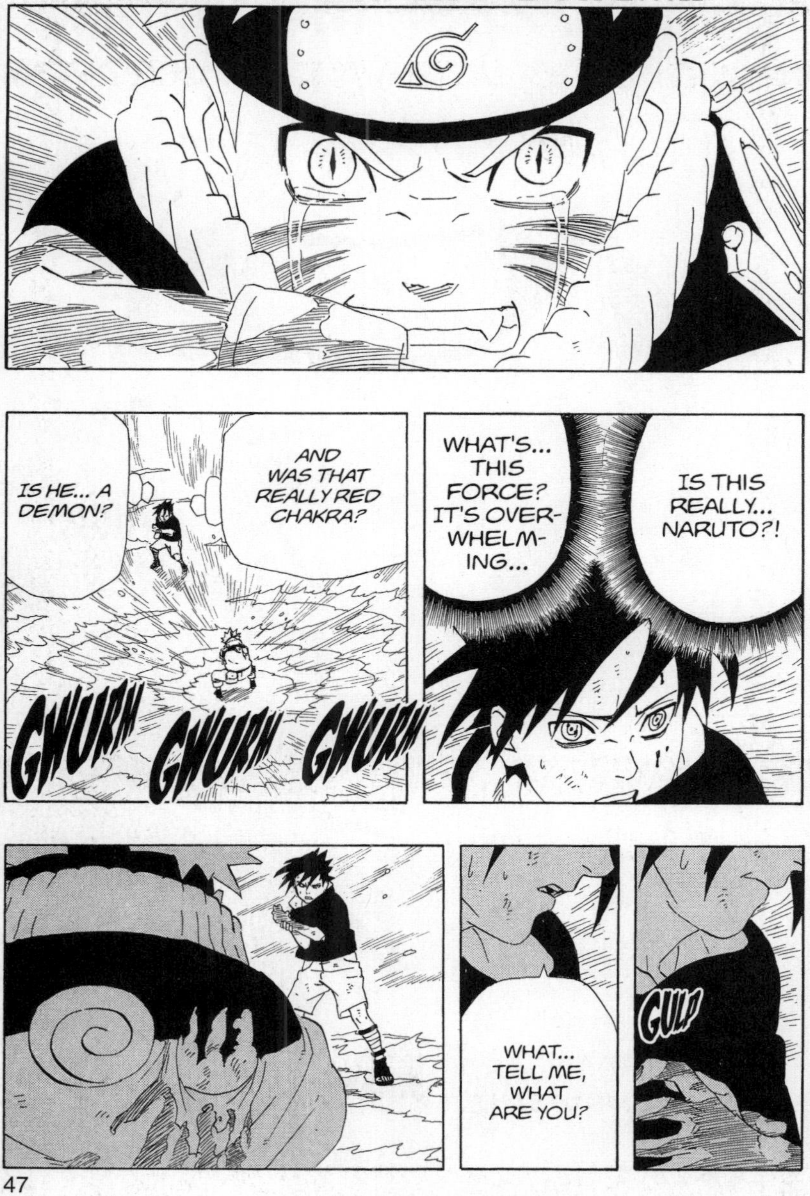
IS THIS REALLY... NARUTO?!
WHAT'S... THIS FORCE? IT'S OVER-WHELMING...
AND WAS THAT REALLY RED CHAKRA?
IS HE... A DEMON?
GWURH GWURH GWURH
GULP
WHAT... TELL ME, WHAT ARE YOU?

Number 229: The Bond...!!

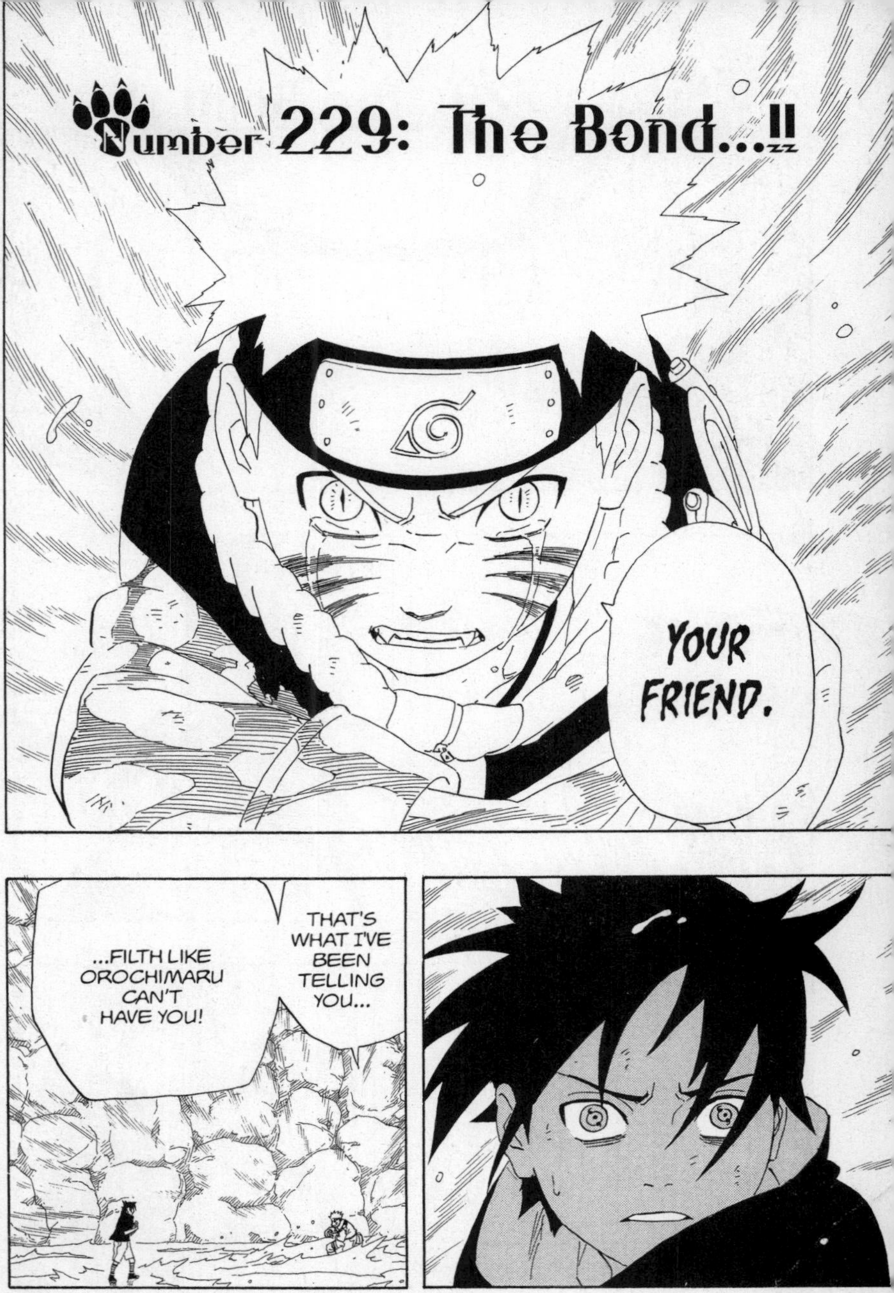
YOUR FRIEND.
THAT'S WHAT I'VE BEEN TELLING YOU...
...FILTH LIKE OROCHIMARU CAN'T HAVE YOU!

READ THIS WAY

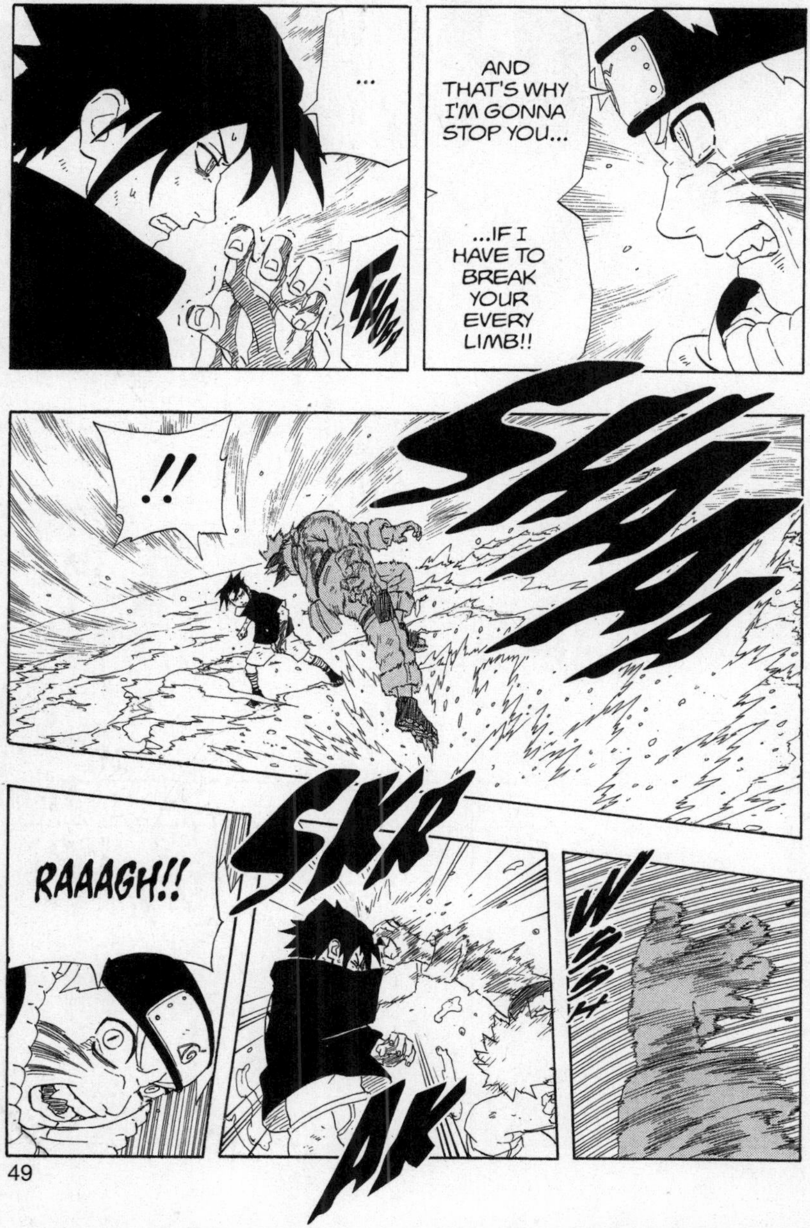
AND THAT'S WHY I'M GONNA STOP YOU...
...IF I HAVE TO BREAK YOUR EVERY LIMB!!
...
!!
RAAAGH!!

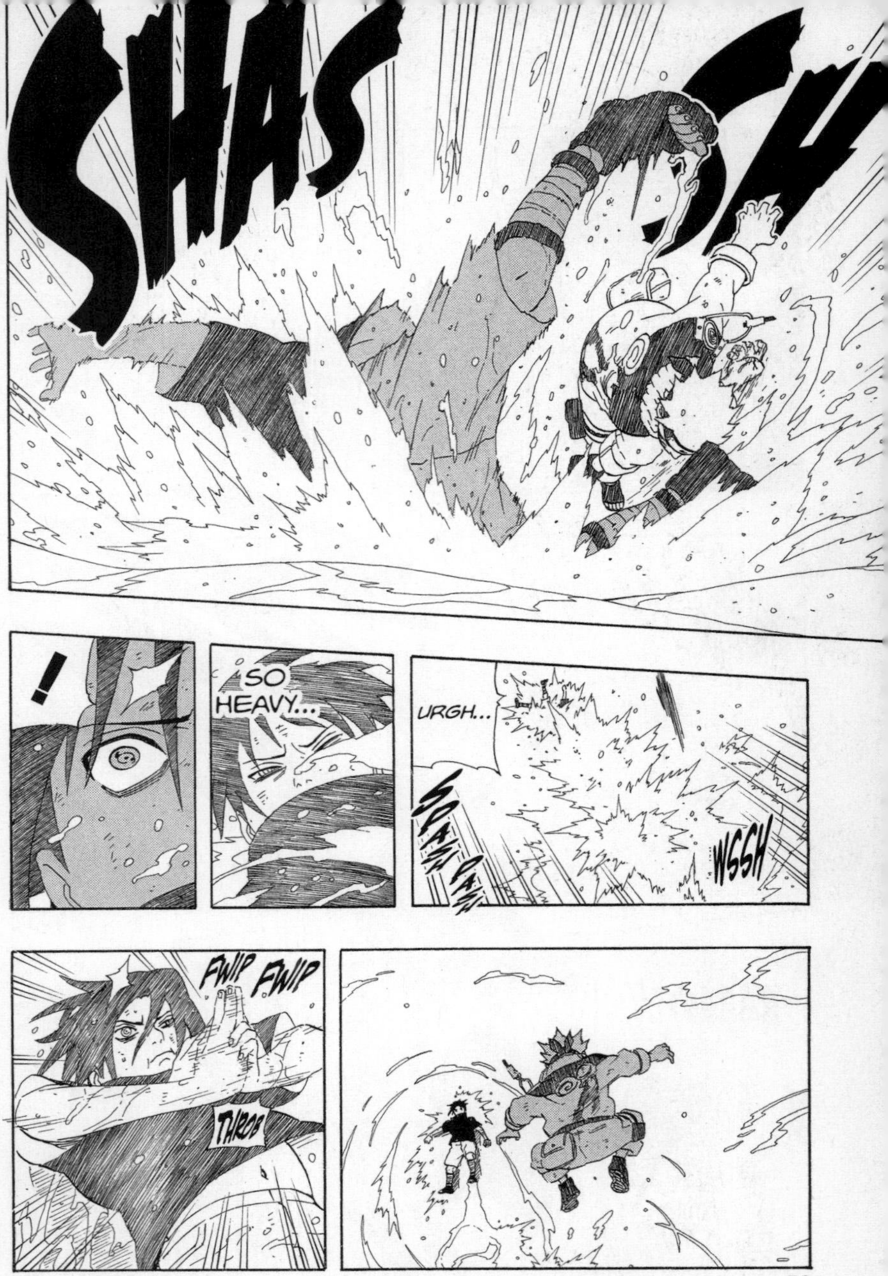
SHAS
SH
URGH...
WSSH
SO HEAVY...
!
FWIP FWIP
THROB

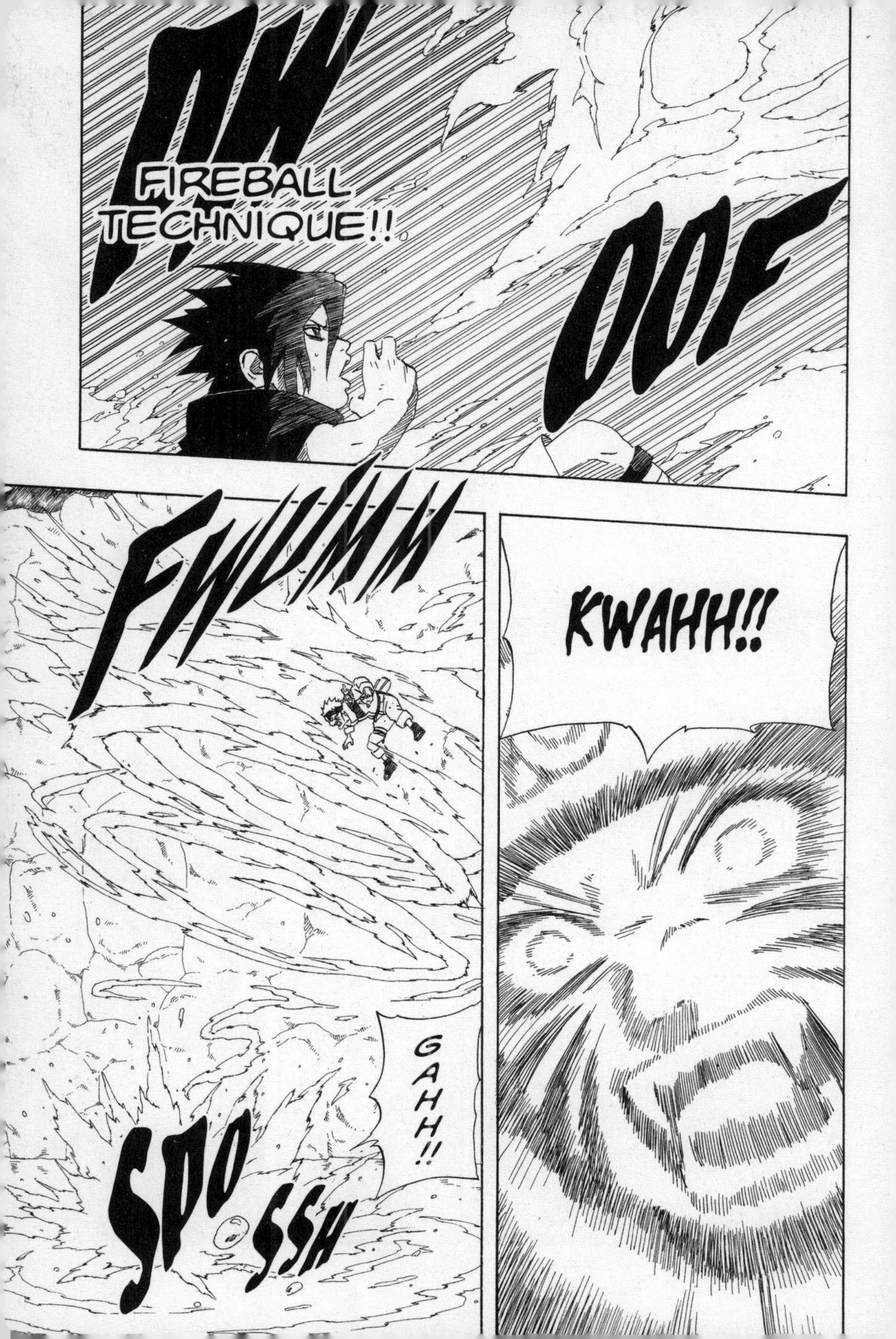
FIREBALL TECHNIQUE!!
OOF
KWAHH!!
FWUMM
GAHH!!
SPO SSH

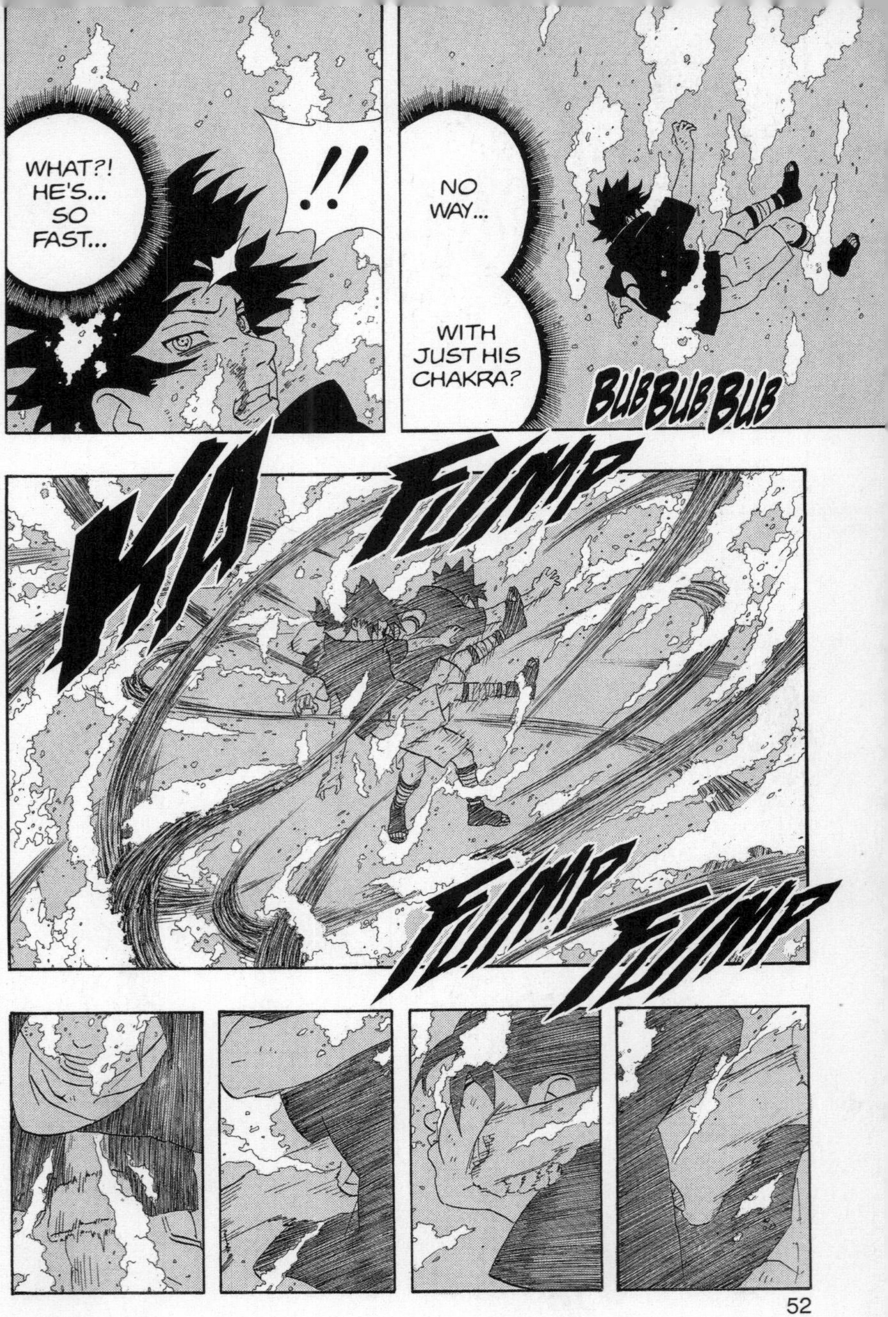
NO WAY...
WITH JUST HIS CHAKRA?
BUB BUB BUB
!!
WHAT?! HE'S... SO FAST...
FUMP
FUMP
FUMP

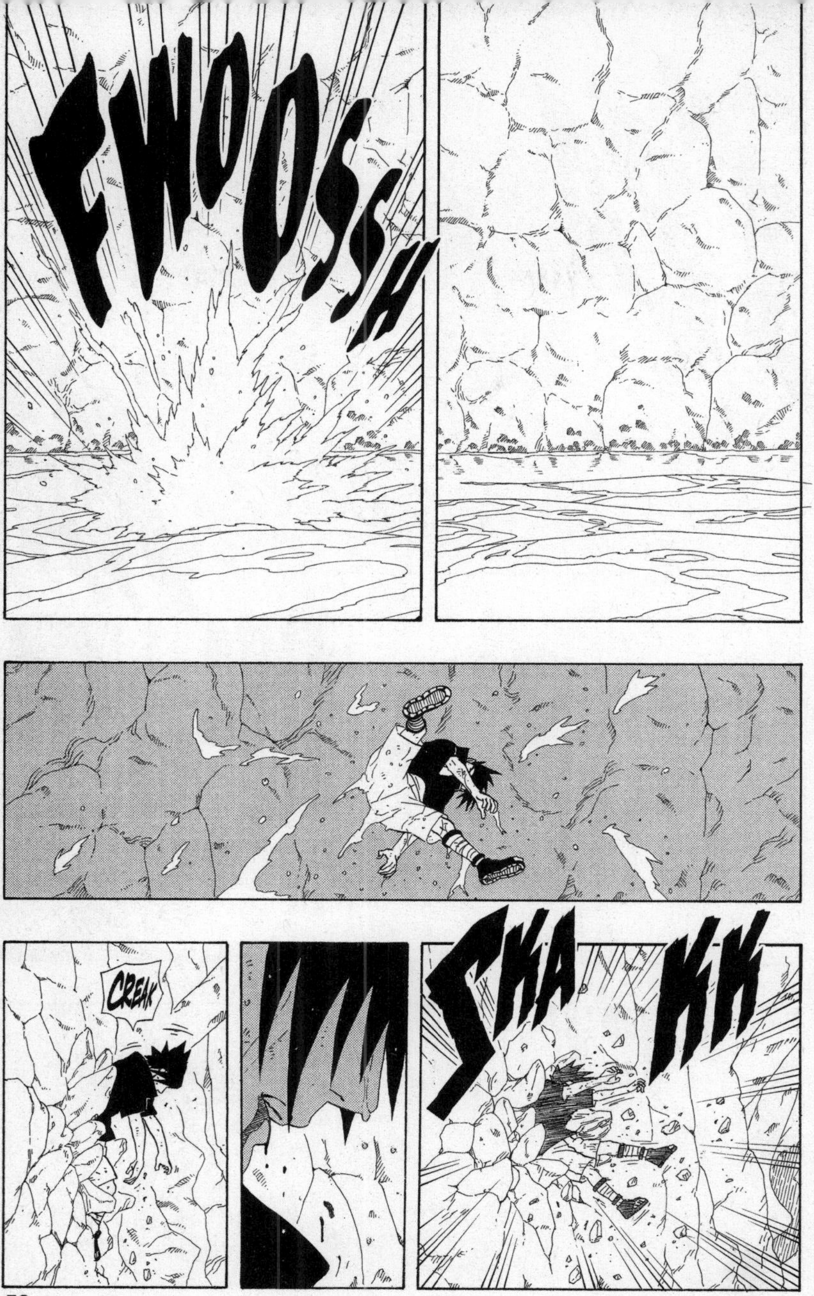
FWOOSSH
CREAK
SKAKKK

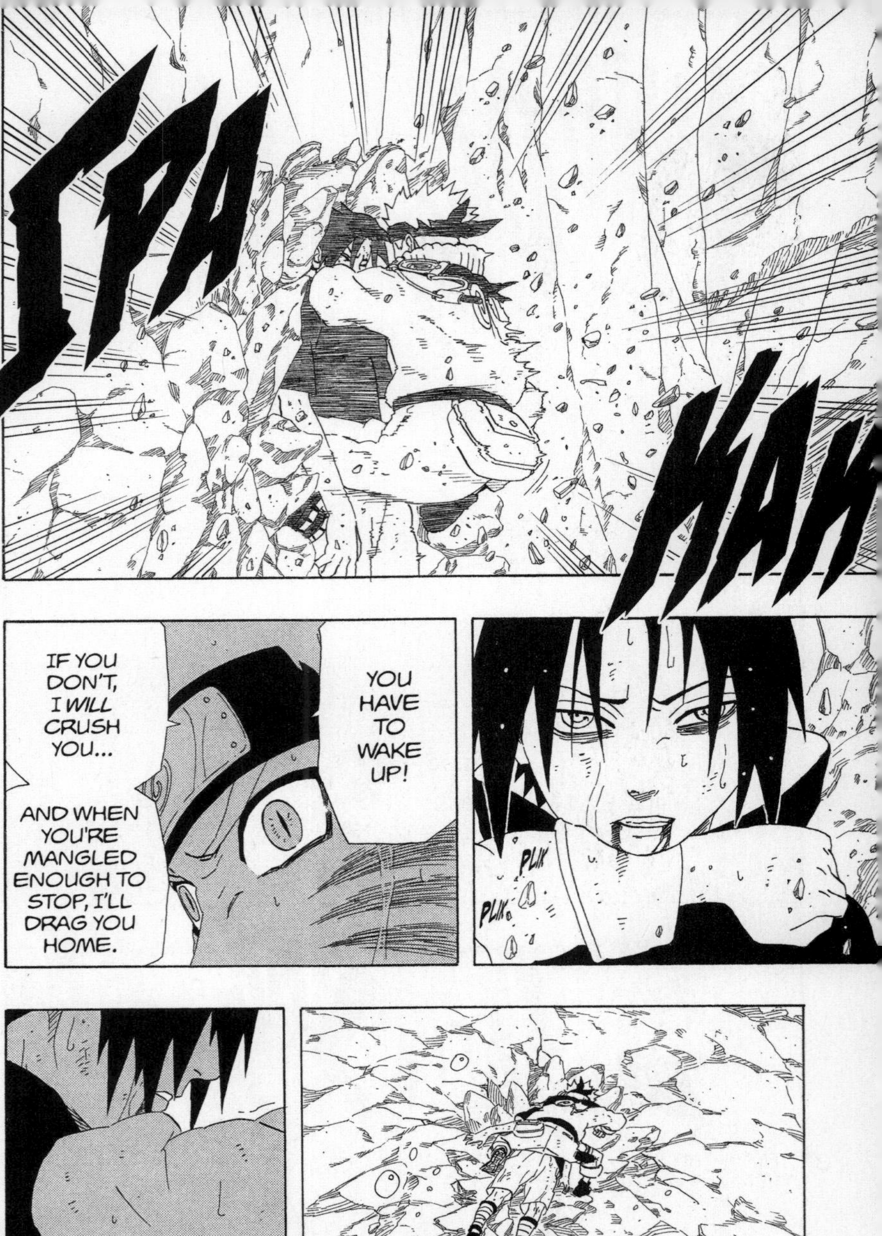
PLIK
PLIK
YOU HAVE TO WAKE UP!
IF YOU DON'T, I WILL CRUSH YOU...
AND WHEN YOU'RE MANGLED ENOUGH TO STOP, I'LL DRAG YOU HOME.

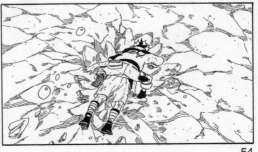

READ THIS WAY

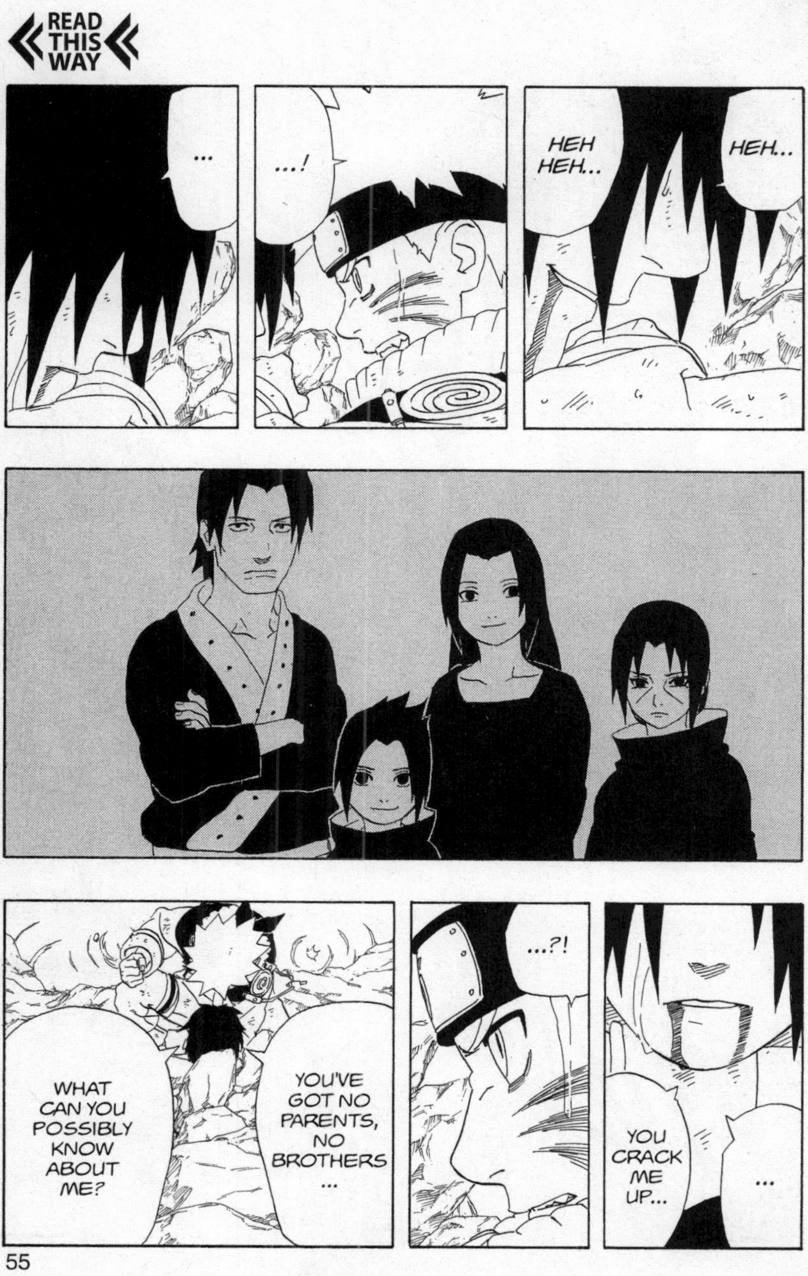
HEH...
HEH HEH...
...!
...
...
YOU CRACK ME UP...
...?!
YOU'VE GOT NO PARENTS, NO BROTHERS...
WHAT CAN YOU POSSIBLY KNOW ABOUT ME?

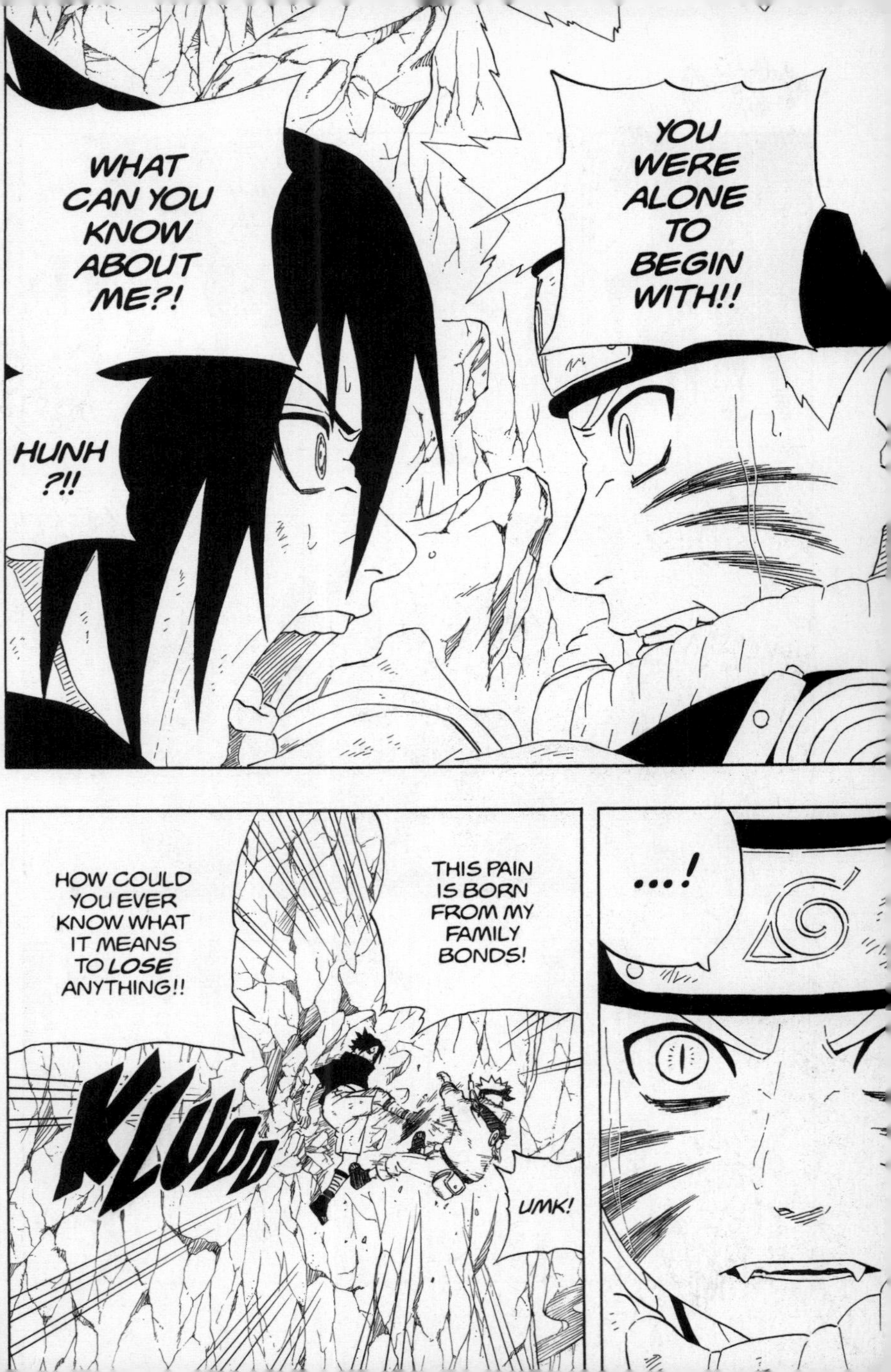

YOU WERE ALONE TO BEGIN WITH!!
WHAT CAN YOU KNOW ABOUT ME?!
HUNH ?!!
...!
THIS PAIN IS BORN FROM MY FAMILY BONDS!
HOW COULD YOU EVER KNOW WHAT IT MEANS TO *LOSE* ANYTHING!!
KLUDD
UMK!

READ THIS WAY

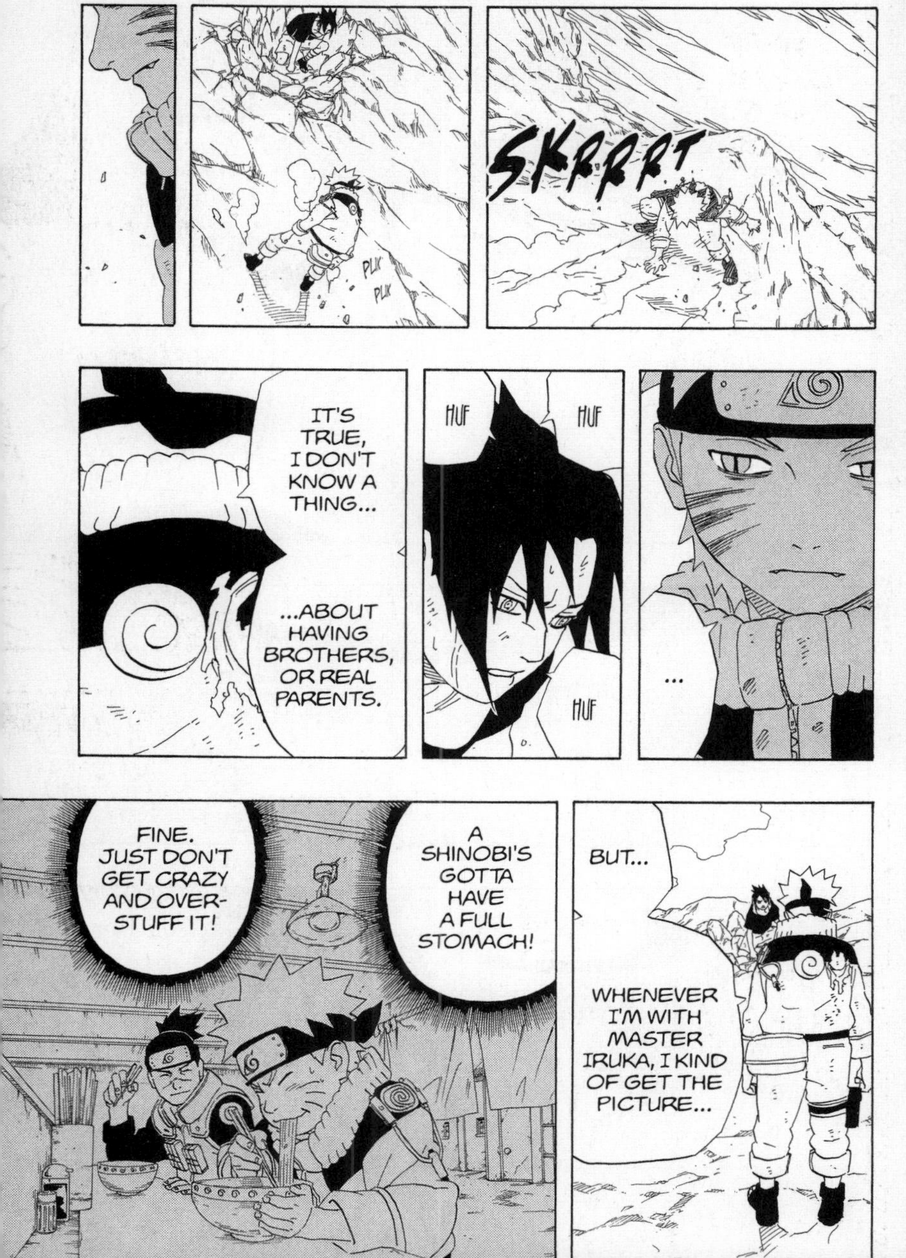
SKRRRT
PLIK
PLIK
...
HUF
HUF
HUF
IT'S TRUE, I DON'T KNOW A THING...
...ABOUT HAVING BROTHERS, OR REAL PARENTS.
BUT...
WHENEVER I'M WITH MASTER IRUKA, I KIND OF GET THE PICTURE...
A SHINOBI'S GOTTA HAVE A FULL STOMACH!
FINE. JUST DON'T GET CRAZY AND OVER-STUFF IT!

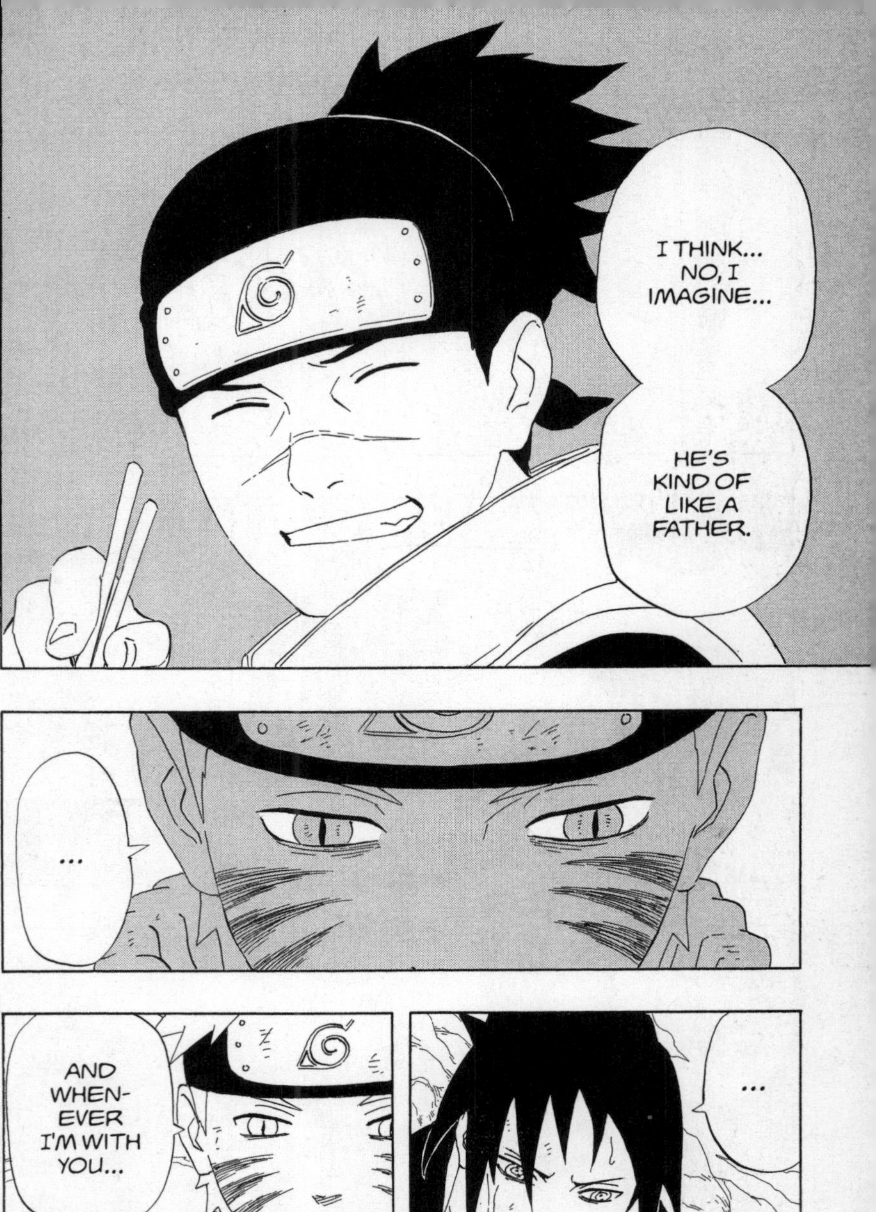
I THINK... NO, I IMAGINE...
HE'S KIND OF LIKE A FATHER.
...
...
AND WHENEVER I'M WITH YOU...

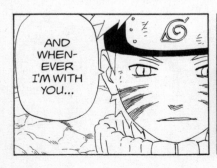

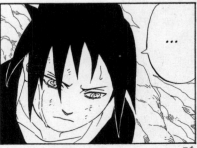

READ THIS WAY

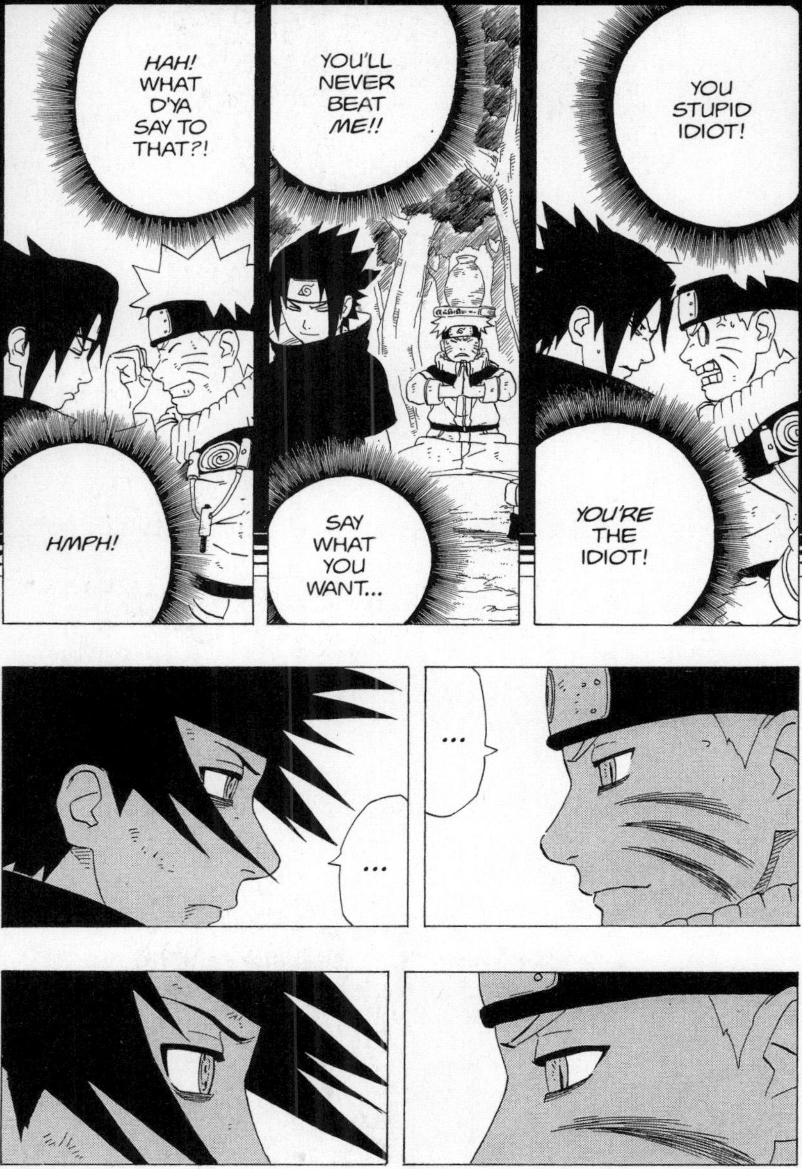
YOU STUPID IDIOT!
YOU'RE THE IDIOT!
YOU'LL NEVER BEAT ME!!
SAY WHAT YOU WANT...
HAH! WHAT D'YA SAY TO THAT?!
HMPH!
...
...

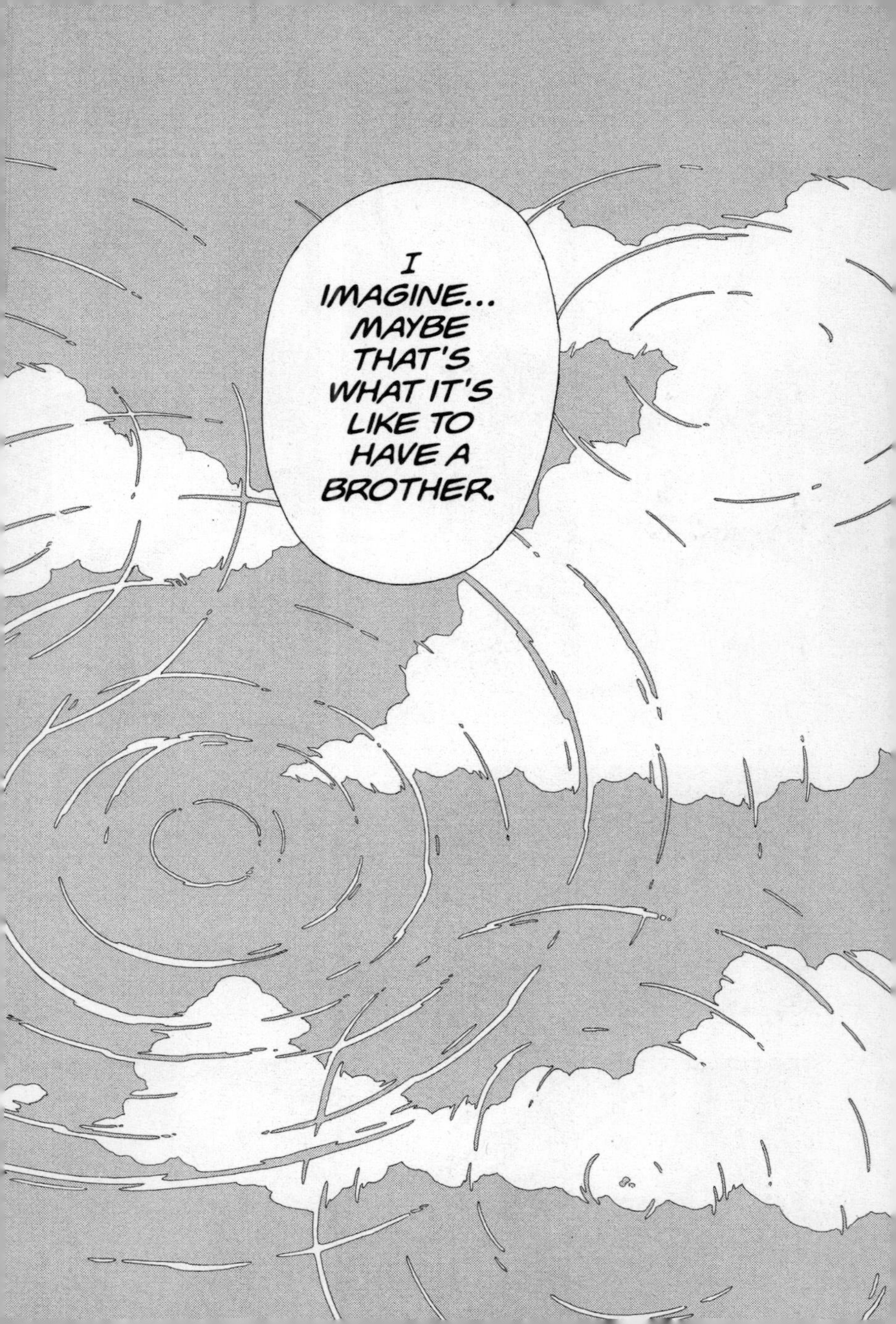
I IMAGINE... MAYBE THAT'S WHAT IT'S LIKE TO HAVE A BROTHER.

...

WHY?

...

!

WHY DO YOU WASTE SO MUCH EFFORT ON... ME?

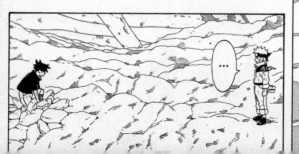

...

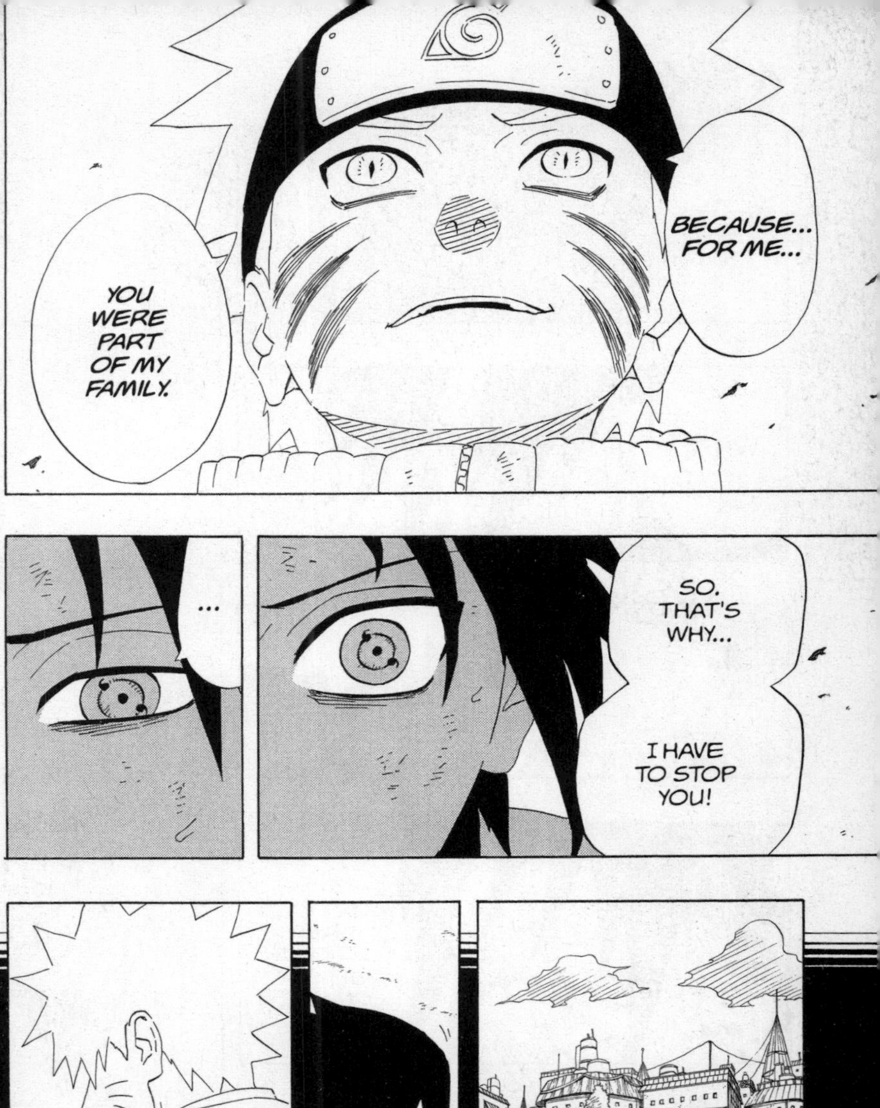
BECAUSE... FOR ME...
YOU WERE PART OF MY FAMILY.
SO. THAT'S WHY...
I HAVE TO STOP YOU!
...
PEEK

SHKK

...

...!

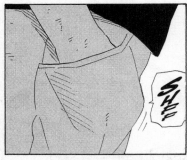

SHFF

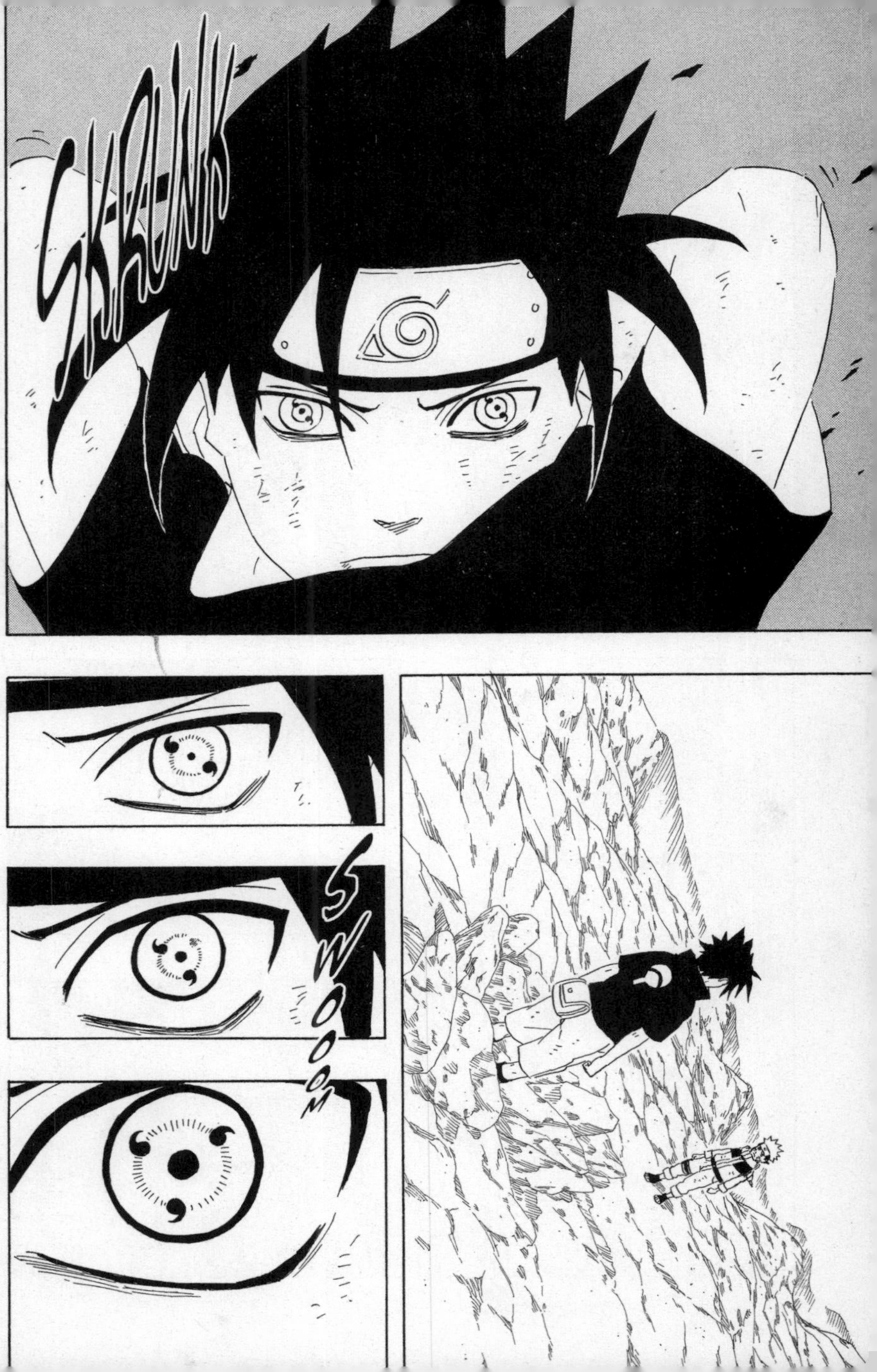
SWOOOOM

READ THIS WAY

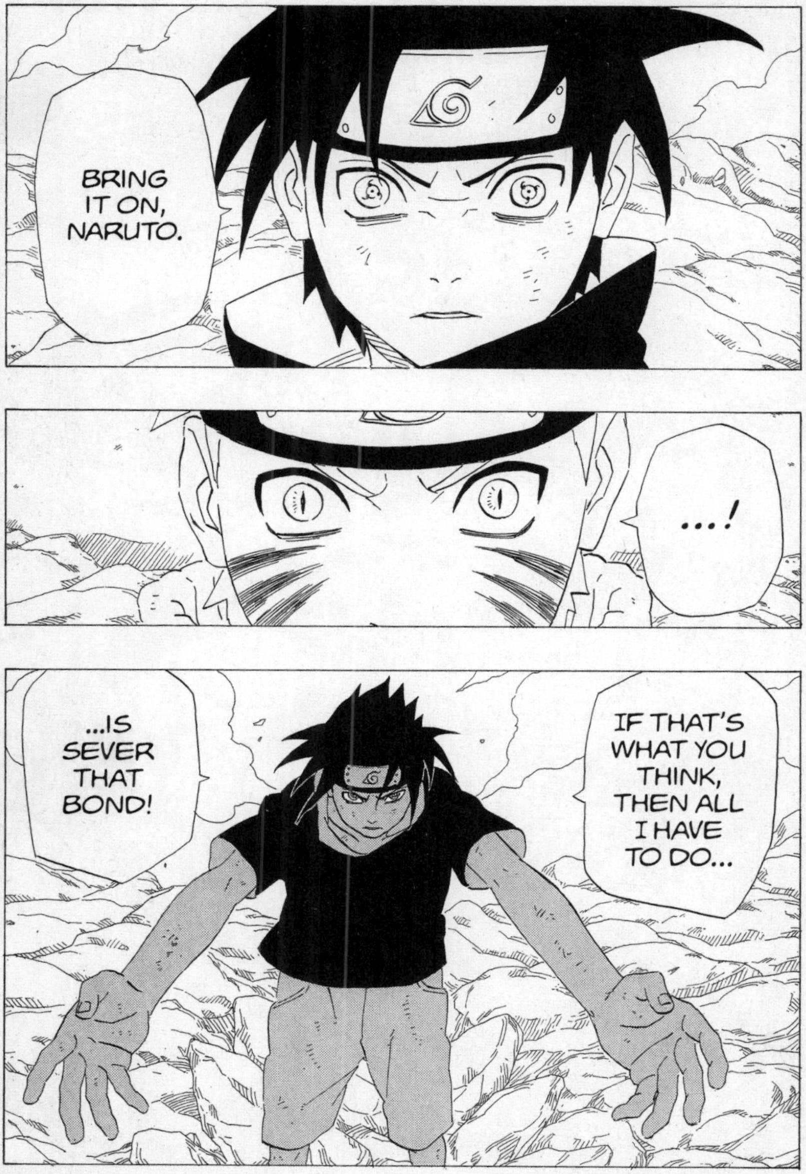
BRING IT ON, NARUTO.
...!
IF THAT'S WHAT YOU THINK, THEN ALL I HAVE TO DO...
...IS SEVER THAT BOND!

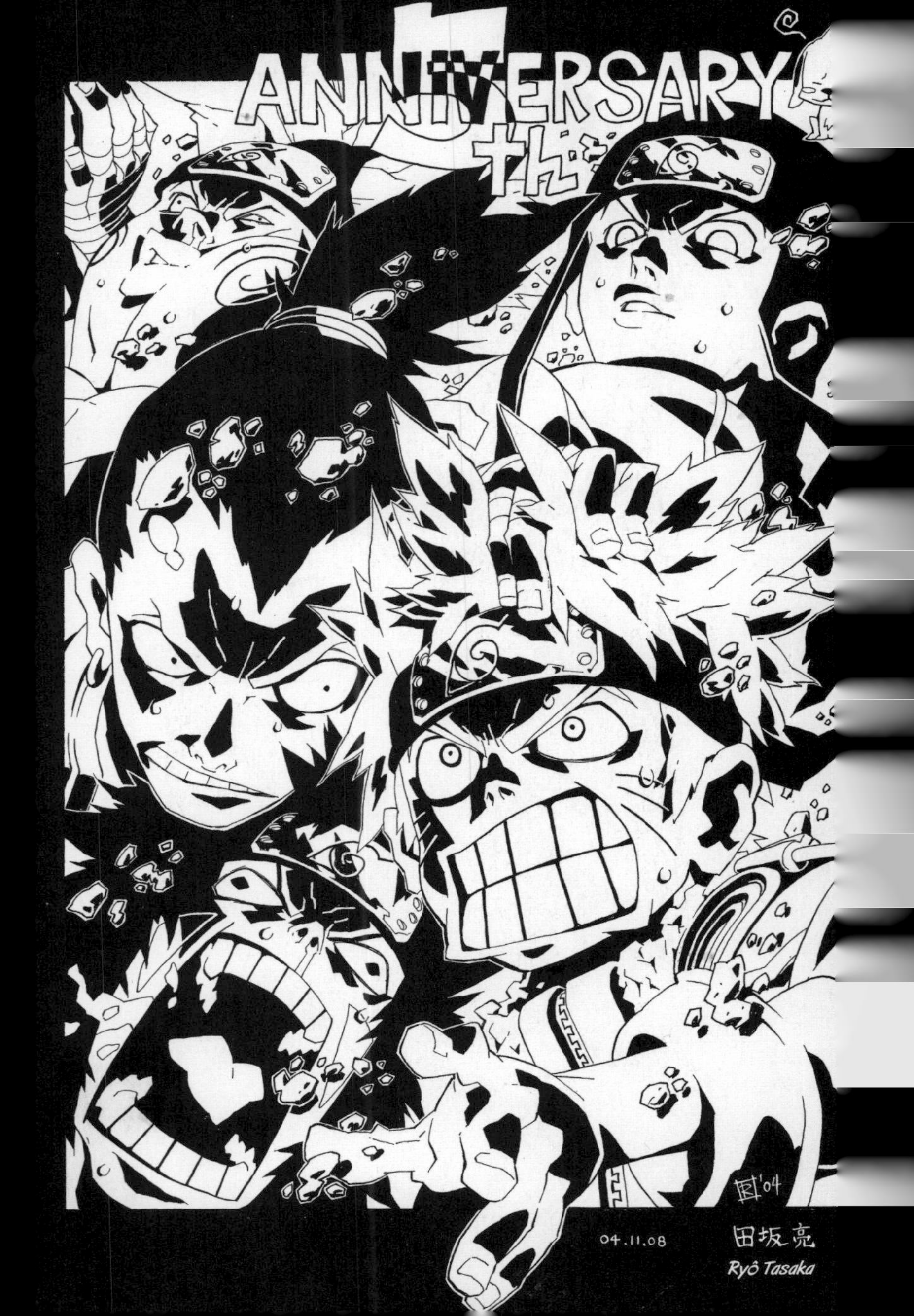
ANNIVERSARY
'04

04.11.08

田坂亮
Ryô Tasaka

Number 230: Awakening!!

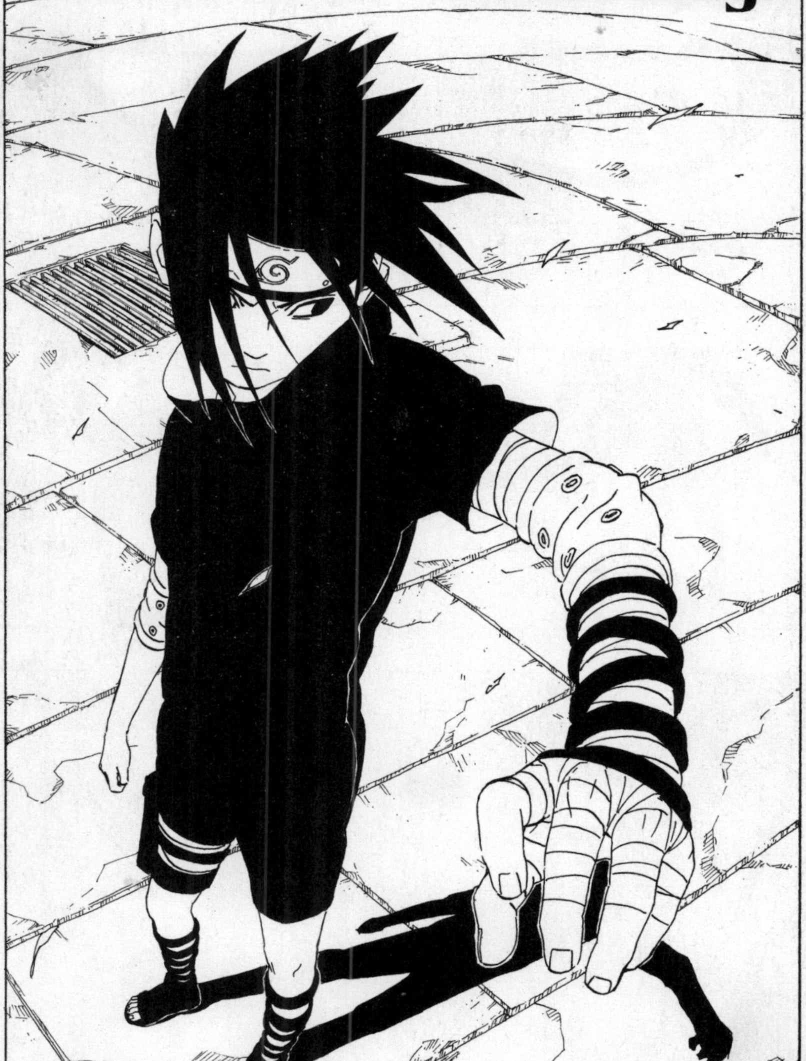

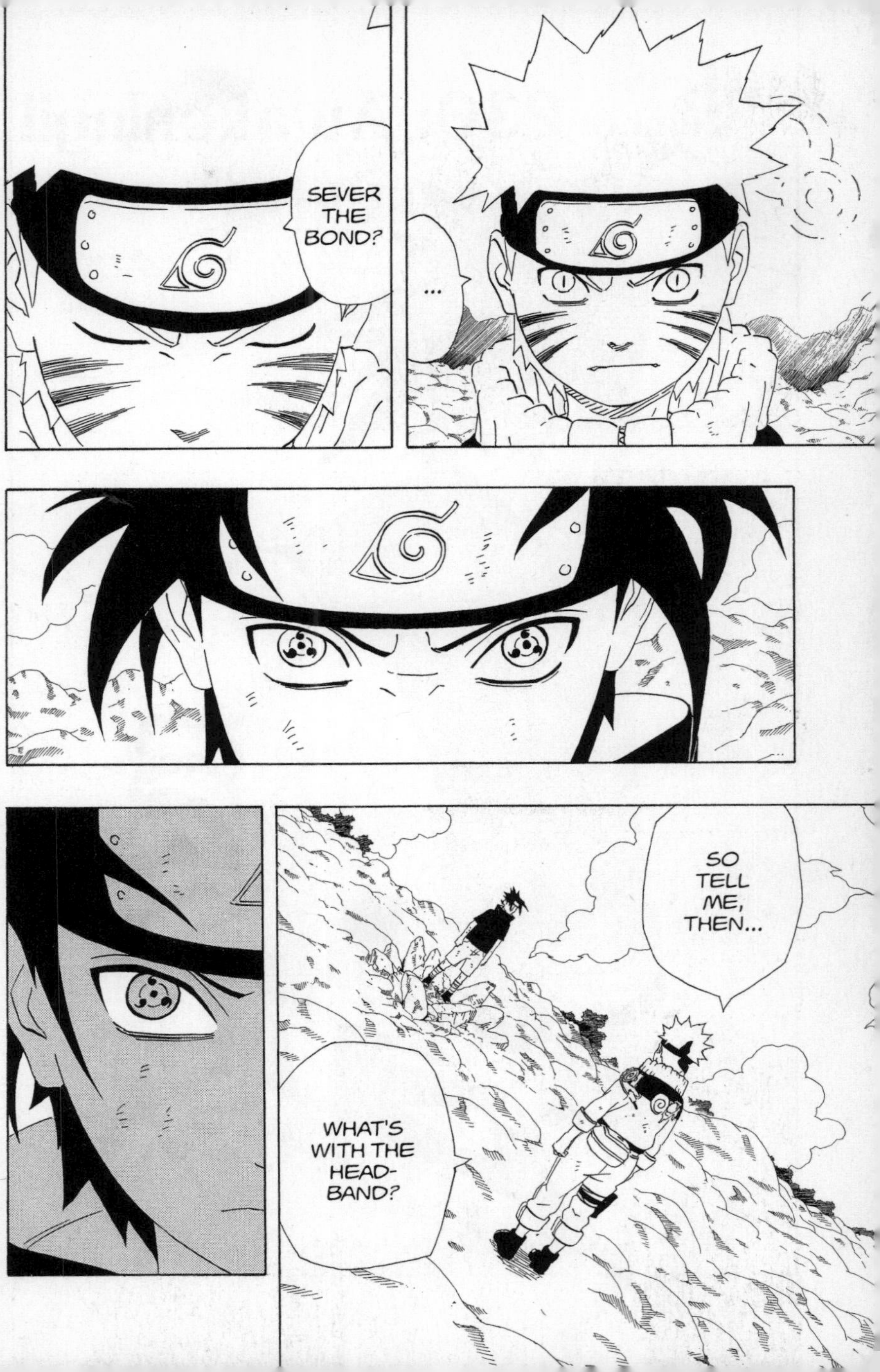
...
SEVER THE BOND?
SO TELL ME, THEN...
WHAT'S WITH THE HEAD-BAND?

READ THIS WAY

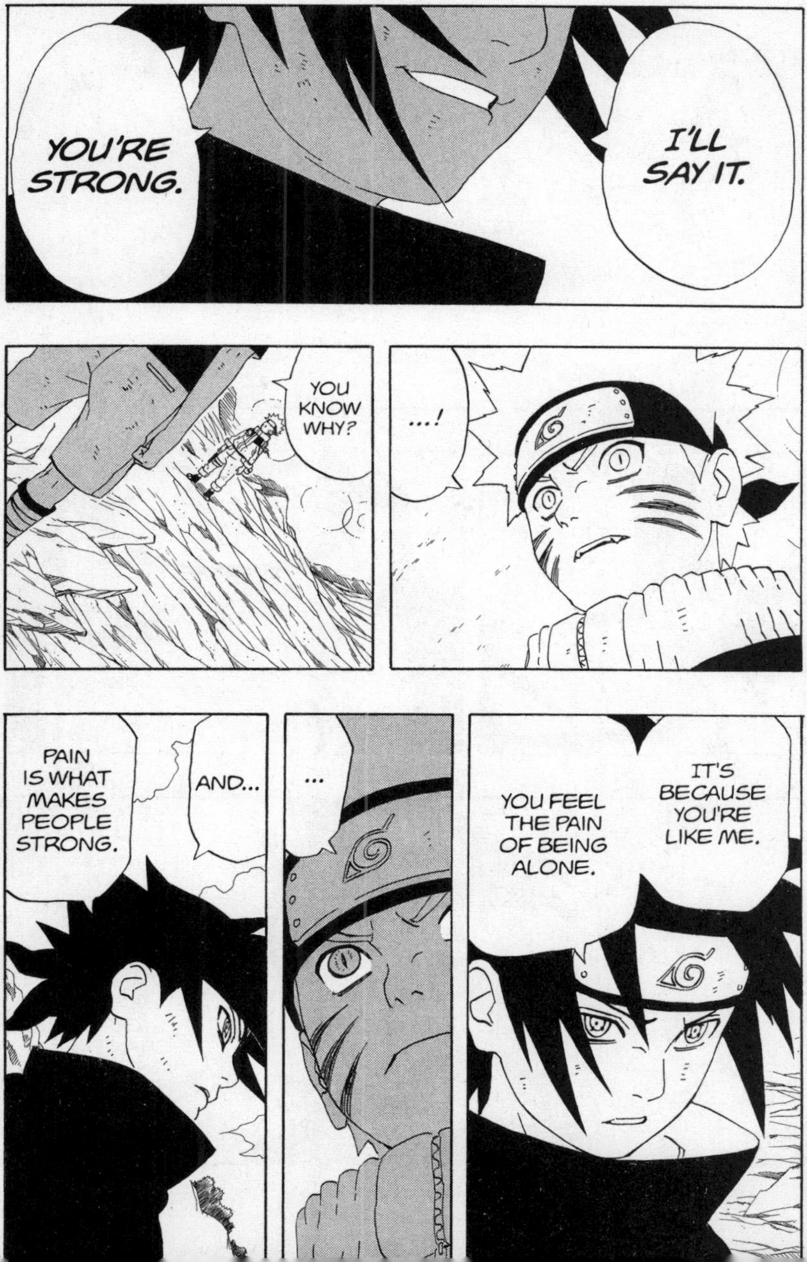

I'LL SAY IT.
YOU'RE STRONG.
...!
YOU KNOW WHY?
IT'S BECAUSE YOU'RE LIKE ME.
YOU FEEL THE PAIN OF BEING ALONE.
...
AND...
PAIN IS WHAT MAKES PEOPLE STRONG.

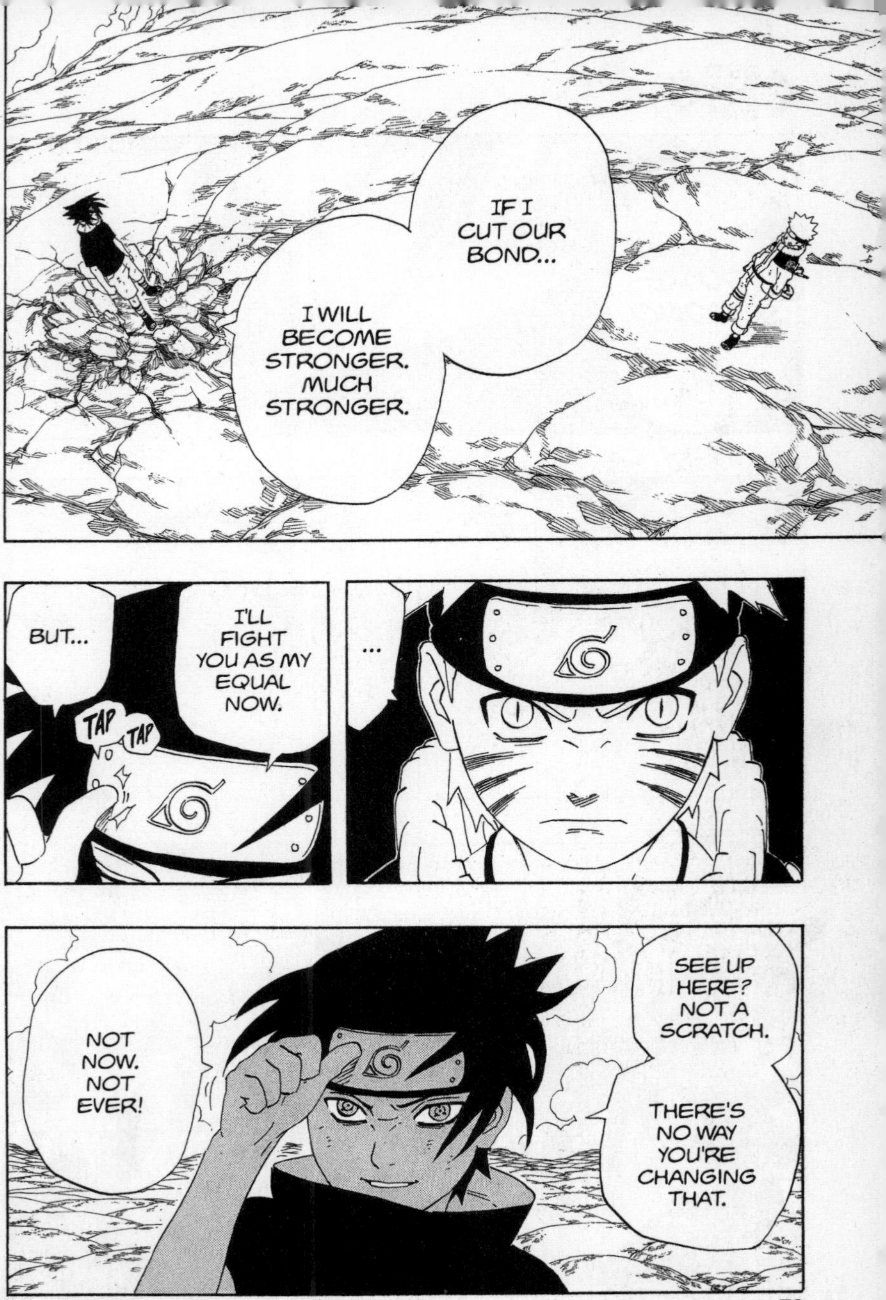
IF I CUT OUR BOND...
I WILL BECOME STRONGER. MUCH STRONGER.
...
BUT...
I'LL FIGHT YOU AS MY EQUAL NOW.
TAP
TAP
SEE UP HERE? NOT A SCRATCH.
THERE'S NO WAY YOU'RE CHANGING THAT.
NOT NOW. NOT EVER!

SASUKE
...

NOTHING I SAY'S GONNA SWAY YOU, IS IT...?

YEAH, WE'RE DONE CHATTING. ALL WE HAVE LEFT...

...IS THE FIGHT.

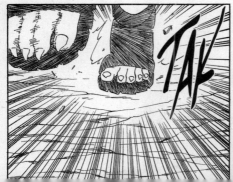

TAK

SO I SAID BRING IT ON.

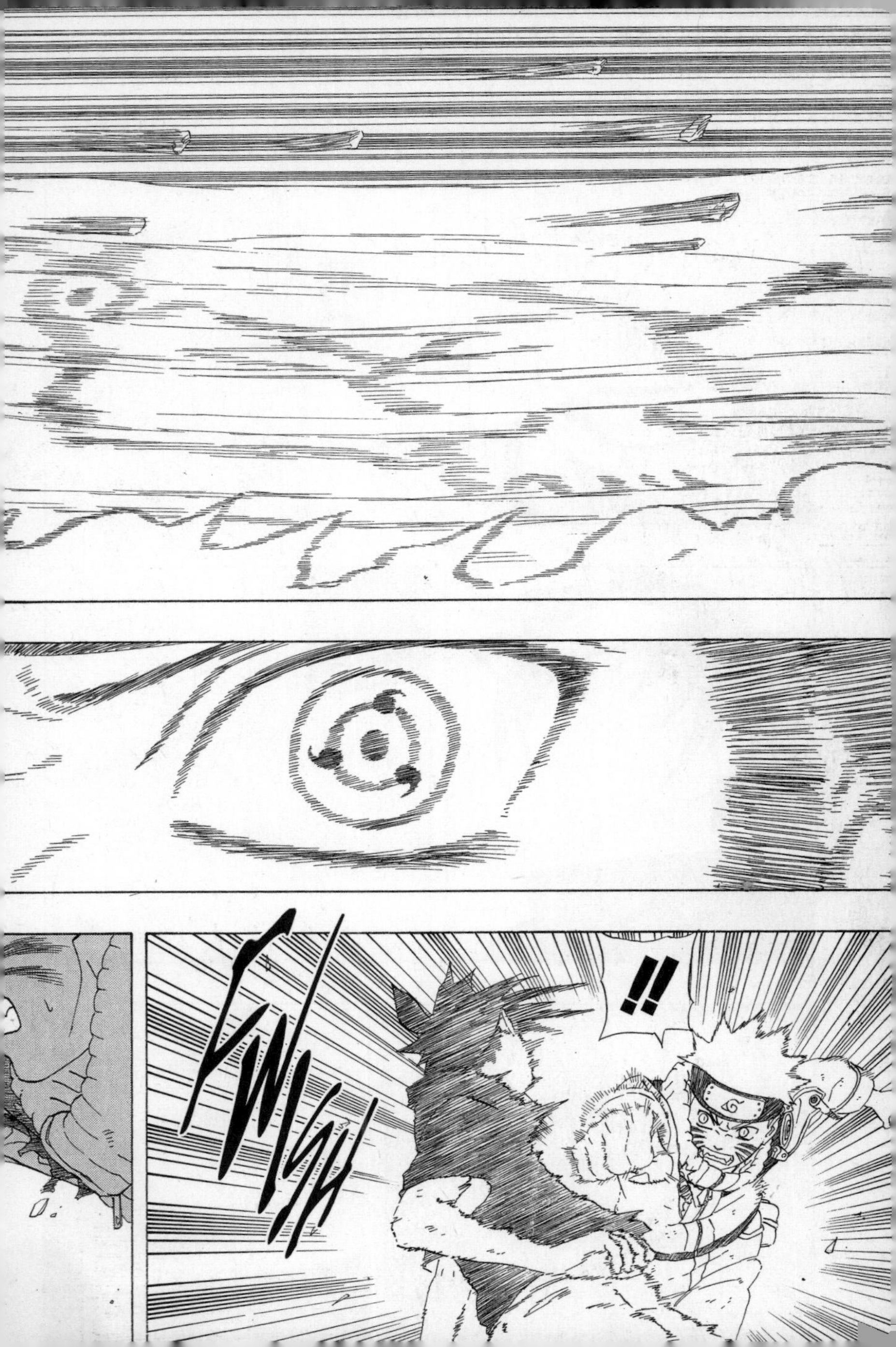
!!
SWISH

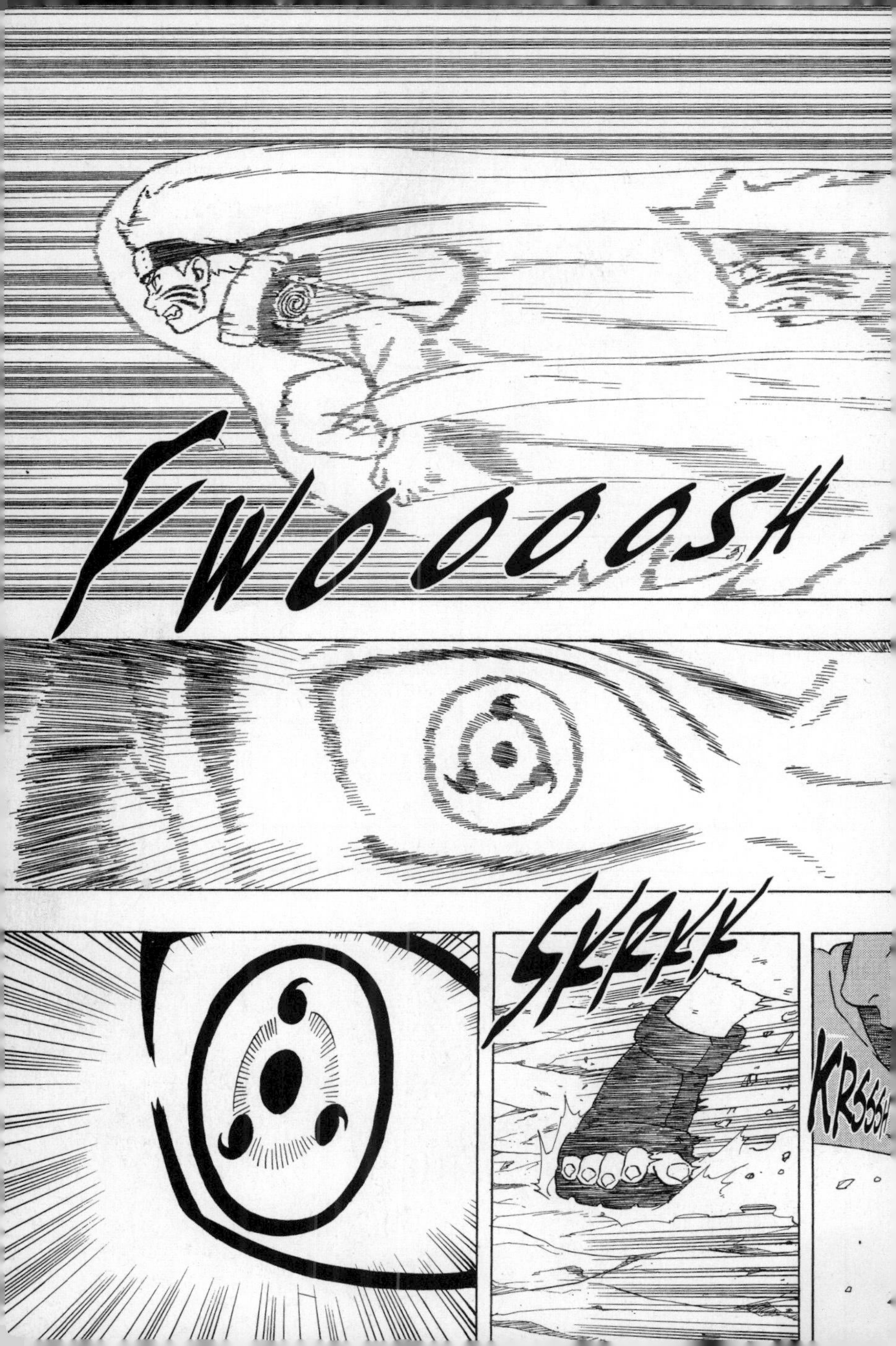
FWOOOOSH
KRSSSH
SKRKK

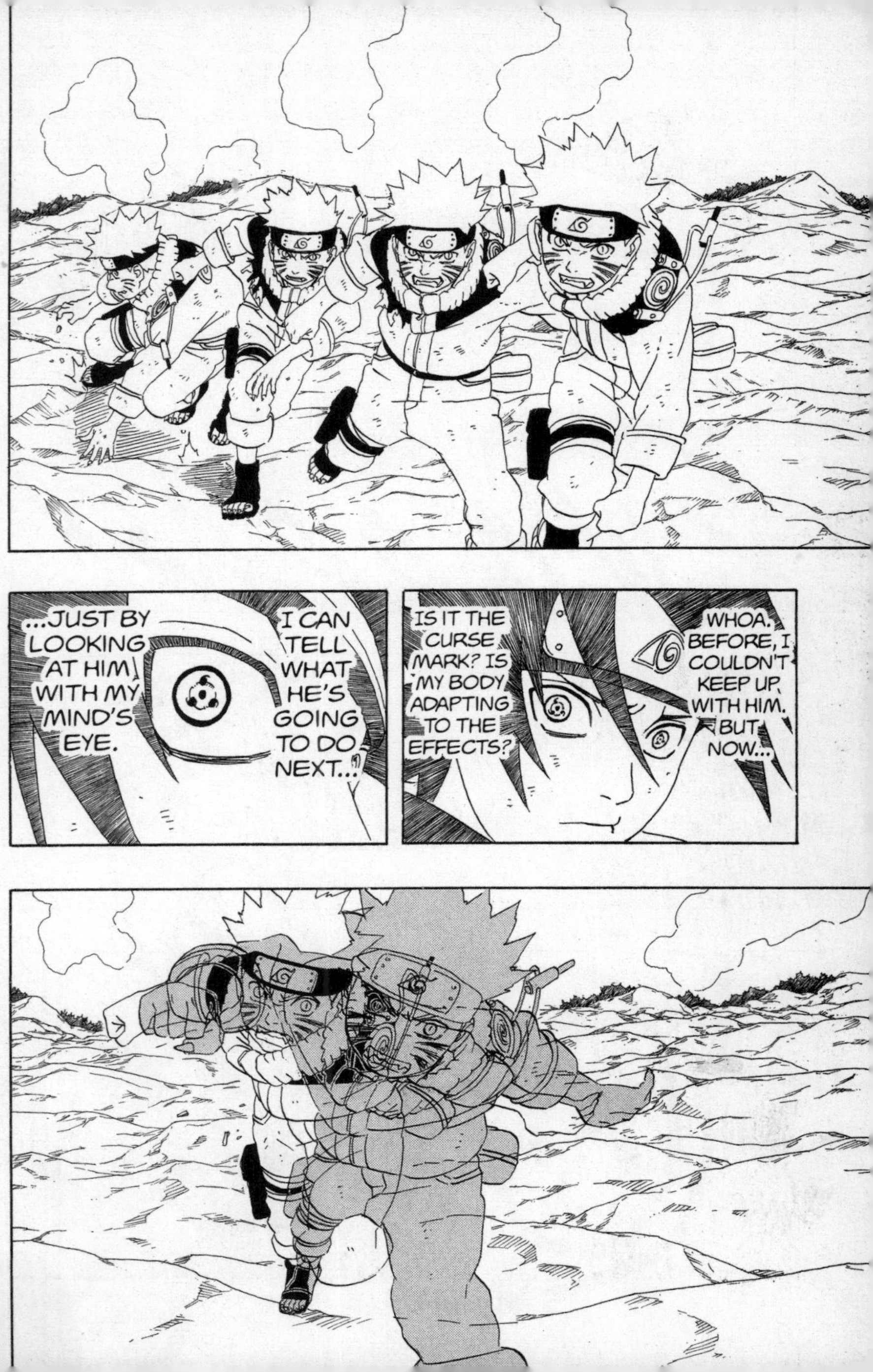
WHOA. BEFORE, I COULDN'T KEEP UP WITH HIM. BUT NOW...
IS IT THE CURSE MARK? IS MY BODY ADAPTING TO THE EFFECTS?
I CAN TELL WHAT HE'S GOING TO DO NEXT...
...JUST BY LOOKING AT HIM WITH MY MIND'S EYE.

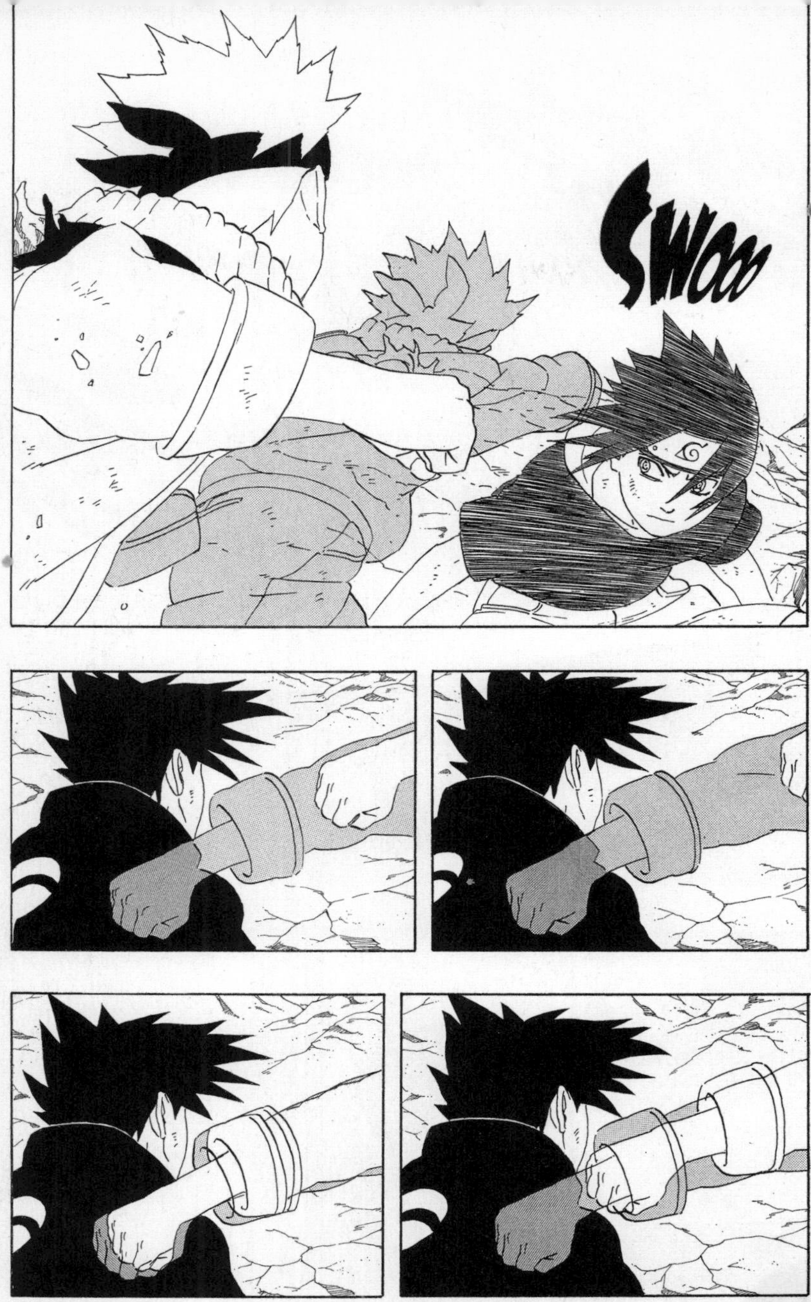
SWOOO

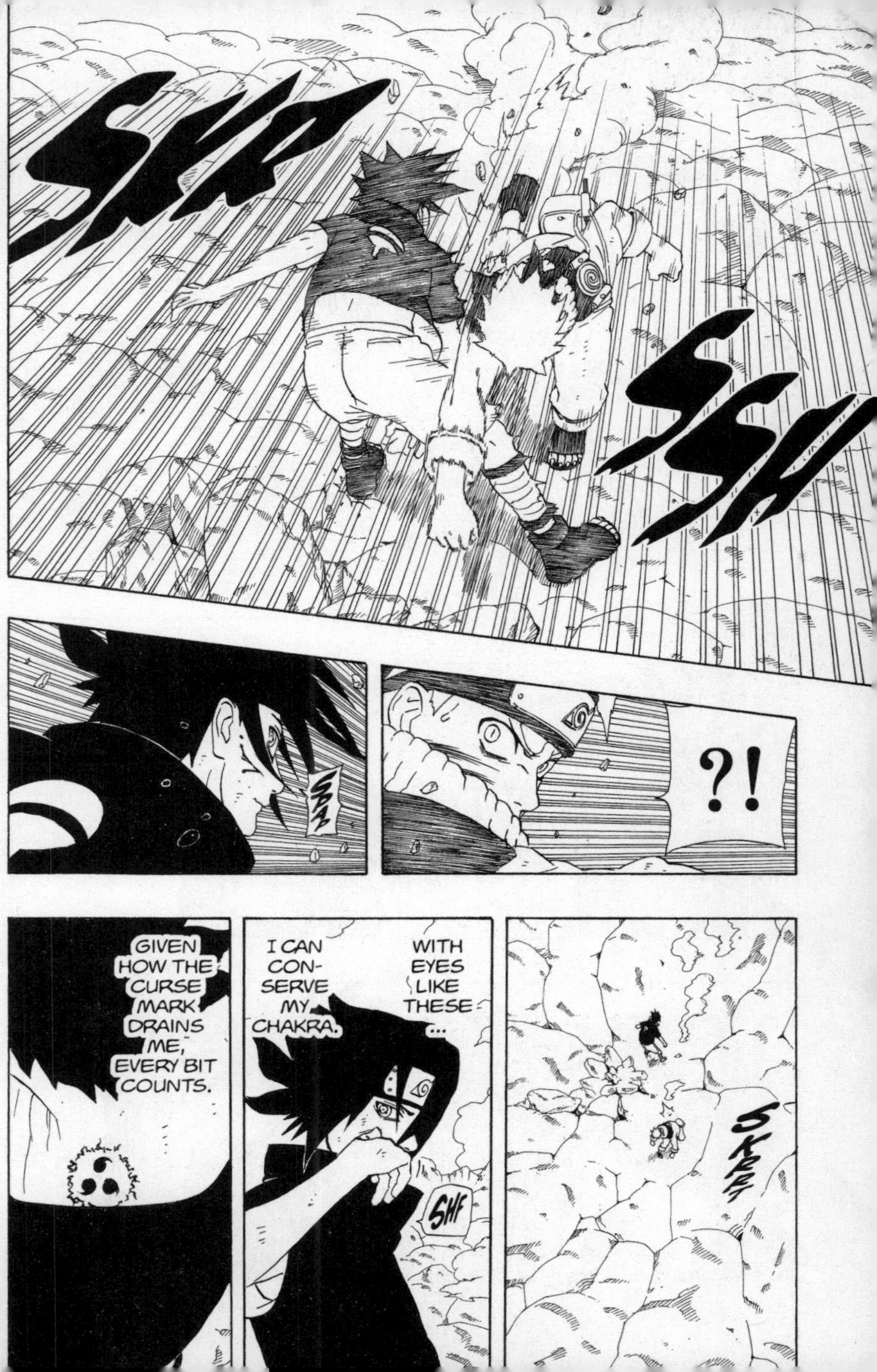
SSH
?!
WITH EYES LIKE THESE...
I CAN CON-SERVE MY CHAKRA.
SHF
GIVEN HOW THE CURSE MARK DRAINS ME, EVERY BIT COUNTS.

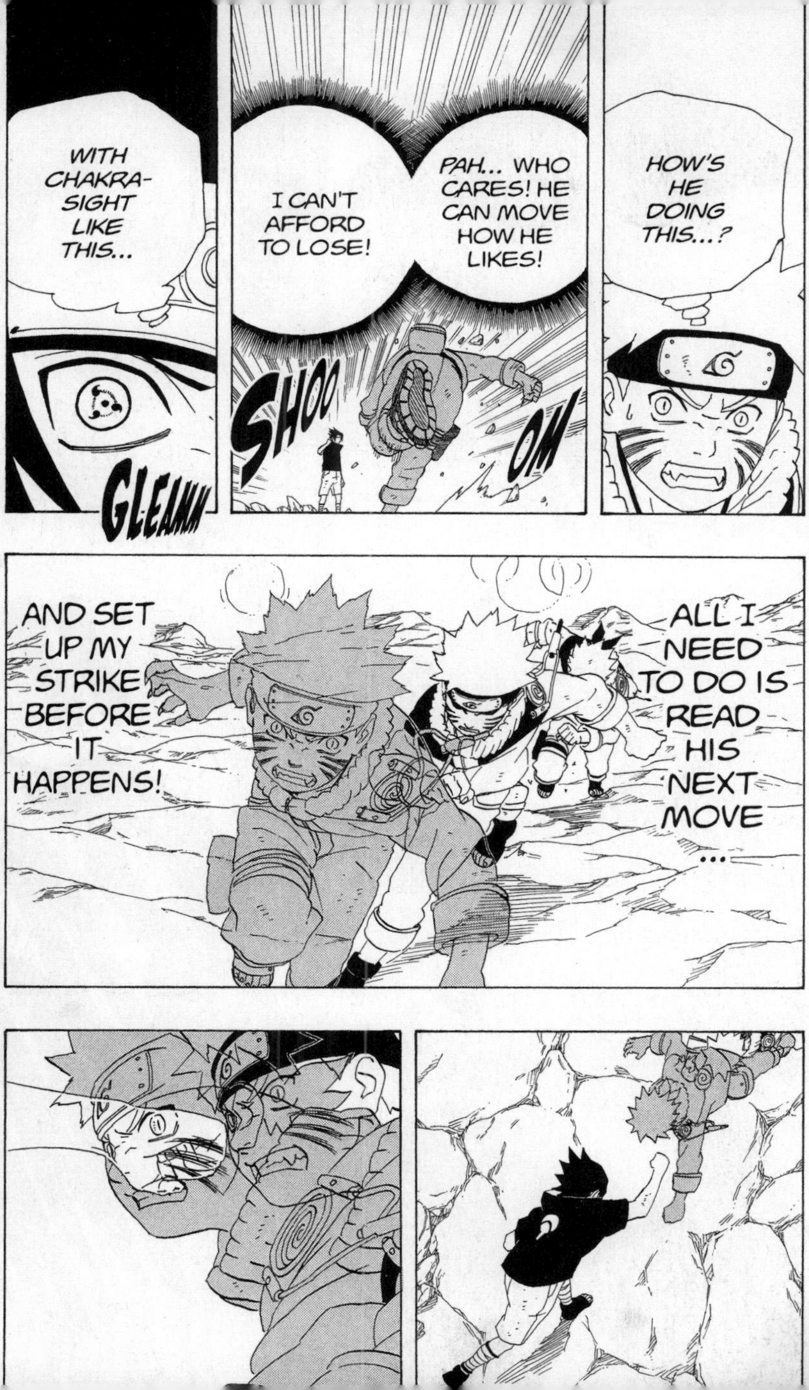
HOW'S HE DOING THIS...?
PAH... WHO CARES! HE CAN MOVE HOW HE LIKES!
I CAN'T AFFORD TO LOSE!
SHOOOM
WITH CHAKRA-SIGHT LIKE THIS...
GLEAMM
ALL I NEED TO DO IS READ HIS NEXT MOVE...
AND SET UP MY STRIKE BEFORE IT HAPPENS!

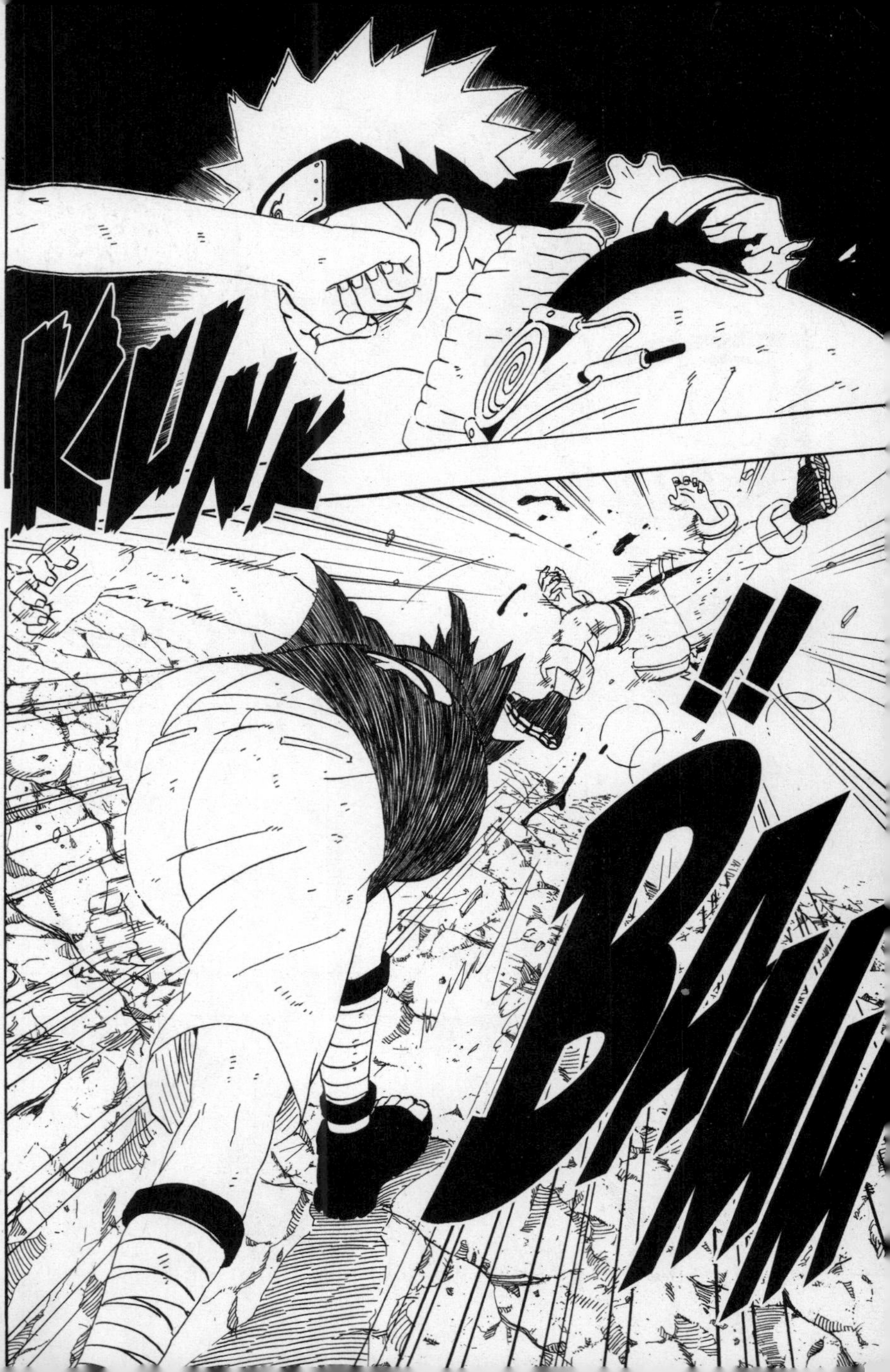
KLUNK
!!
BA

READ THIS WAY

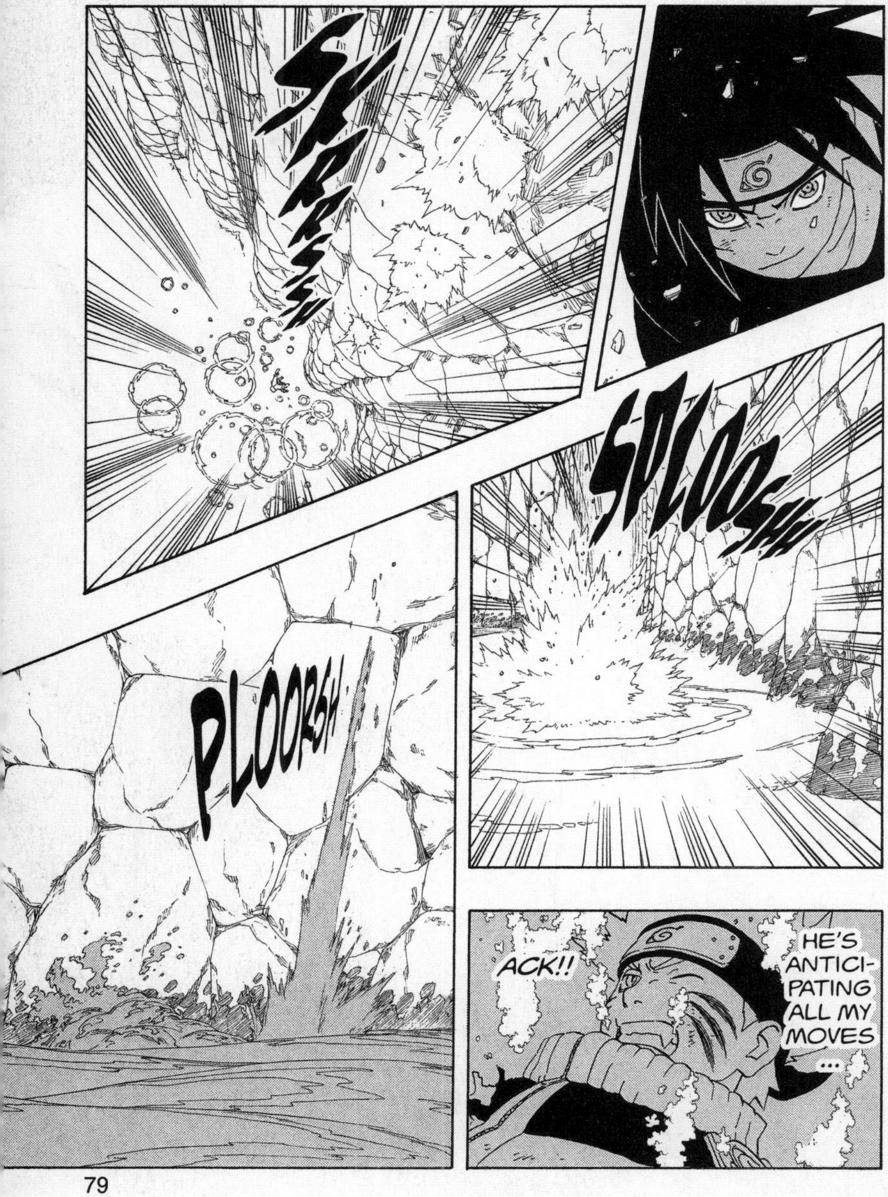
SPLOOSH
PLOORSH
HE'S ANTICI-PATING ALL MY MOVES...
ACK!!

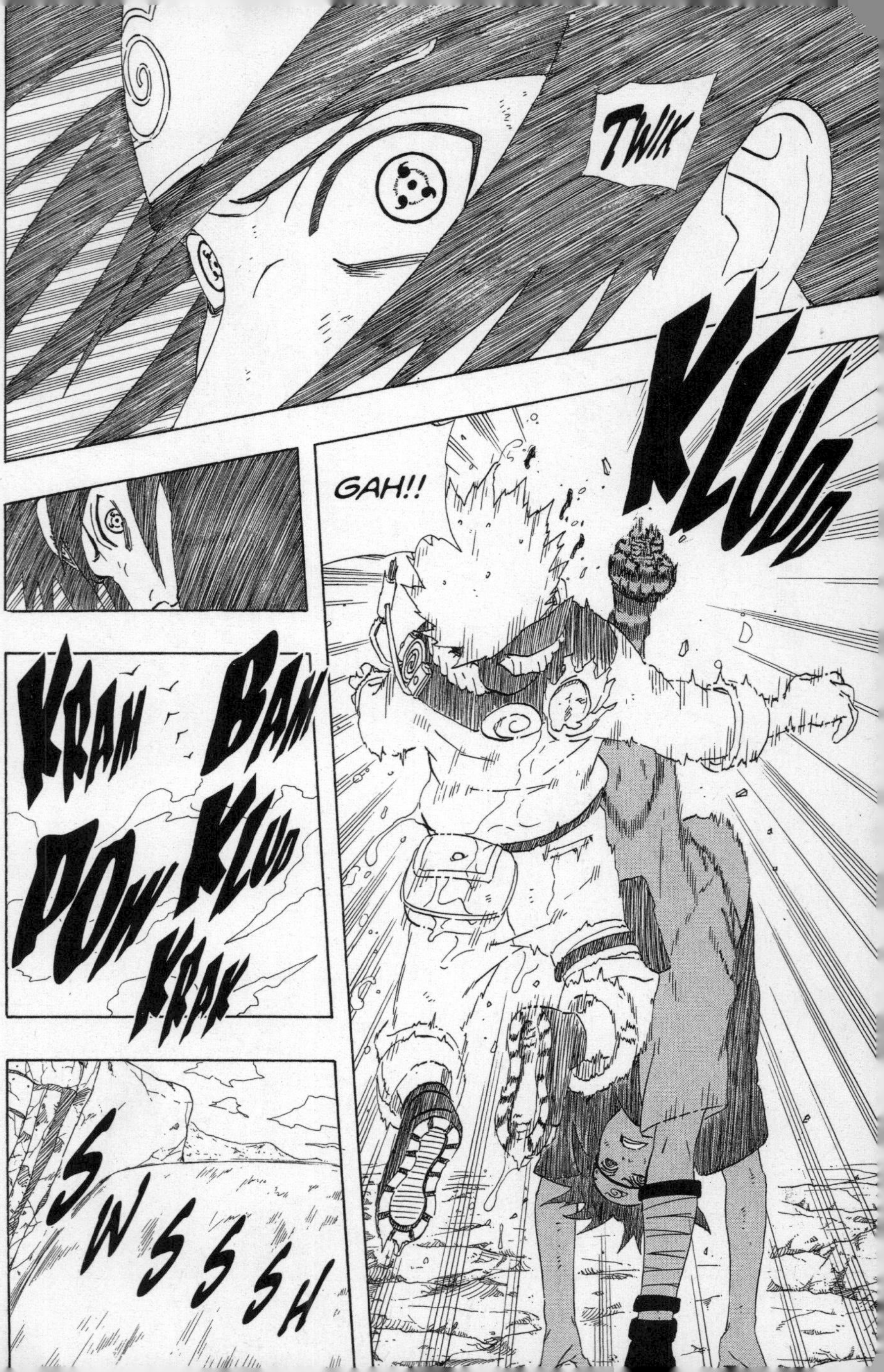
TWIK
KLUD
GAH!!
BAM
KRAM
KLUD
POW
KRAK
SWSSSH

READ THIS WAY

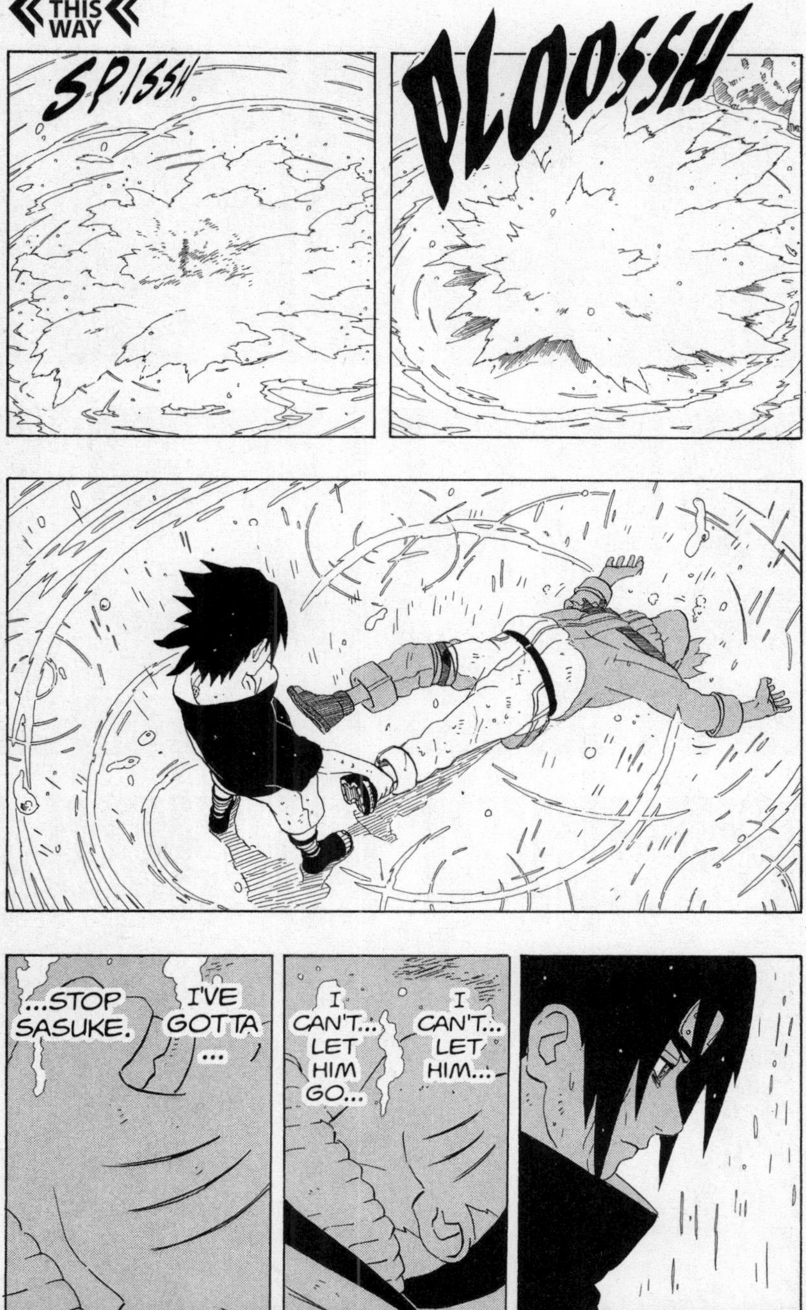
PLOOSSH
SPISSH
I CAN'T... LET HIM...
I CAN'T... LET HIM GO...
I'VE GOTTA ...
...STOP SASUKE.

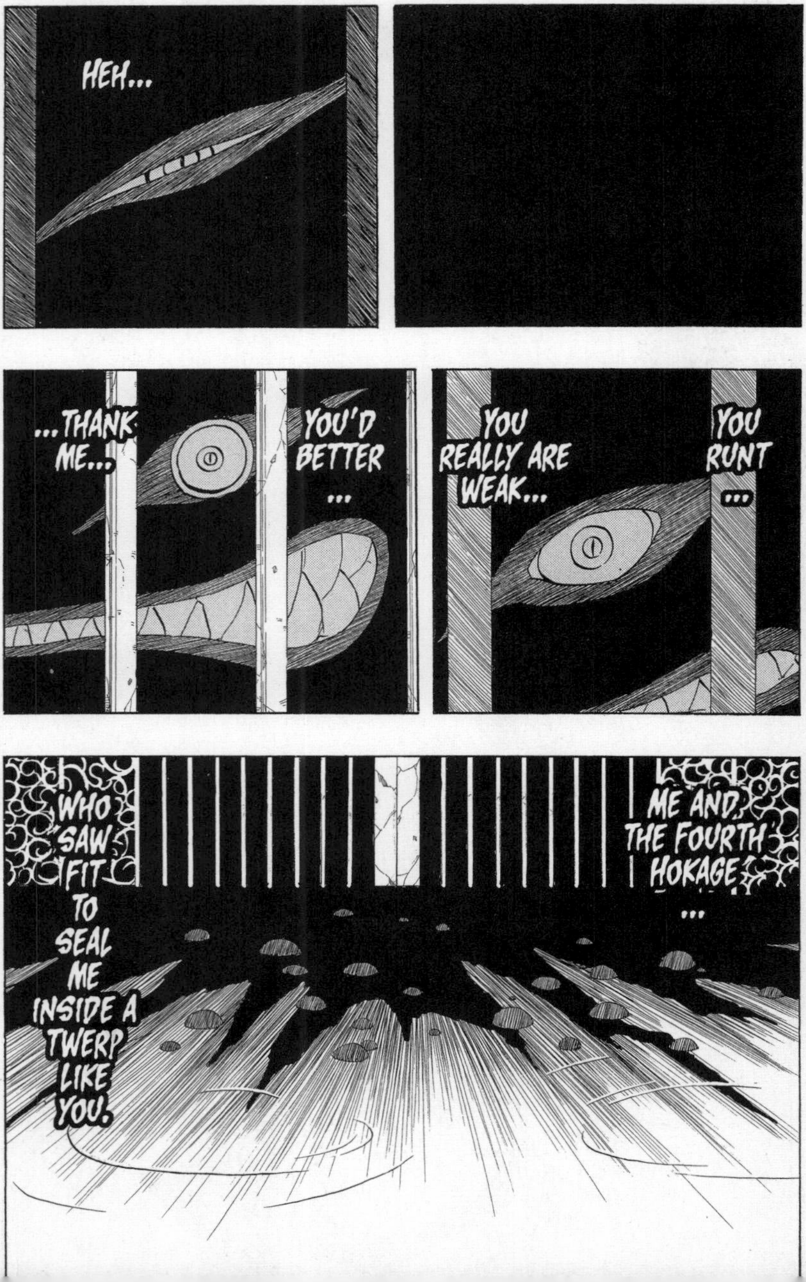
HEH...
YOU RUNT...
YOU REALLY ARE WEAK...
YOU'D BETTER...
...THANK ME...
ME AND THE FOURTH HOKAGE...
WHO SAW FIT TO SEAL ME INSIDE A TWERP LIKE YOU.

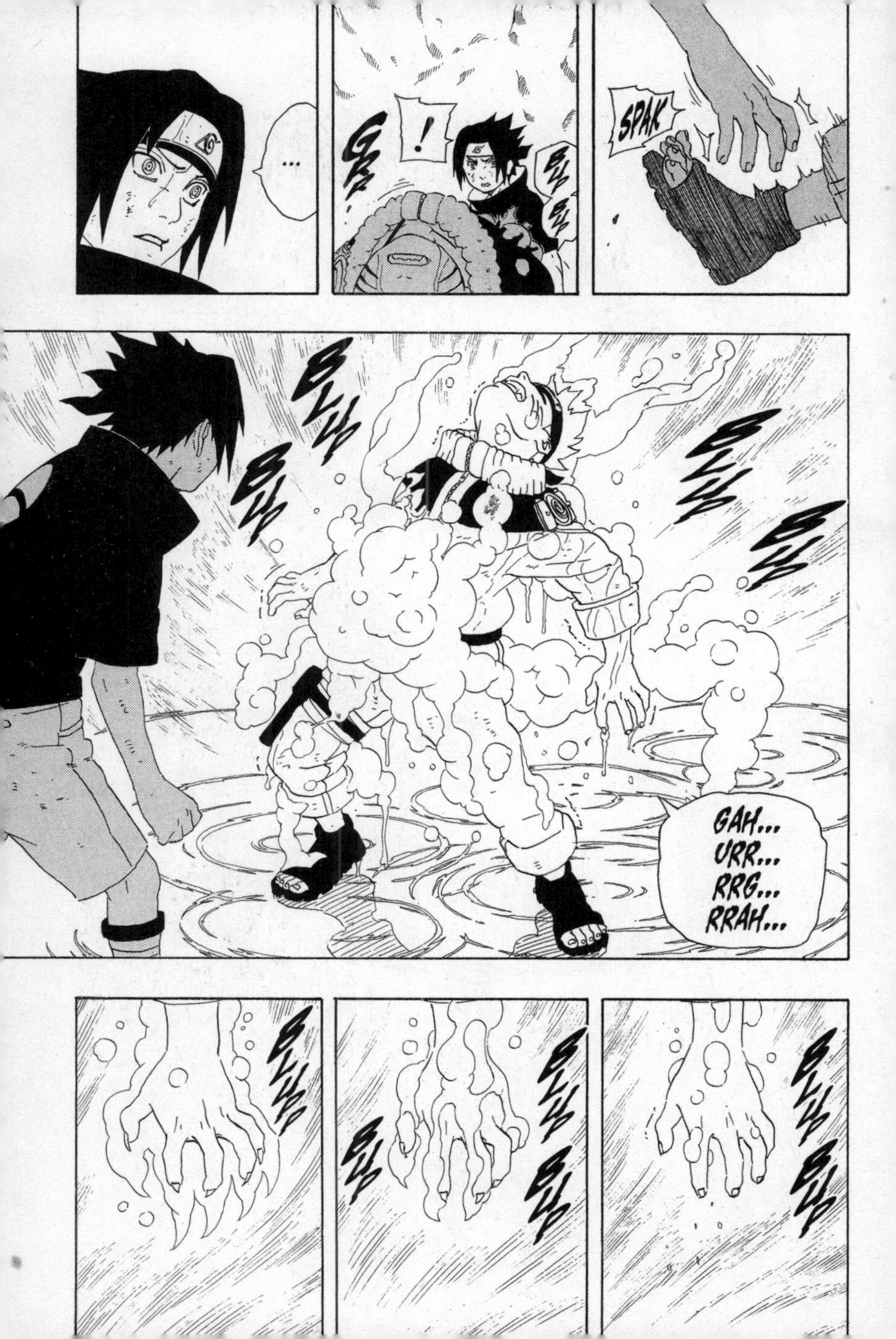
SPAK
!
...
GAH... URR... RRG... RRAH...

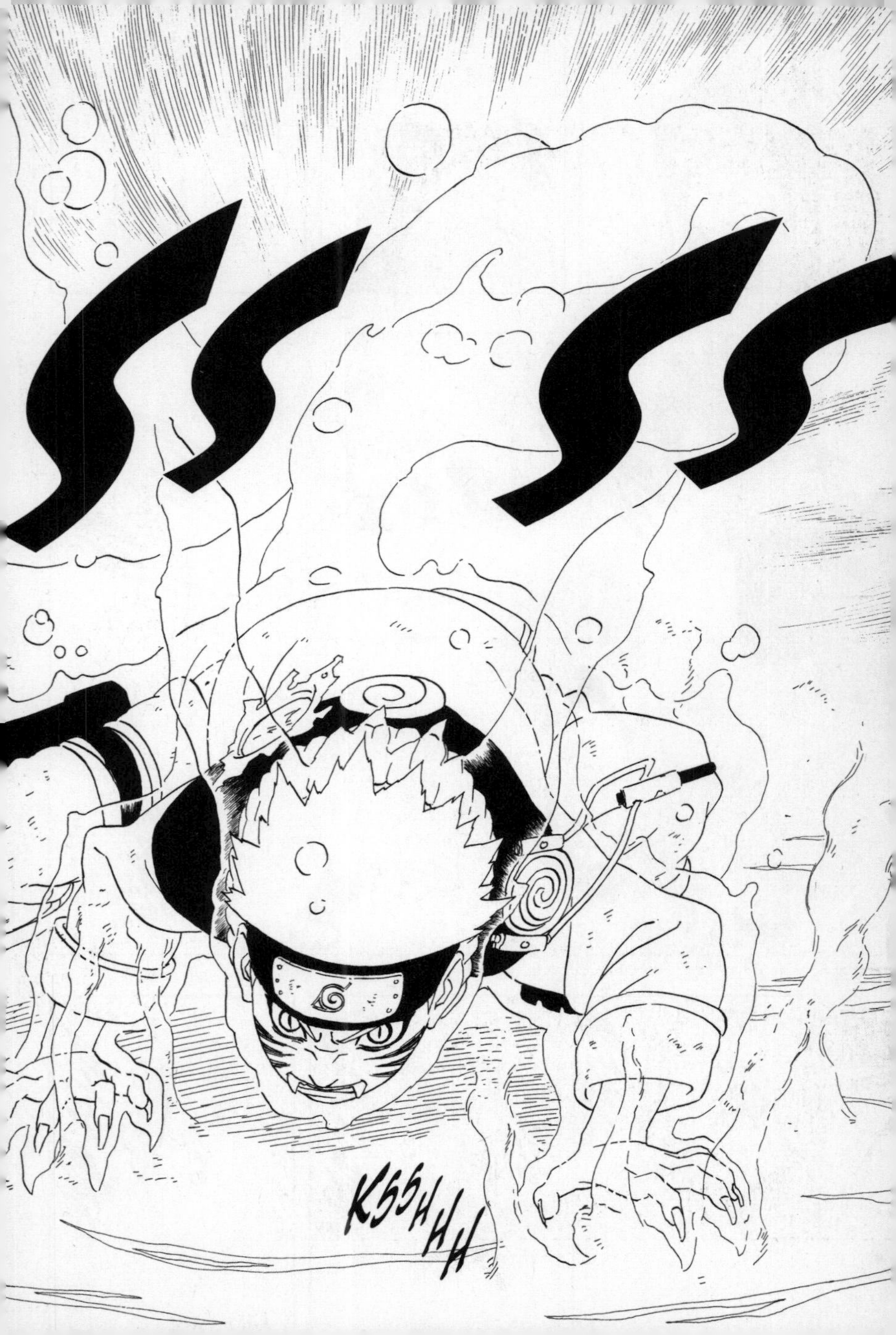
SSSSS
KSSHHH

READ THIS WAY

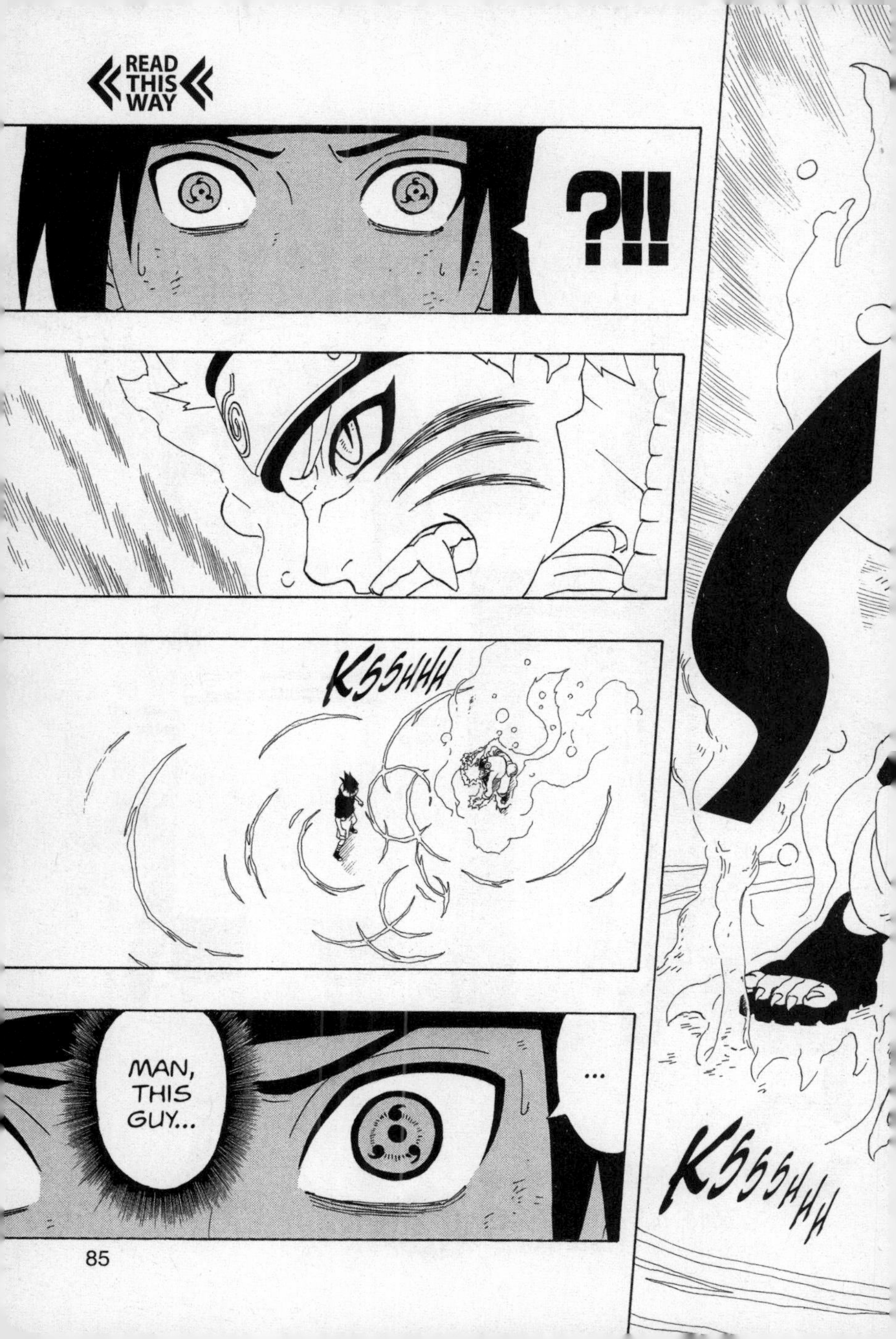
KSSSHHH
?!!
KSSHHH
...
MAN, THIS GUY...

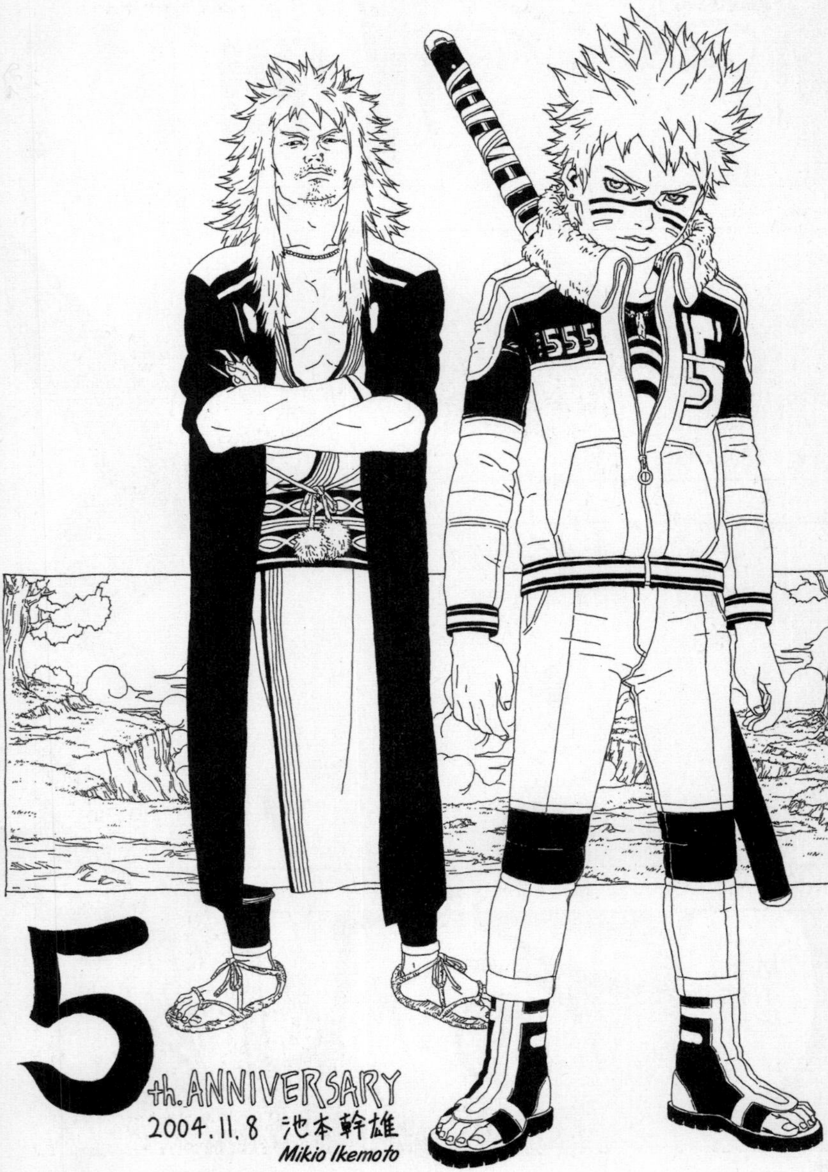
555
5th. ANNIVERSARY
2004.11.8 池本幹雄
Mikio Ikemoto

Number 231: Special!!

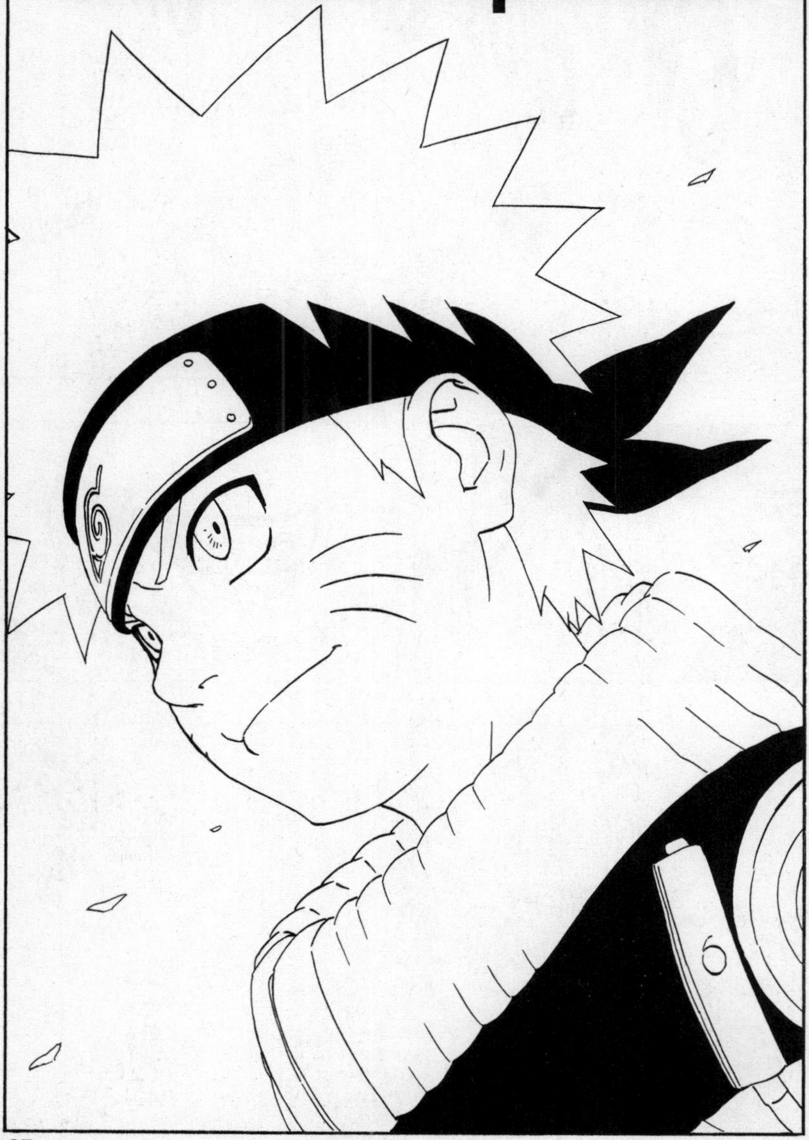

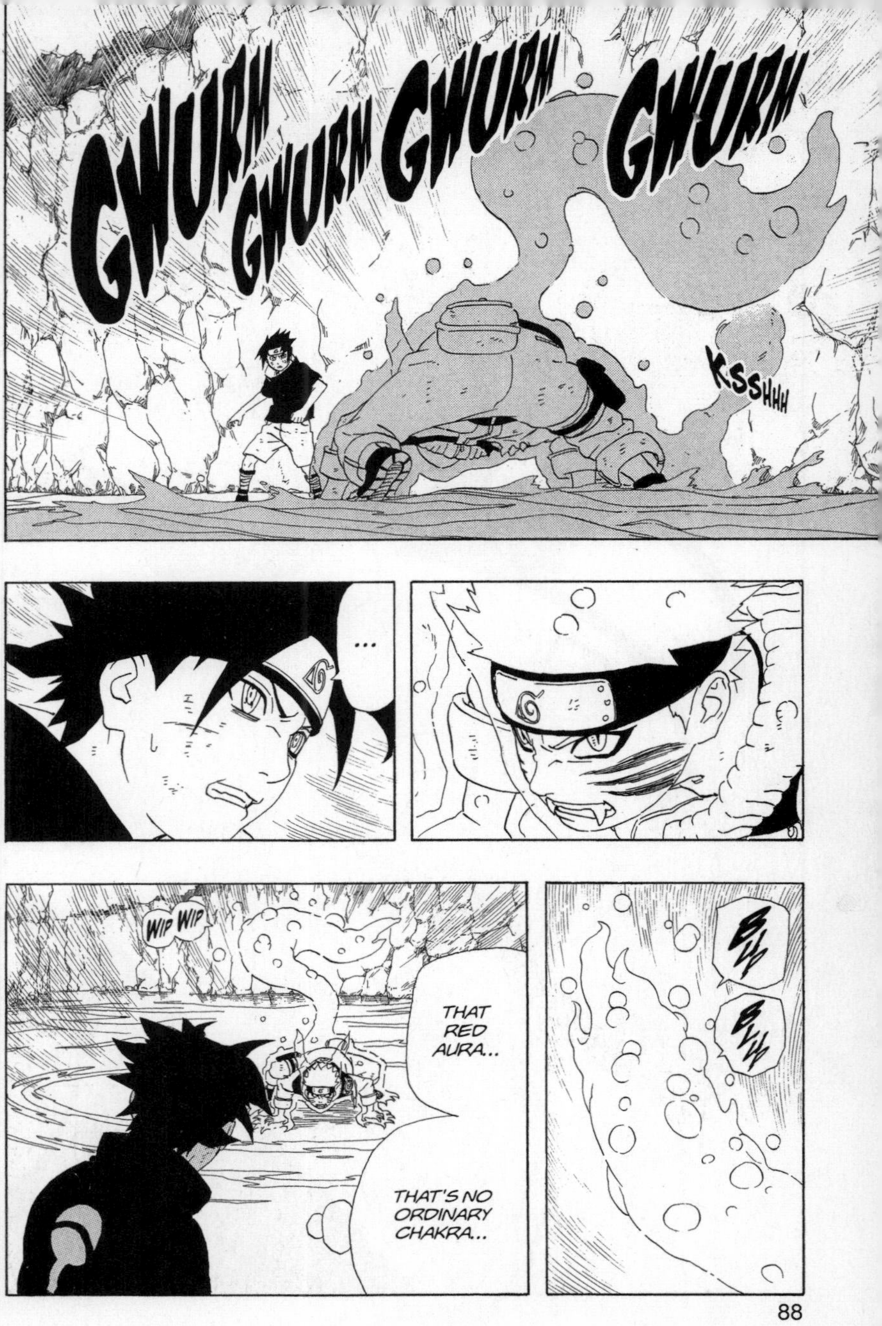
GWURM
GWURM
GWURM
GWURM
K-SSHHH
...
WIP WIP
THAT RED AURA...
THAT'S NO ORDINARY CHAKRA...

READ THIS WAY

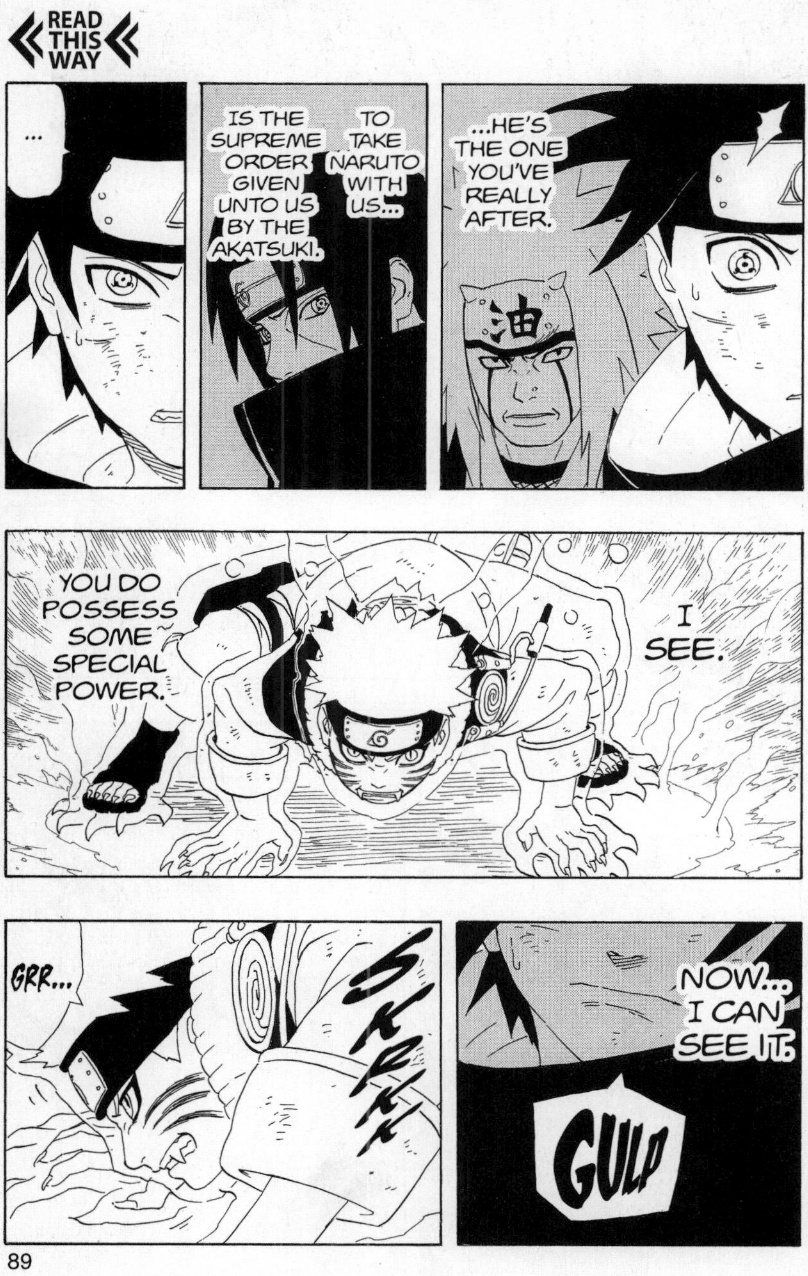

...HE'S THE ONE YOU'VE REALLY AFTER.
TO TAKE NARUTO WITH US...
IS THE SUPREME ORDER GIVEN UNTO US BY THE AKATSUKI.
...
I SEE.
YOU DO POSSESS SOME SPECIAL POWER.
NOW... I CAN SEE IT.
GULP
SKRKK
GRR...

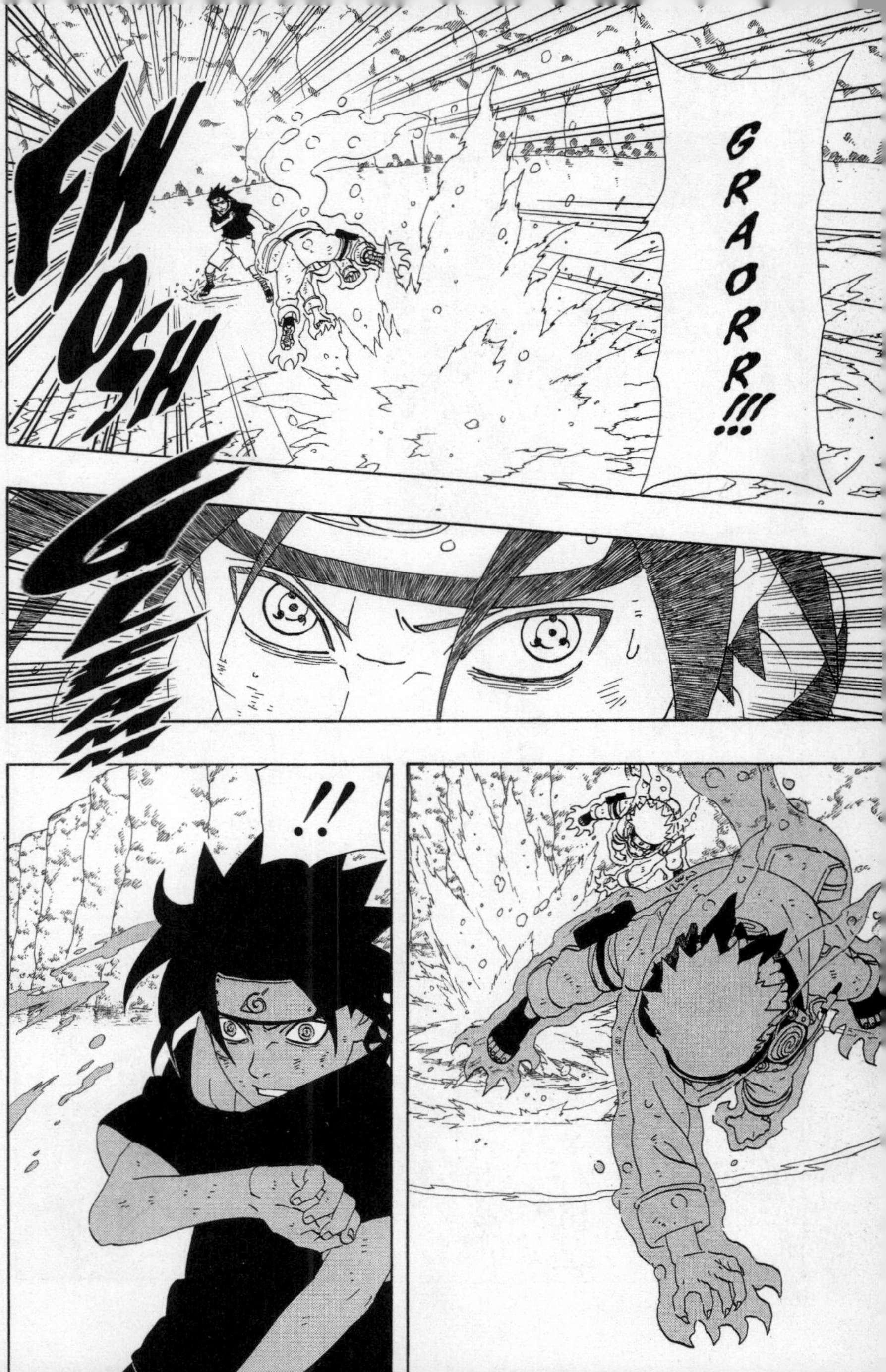
GRAORRR!!!
FWOSH
!!

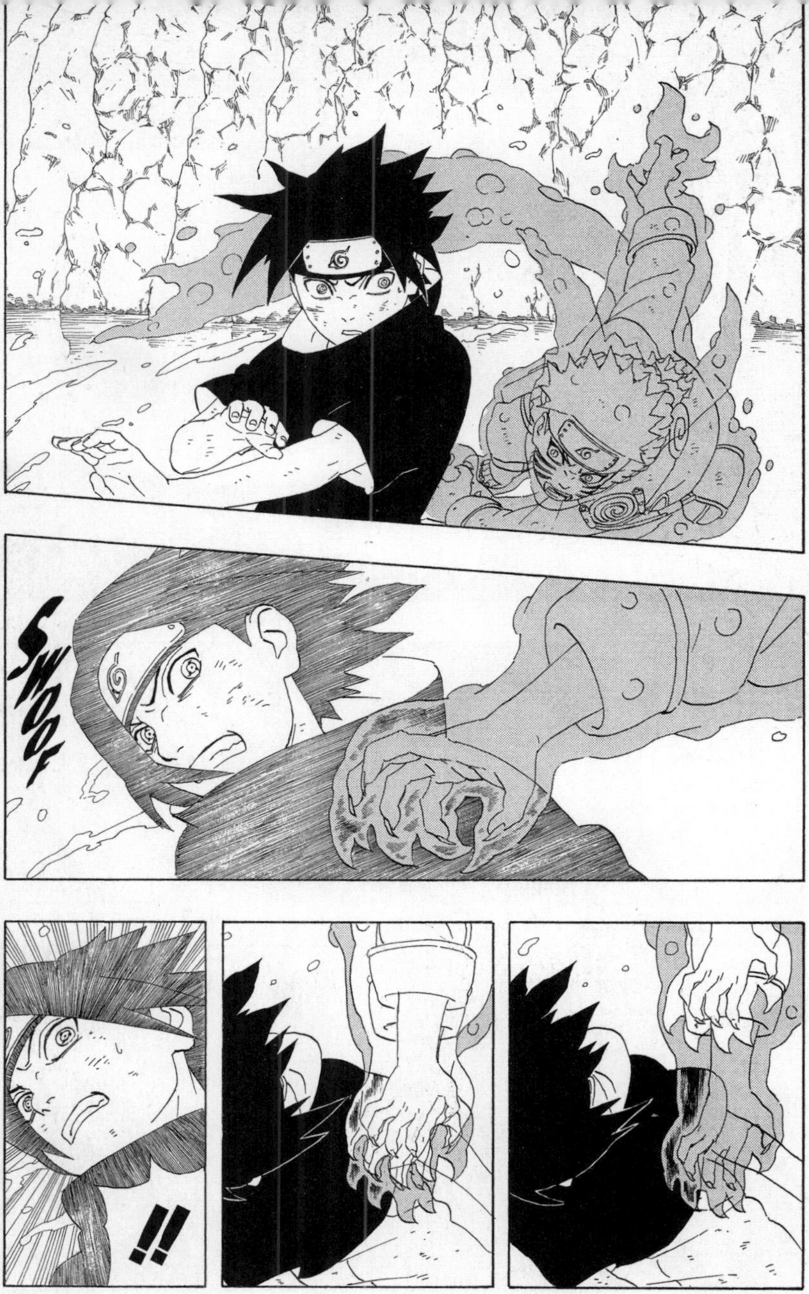
SHOOF
!!

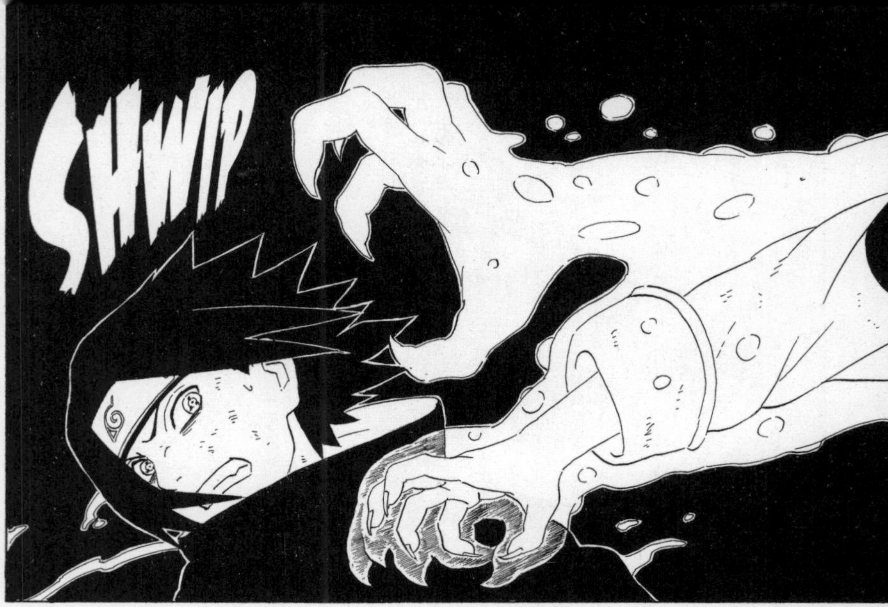
SHWIP

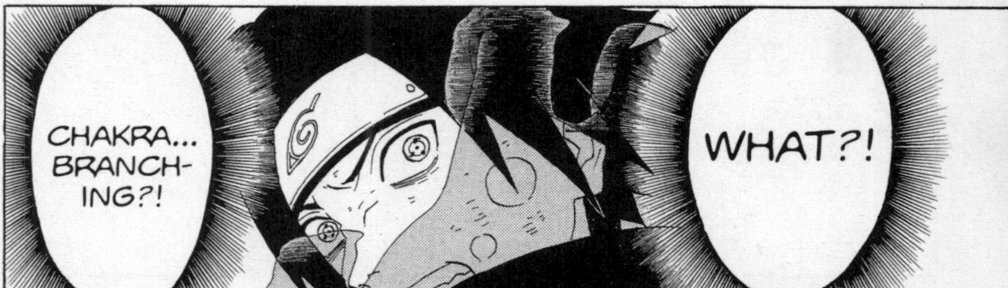
WHAT?!
CHAKRA... BRANCH-ING?!

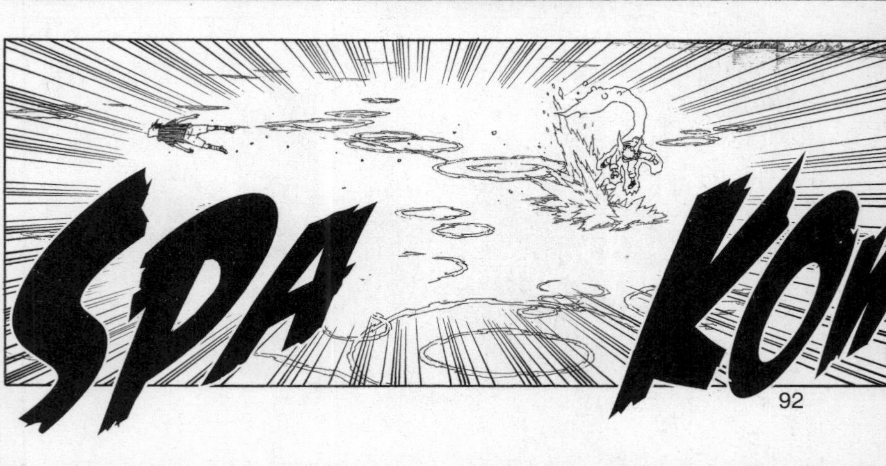
SPA
KOW

READ THIS WAY

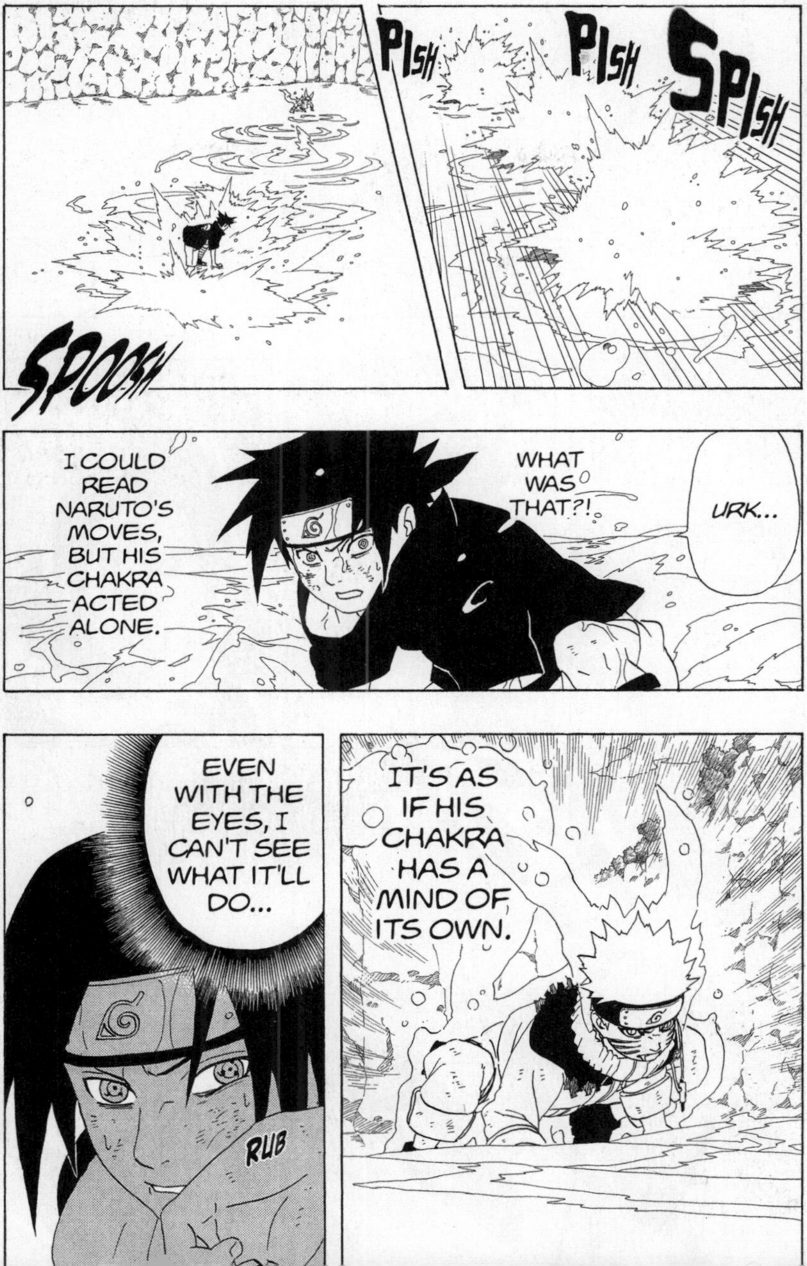
PISH
PISH
SPISH
SPOOSH
URK...
WHAT WAS THAT?!
I COULD READ NARUTO'S MOVES, BUT HIS CHAKRA ACTED ALONE.
IT'S AS IF HIS CHAKRA HAS A MIND OF ITS OWN.
EVEN WITH THE EYES, I CAN'T SEE WHAT IT'LL DO...
RUB

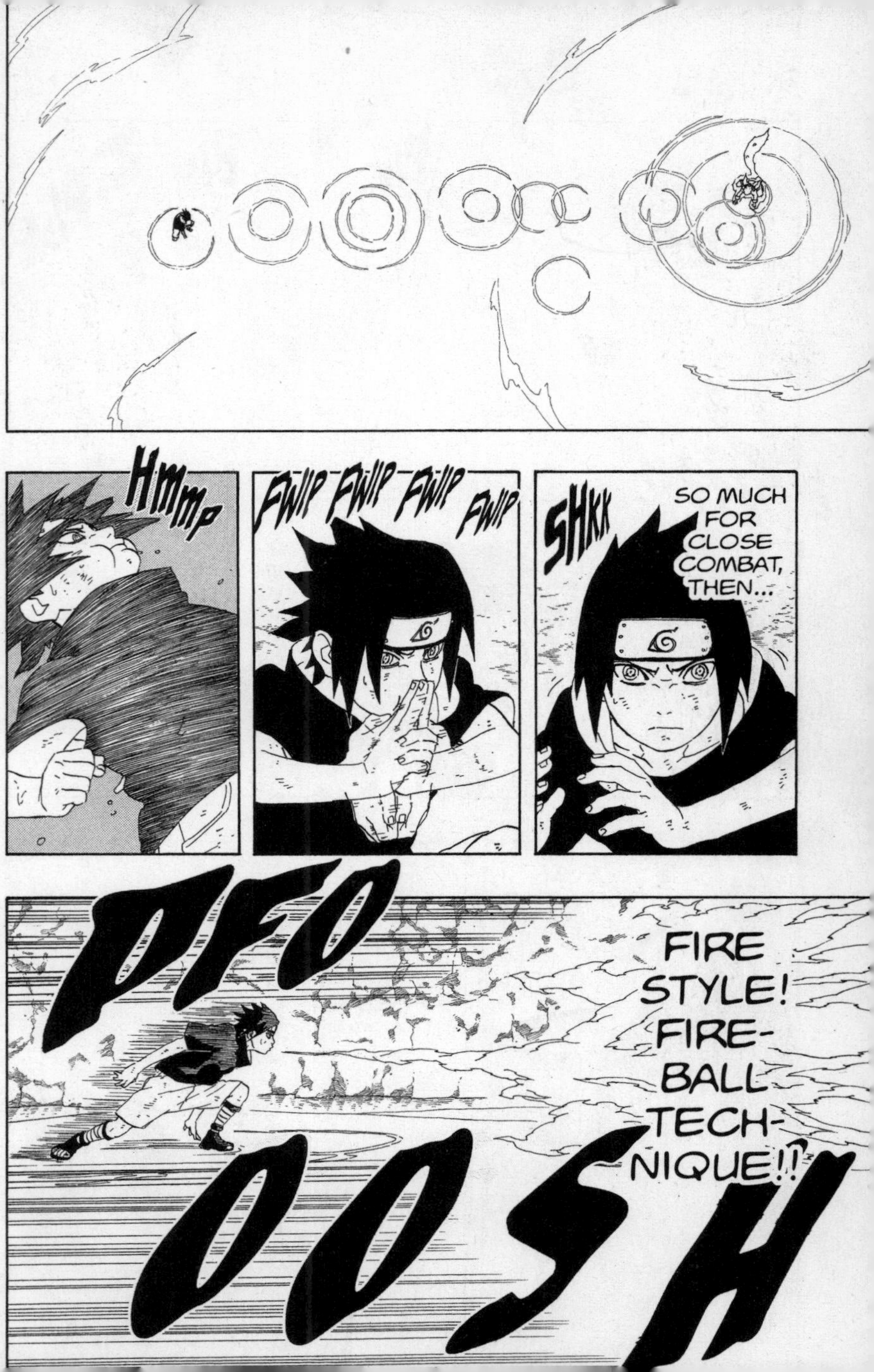
SHKK
SO MUCH FOR CLOSE COMBAT, THEN...
FWIP FWIP FWIP FWIP
HMMP
FIRE STYLE! FIRE-BALL TECH-NIQUE!!
DFOOOSH

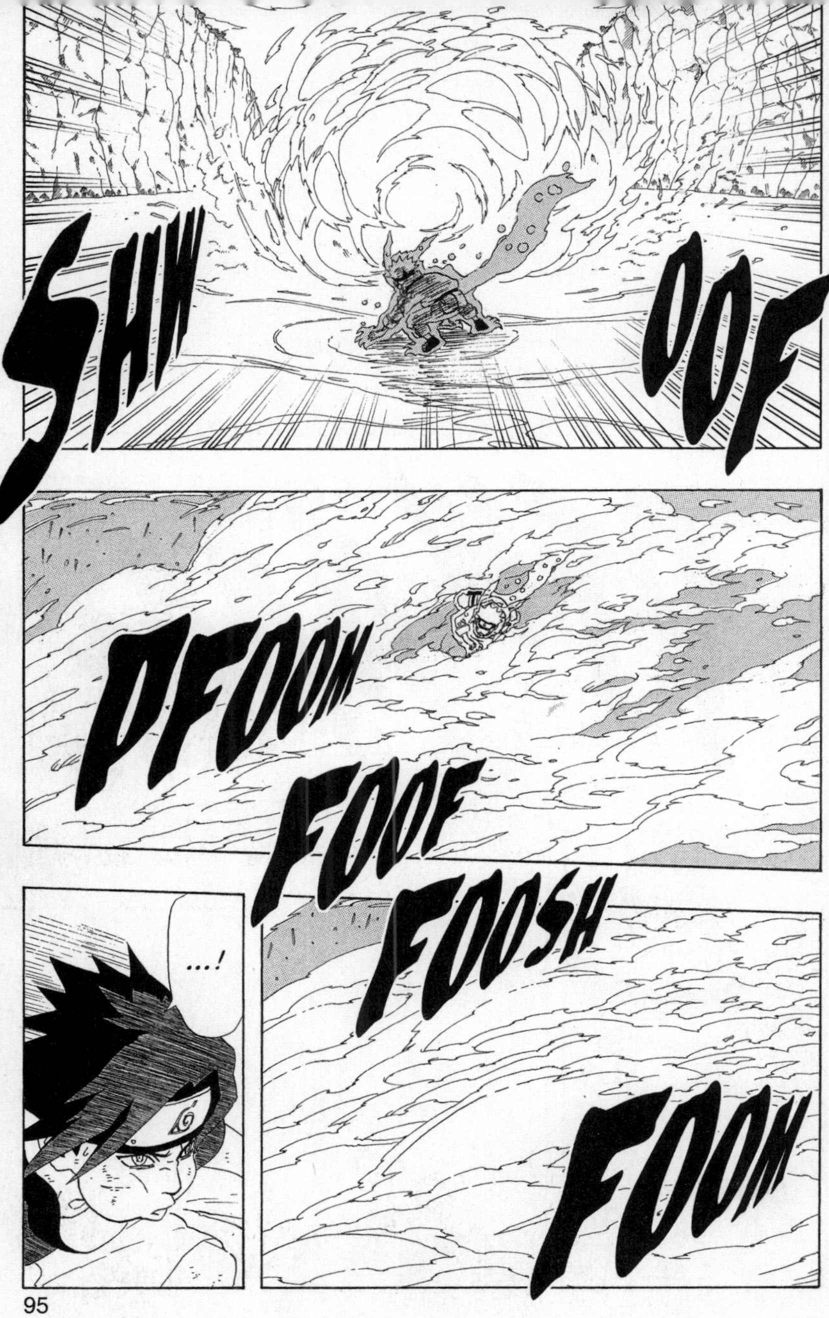
SHWOOF
PFOOM
FOOF
FOOSH
FOOM
...!

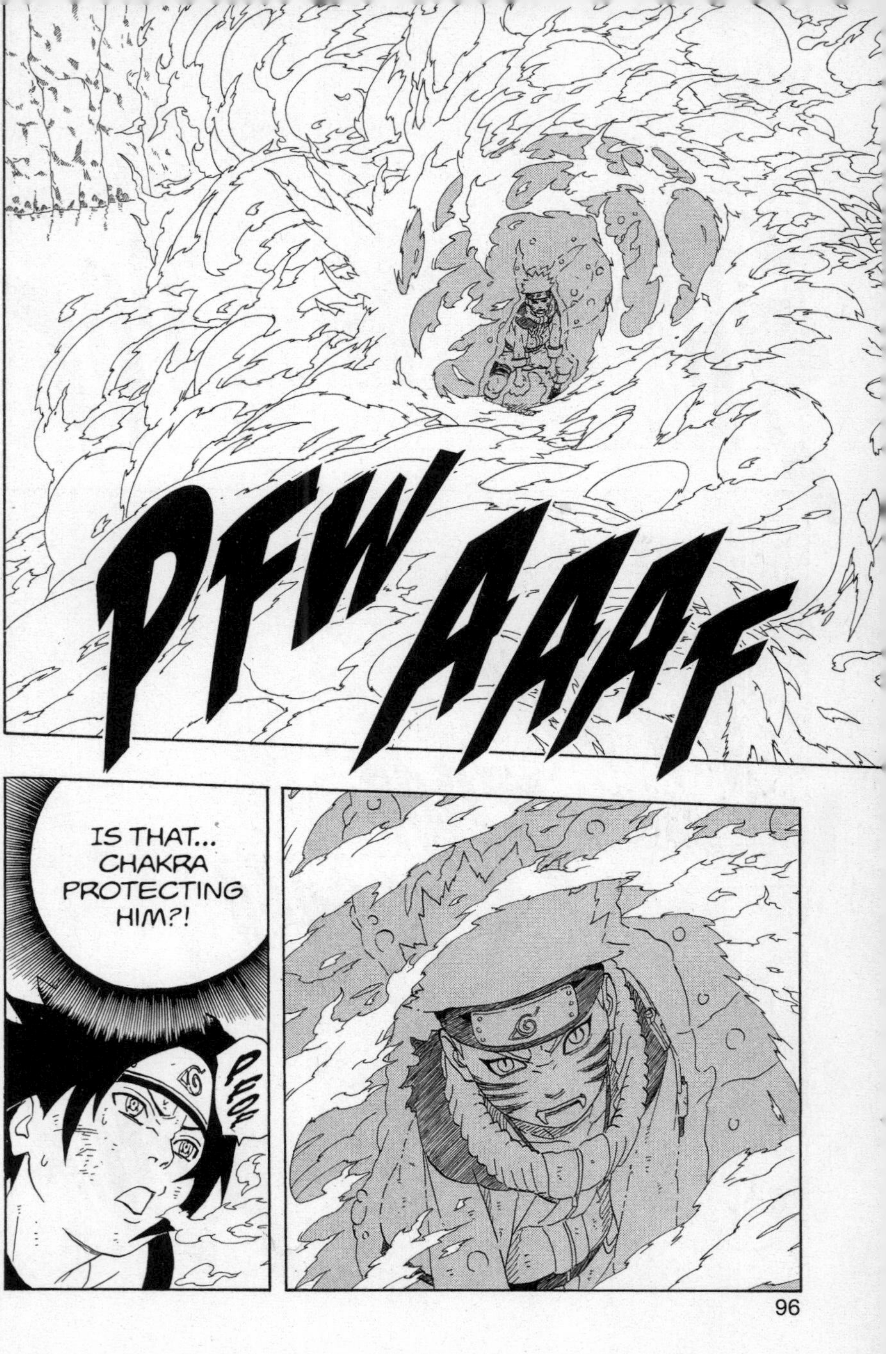
PFWAAAF
IS THAT... CHAKRA PROTECTING HIM?!

READ THIS WAY

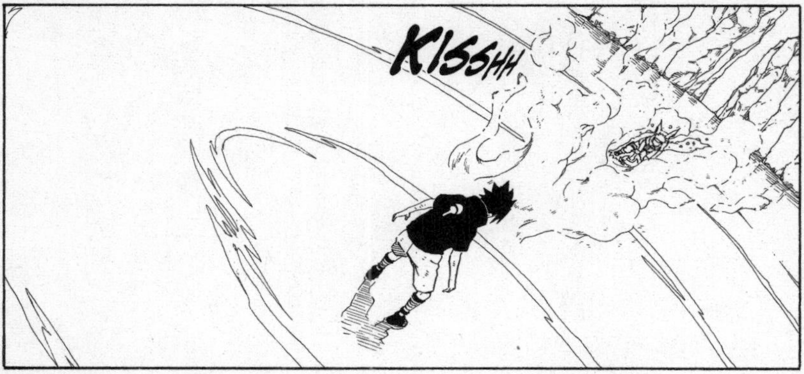
KISSHH

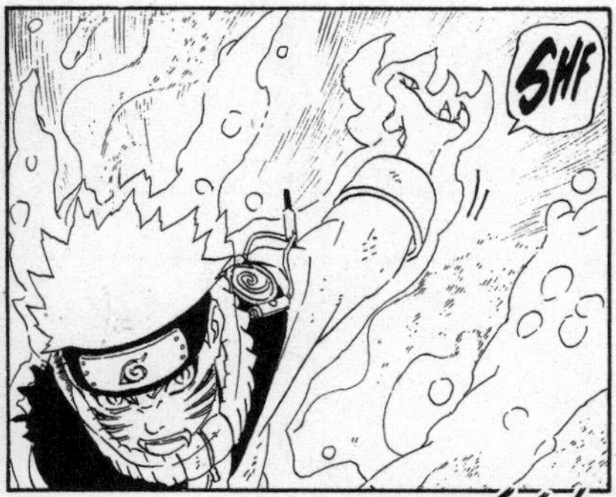
SHF

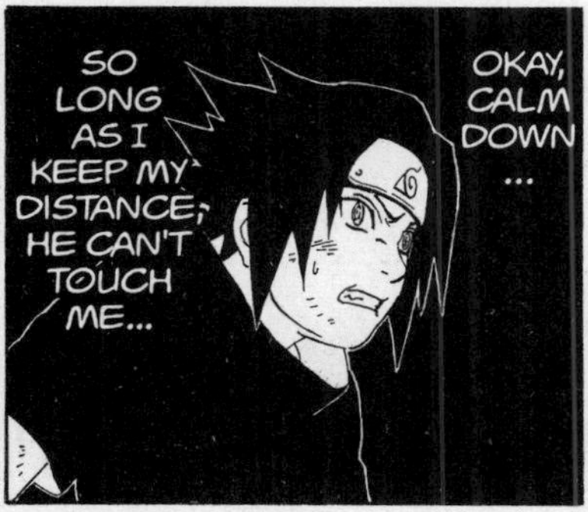
OKAY, CALM DOWN...
SO LONG AS I KEEP MY DISTANCE, HE CAN'T TOUCH ME...

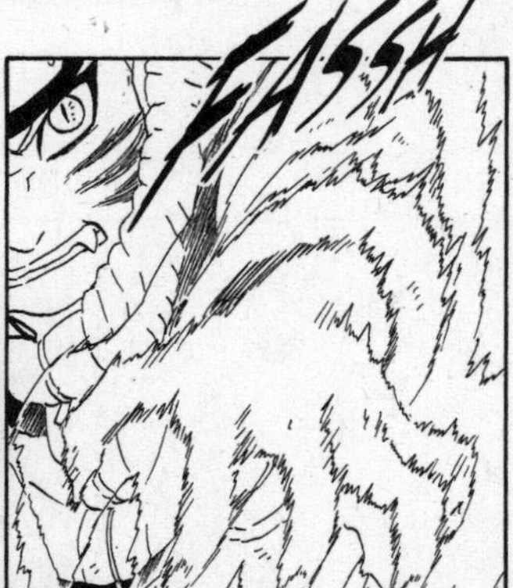
FASSH

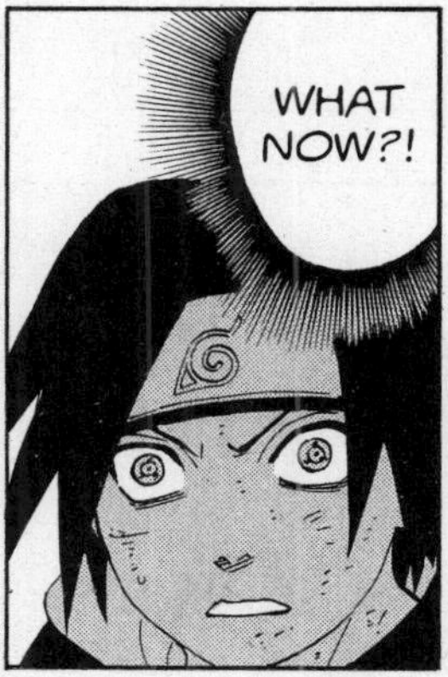
WHAT NOW?!

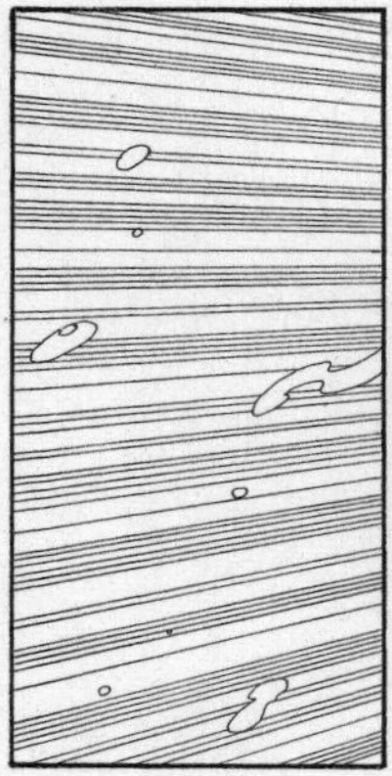

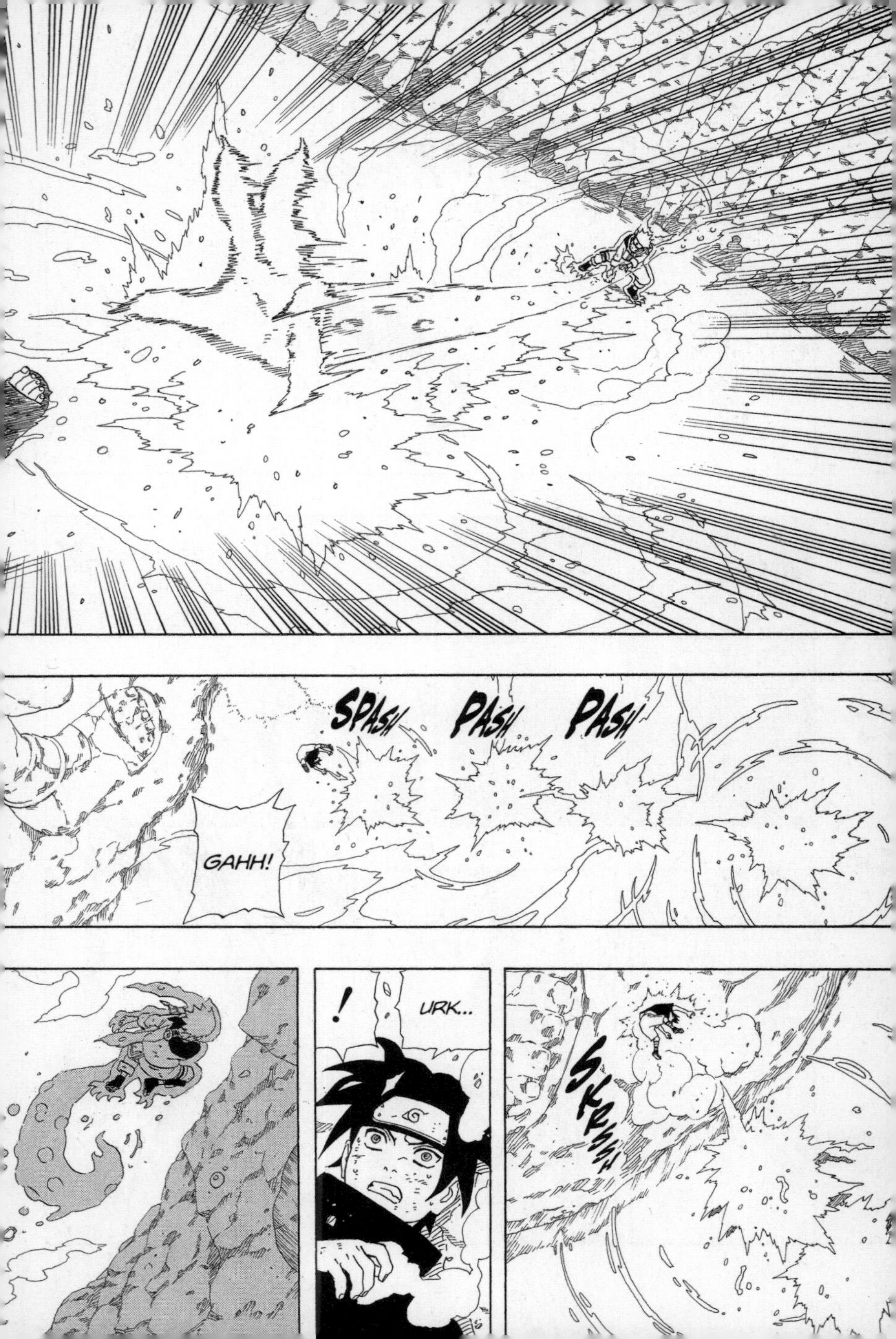
PASH
PASH
SPASH
GAHH!
!
URK...

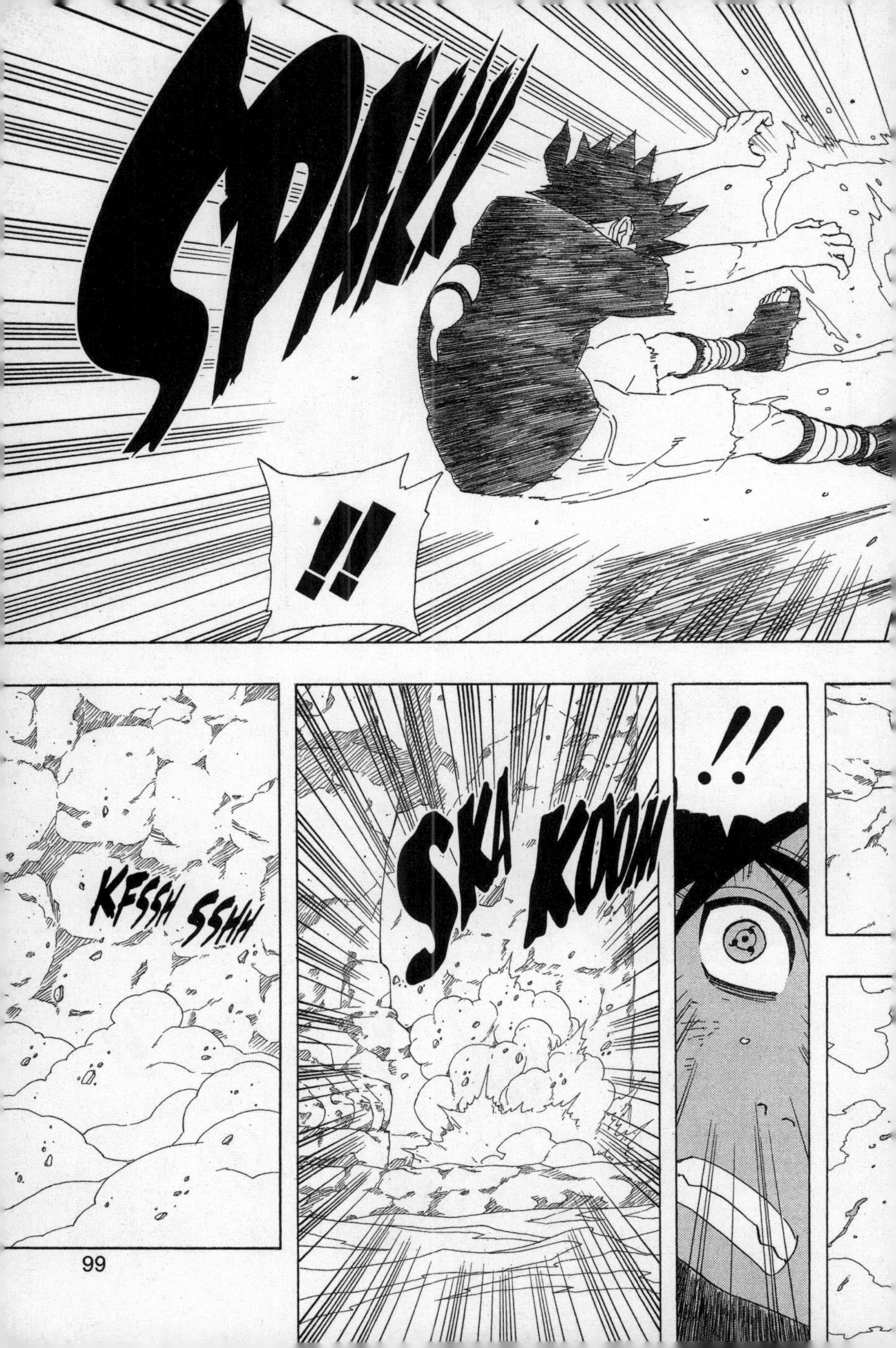
SPAK
!!
!!
SKA KOOM
KFSSH SSHH

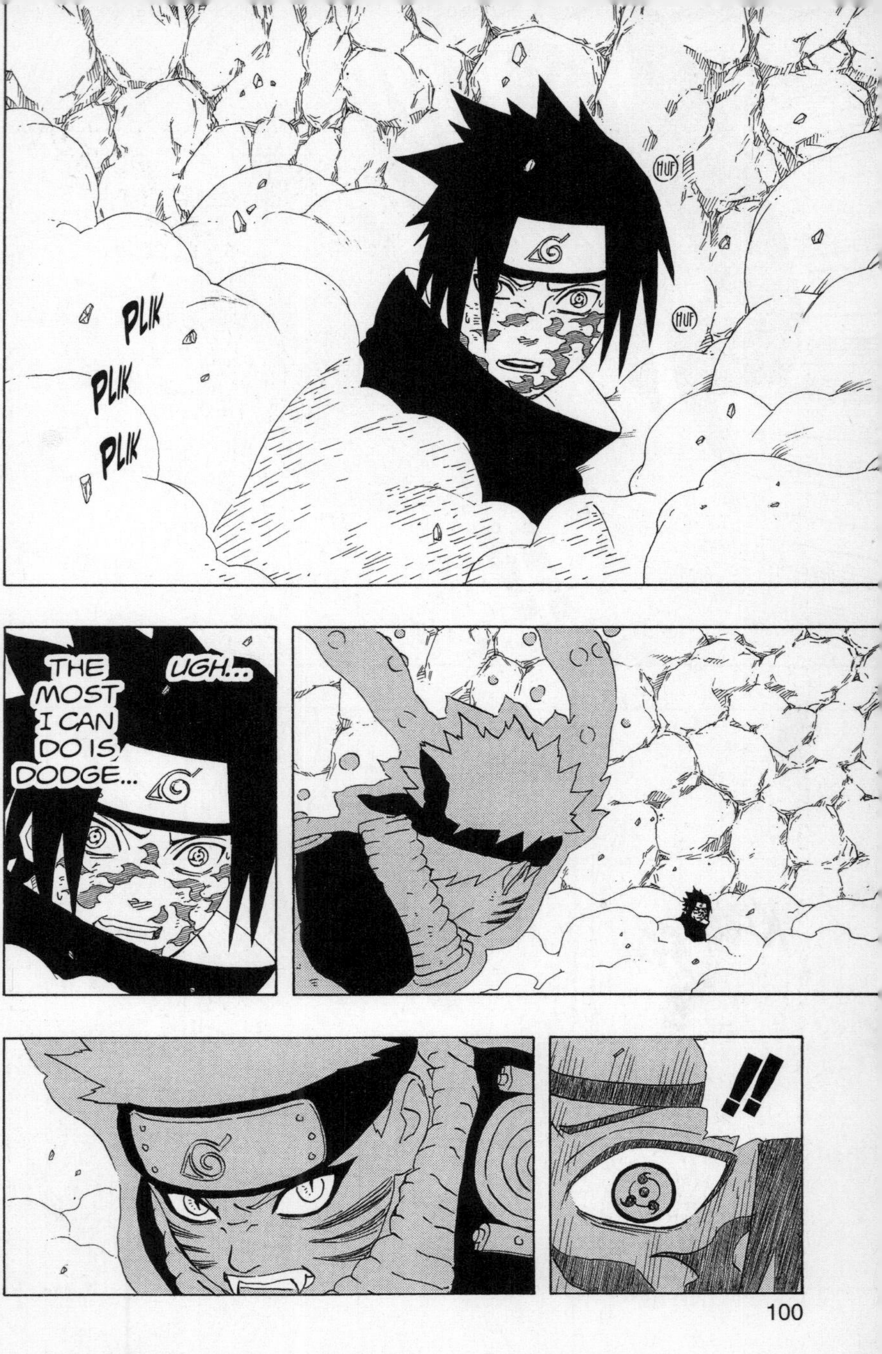
HUF
HUF
PLIK
PLIK
PLIK
UGH...
THE MOST I CAN DO IS DODGE...
!!

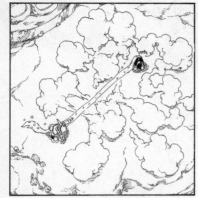

GLOM GLOM

SKRY

WHOAA!

KRSSH

!!

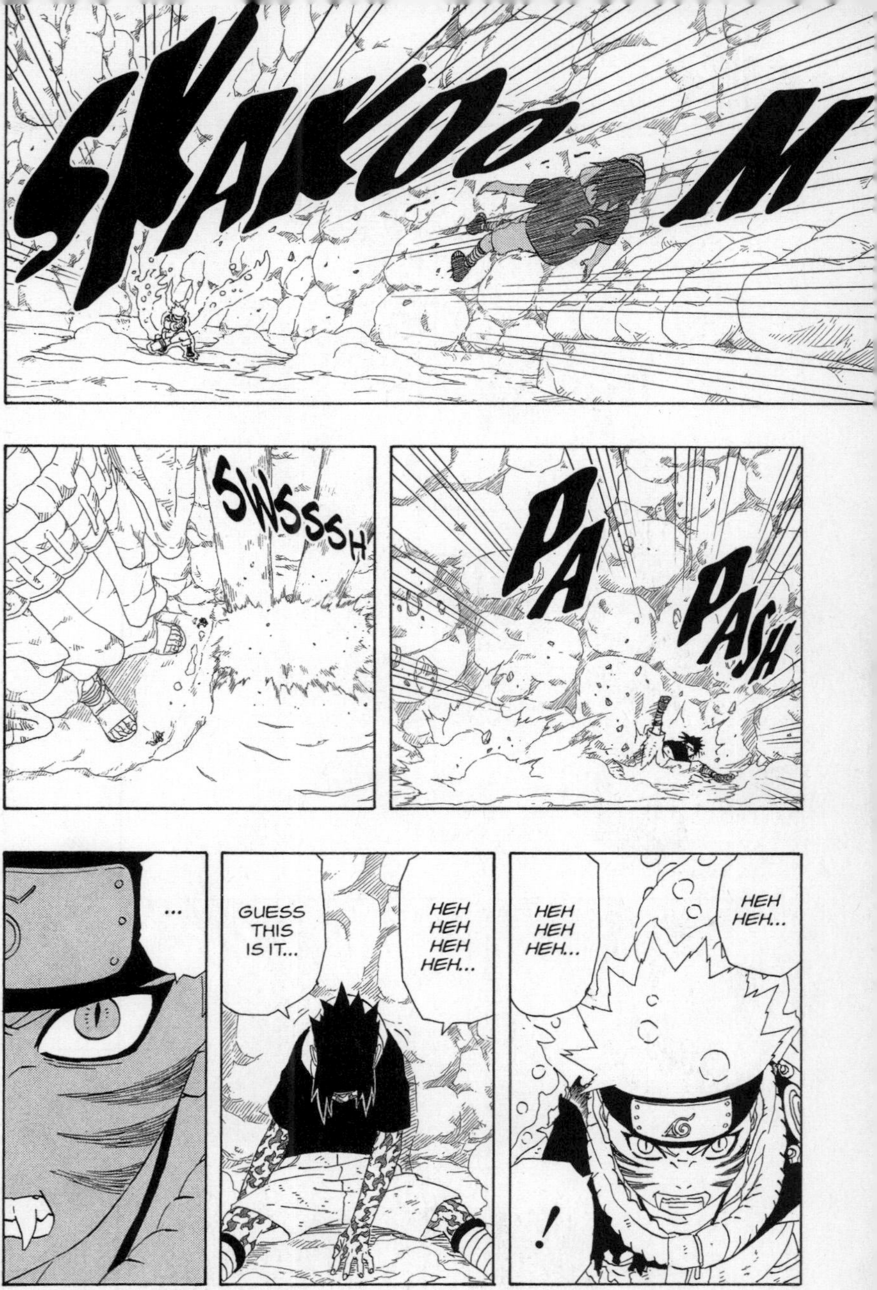
SKADOOM
PA PASH
SWSSSH
HEH HEH...
HEH HEH HEH...
!
HEH HEH HEH HEH...
GUESS THIS IS IT...
...

READ THIS WAY

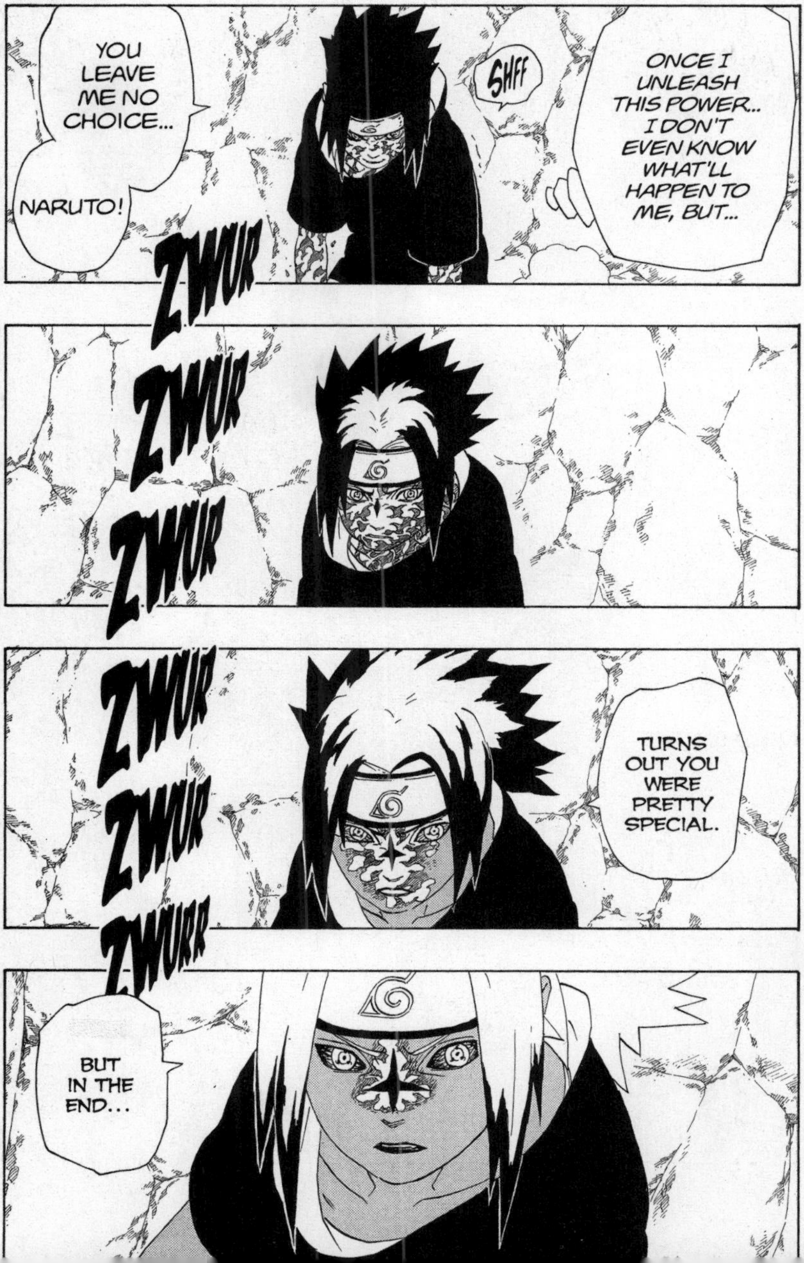
ONCE I UNLEASH THIS POWER... I DON'T EVEN KNOW WHAT'LL HAPPEN TO ME, BUT...
SHFF
YOU LEAVE ME NO CHOICE...
NARUTO!
ZWUR
ZWUR
ZWUR
ZWUR
TURNS OUT YOU WERE PRETTY SPECIAL.
ZWUR
ZWURR
BUT IN THE END...

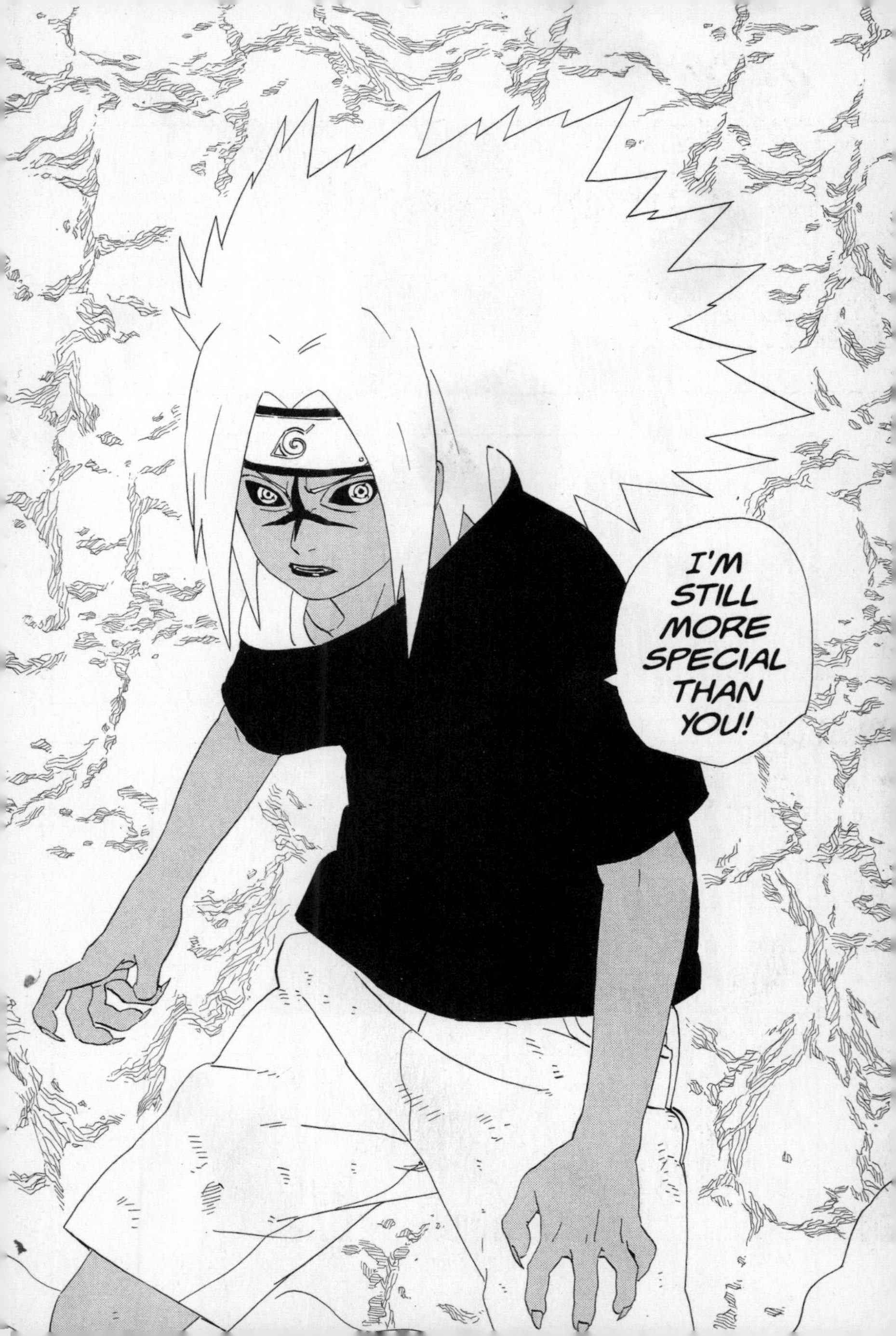
I'M STILL MORE SPECIAL THAN YOU!

READ THIS WAY

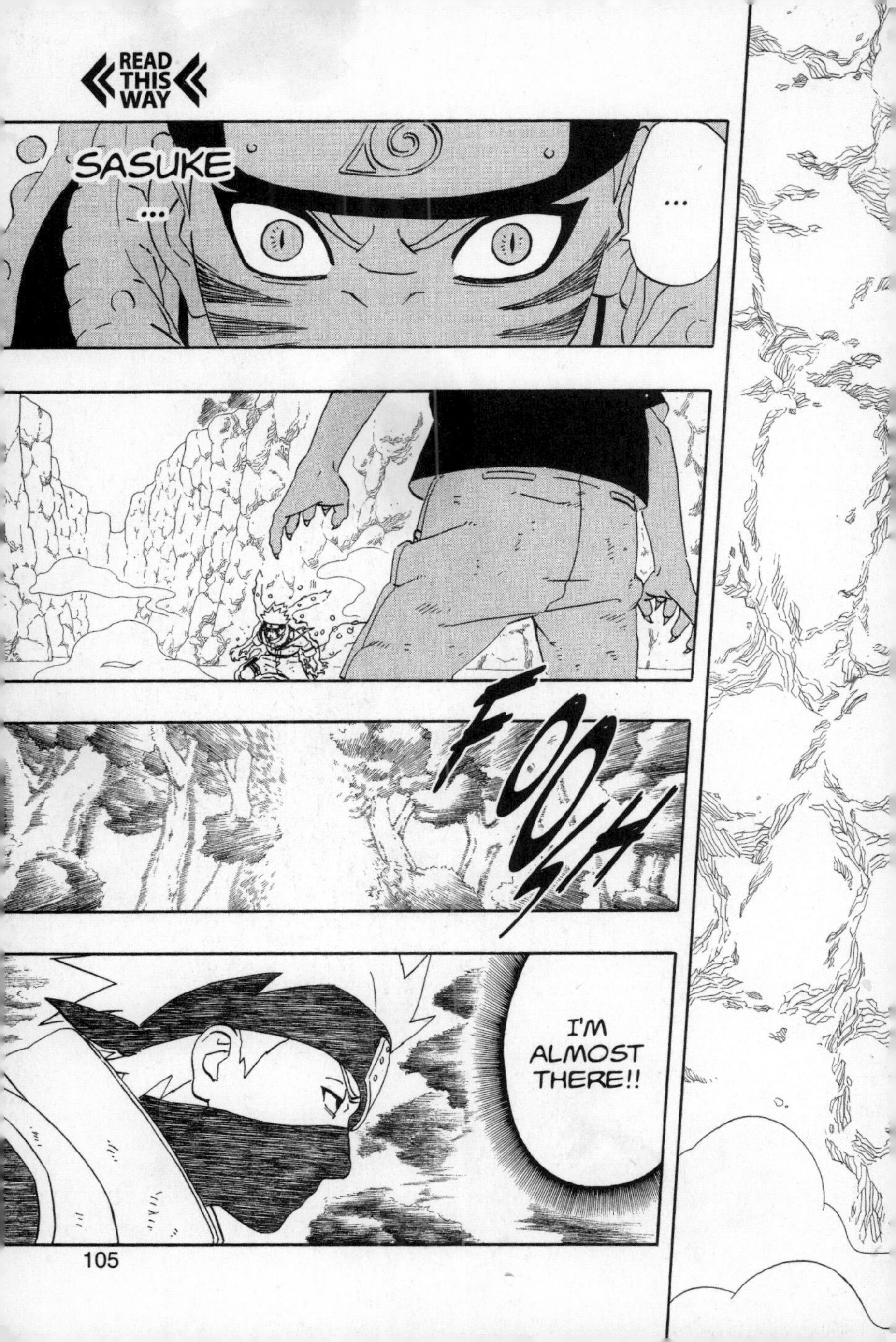
...
SASUKE
...
FOOSH
I'M ALMOST THERE!!

Mr. Kishimoto, congrats on the 5th anniversary!
My hats off to you for the efforts you put in!!

by. 西谷浩一
Koichi Nishitani

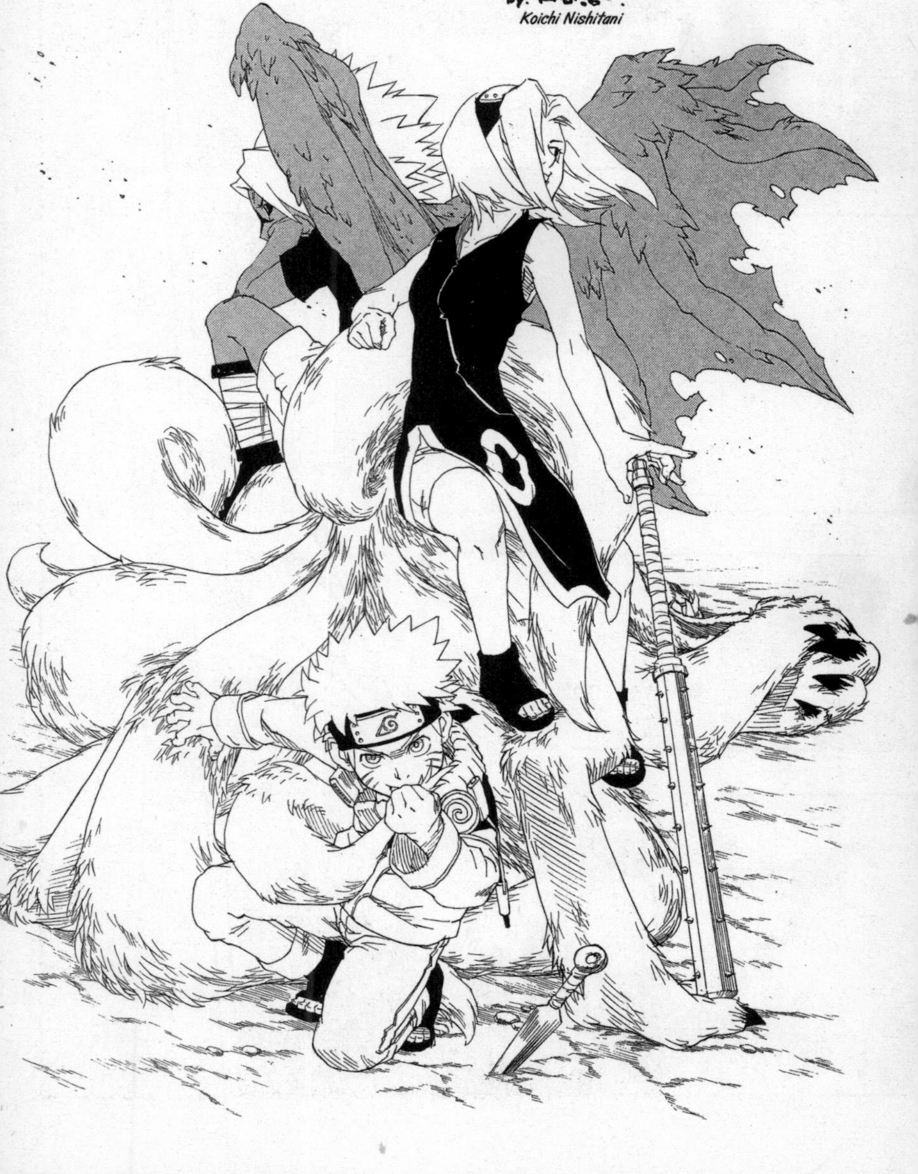

Number 232: The Final Valley

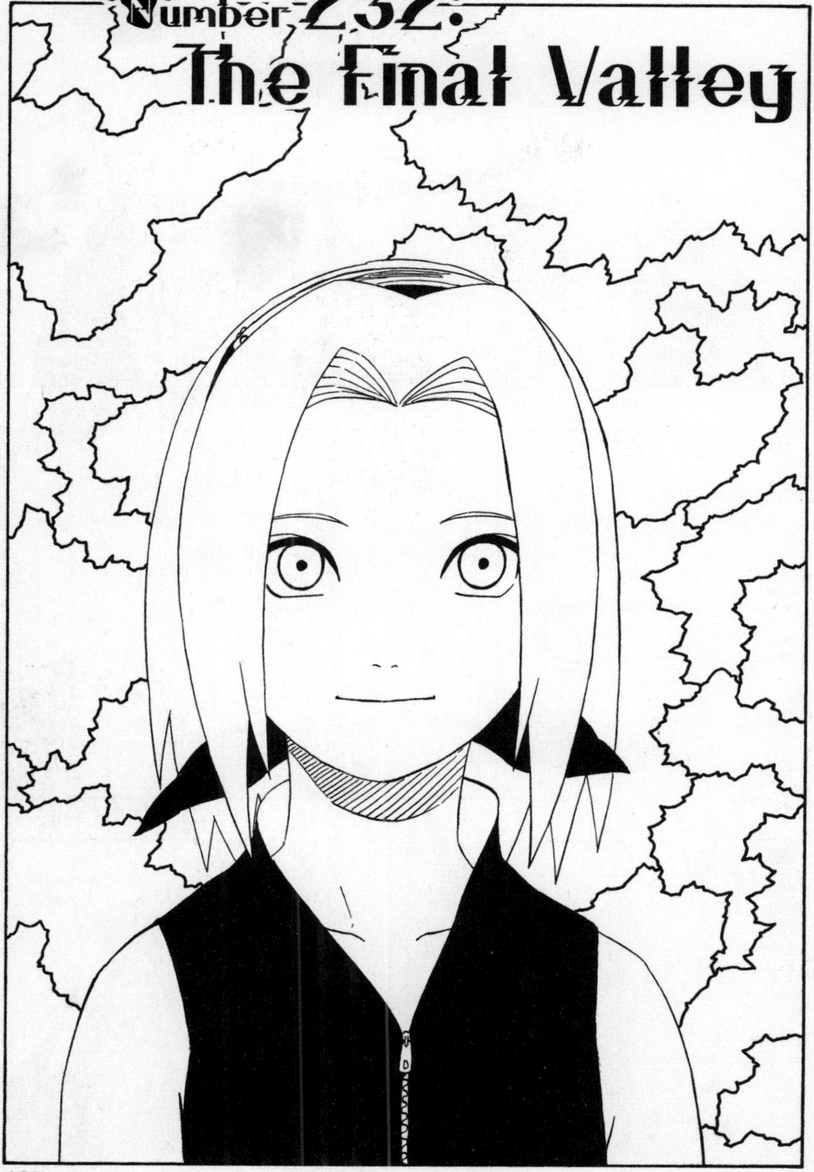

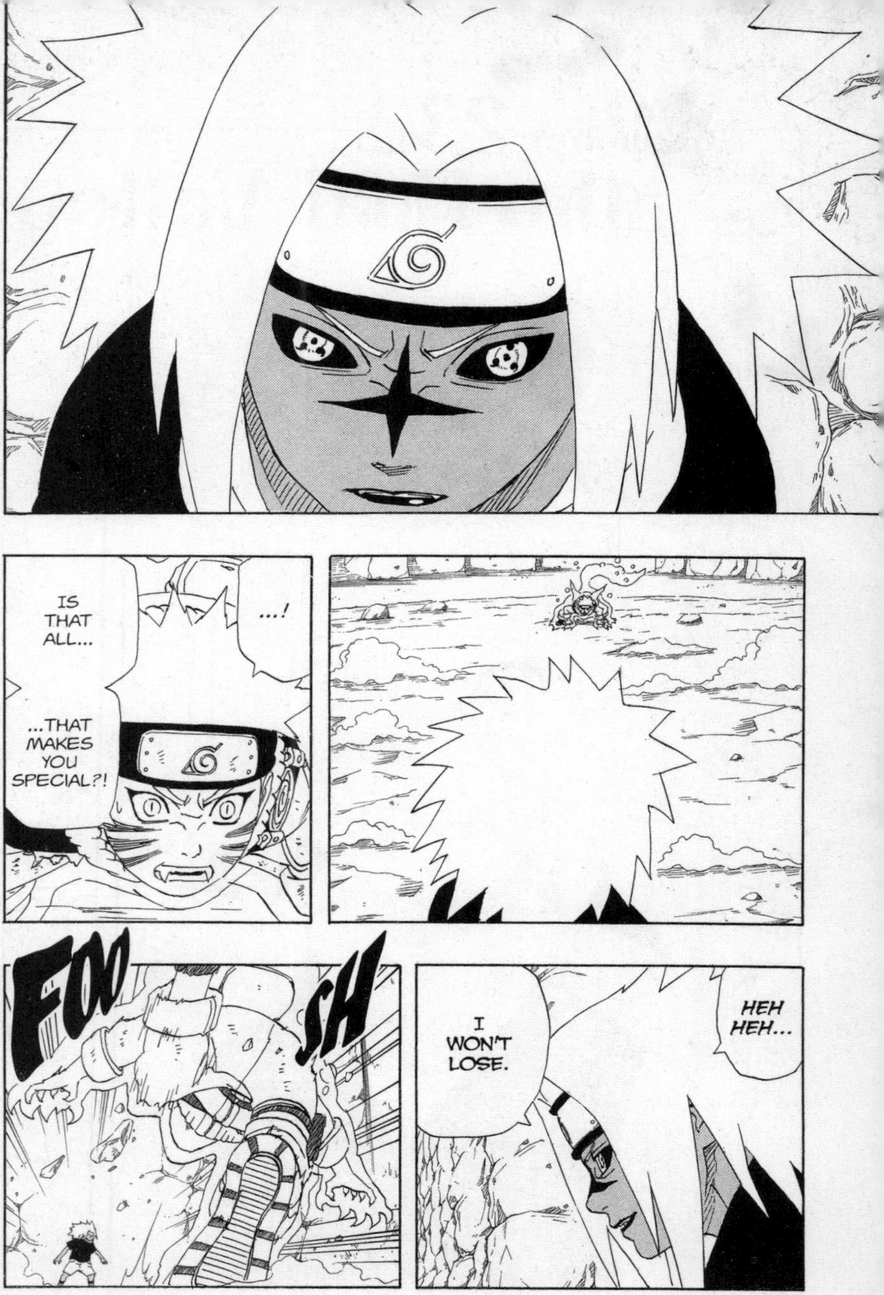
...!
IS THAT ALL...
...THAT MAKES YOU SPECIAL?!
HEH HEH...
I WON'T LOSE.
FOOSH

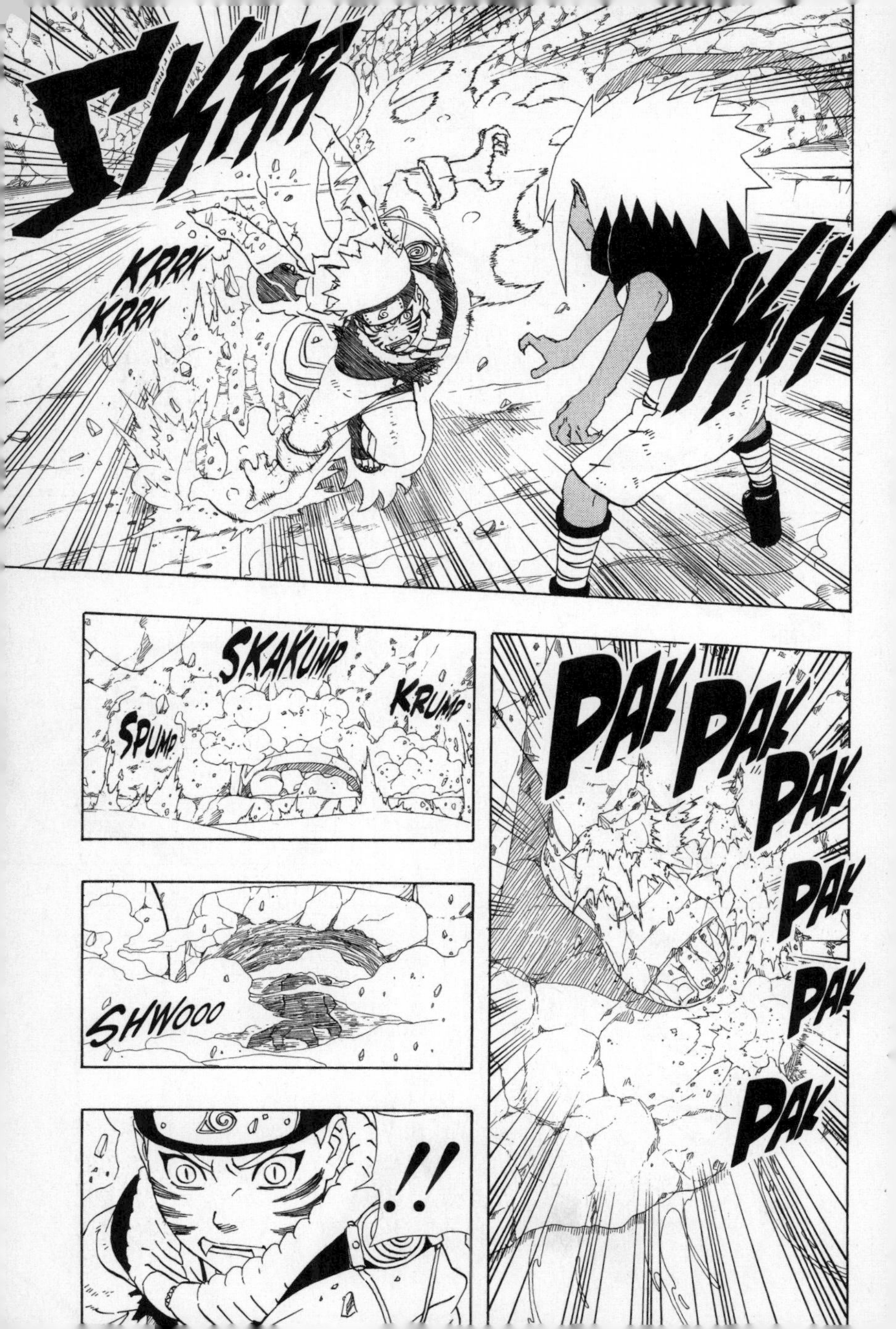
KRRK
KRRK
PAK PAK PAK PAK PAK PAK
SKAKUMP
KRUMP
SPUMP
SHWOOO
!!

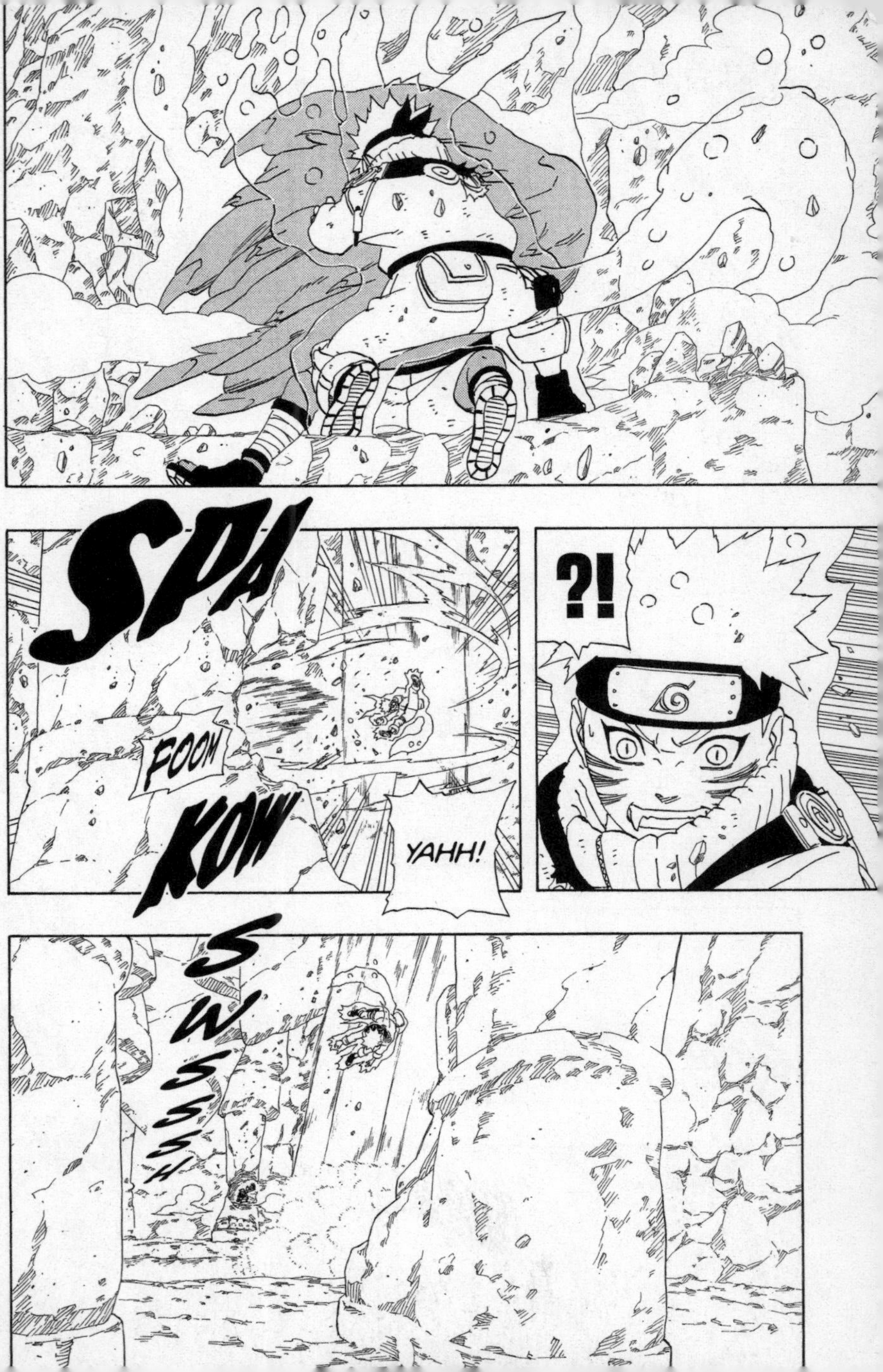
?!
SPA
FOOM
KOW
YAHH!
SWSSSH

READ THIS WAY

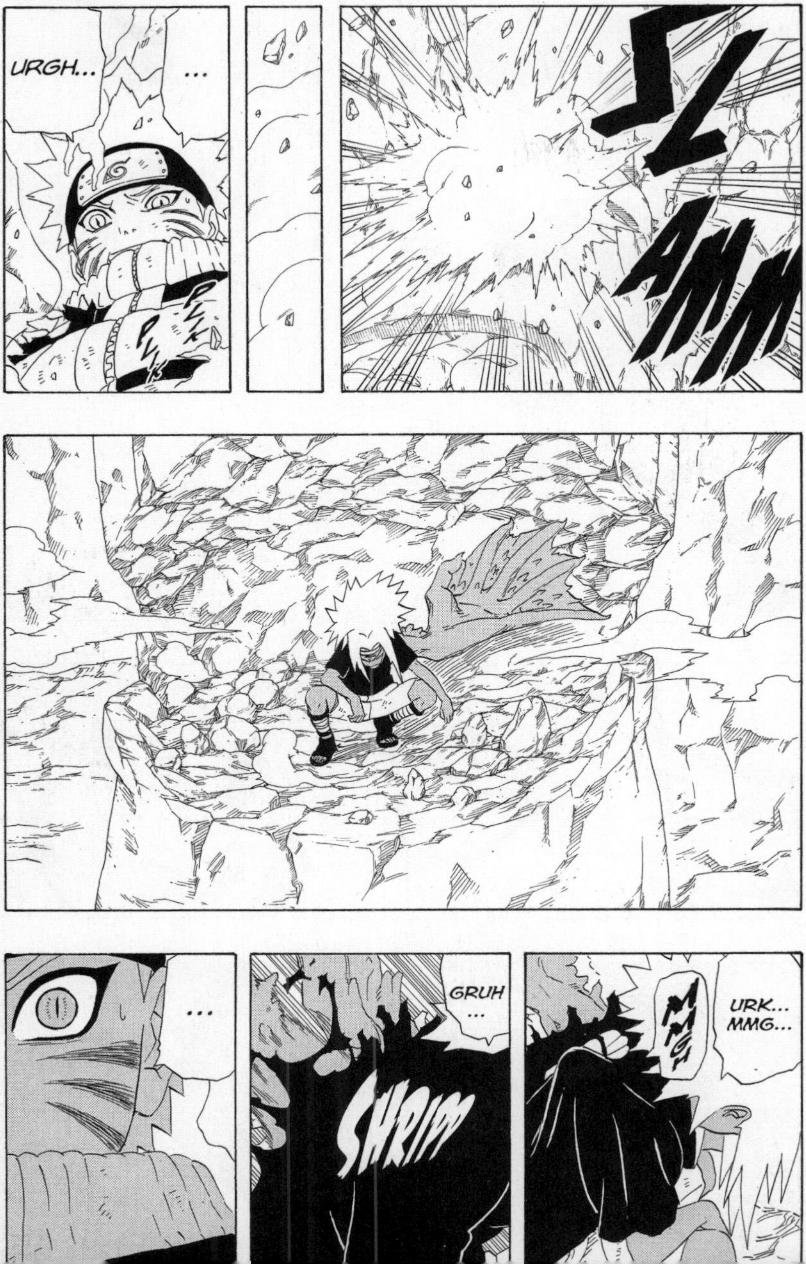
SLAMM
...
URGH...
PLIK
PLIK
URK...
MMG...
MMGH
GRUH
...
SHRIPP
...

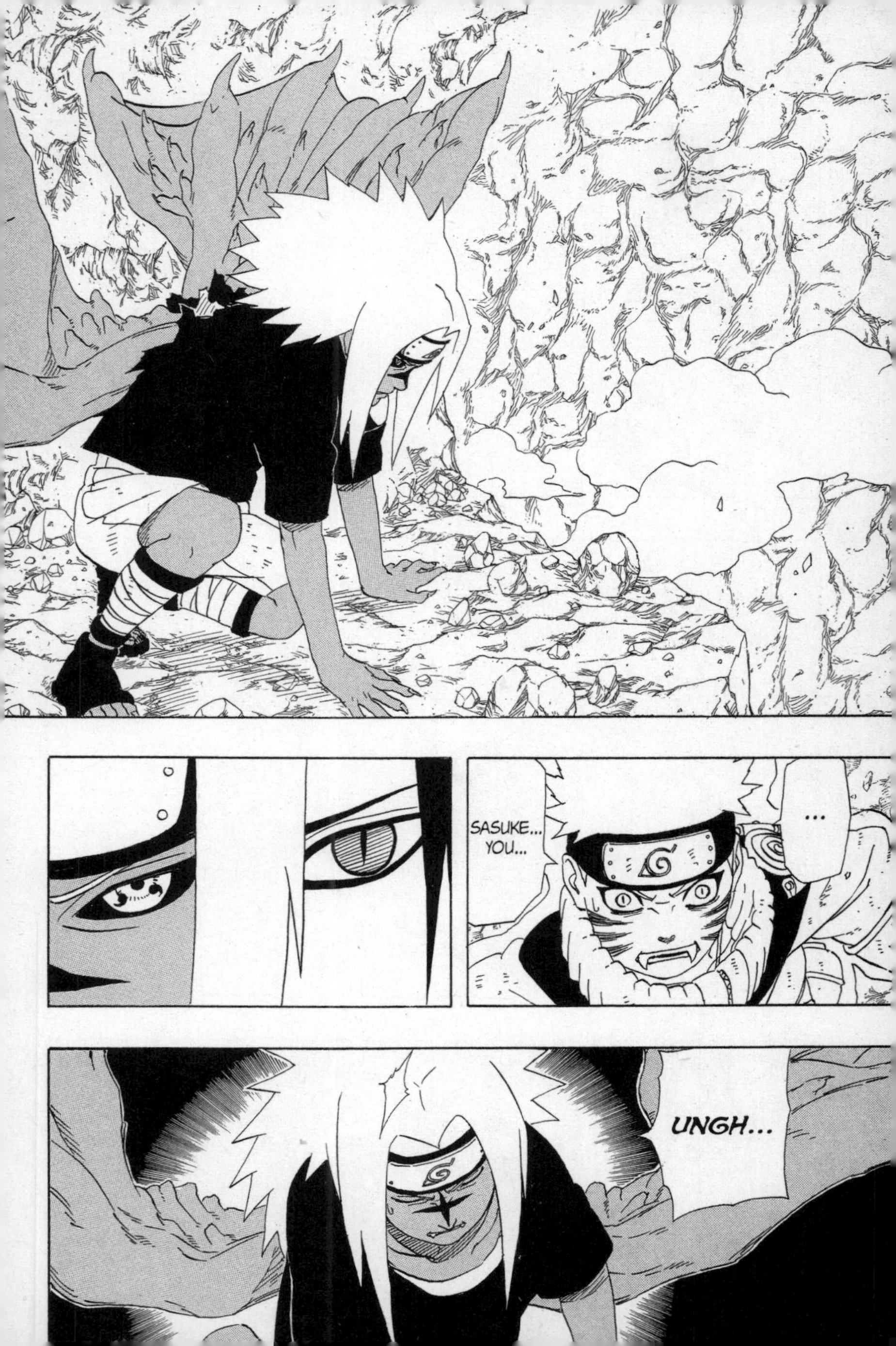
...
SASUKE... YOU...
UNGH...

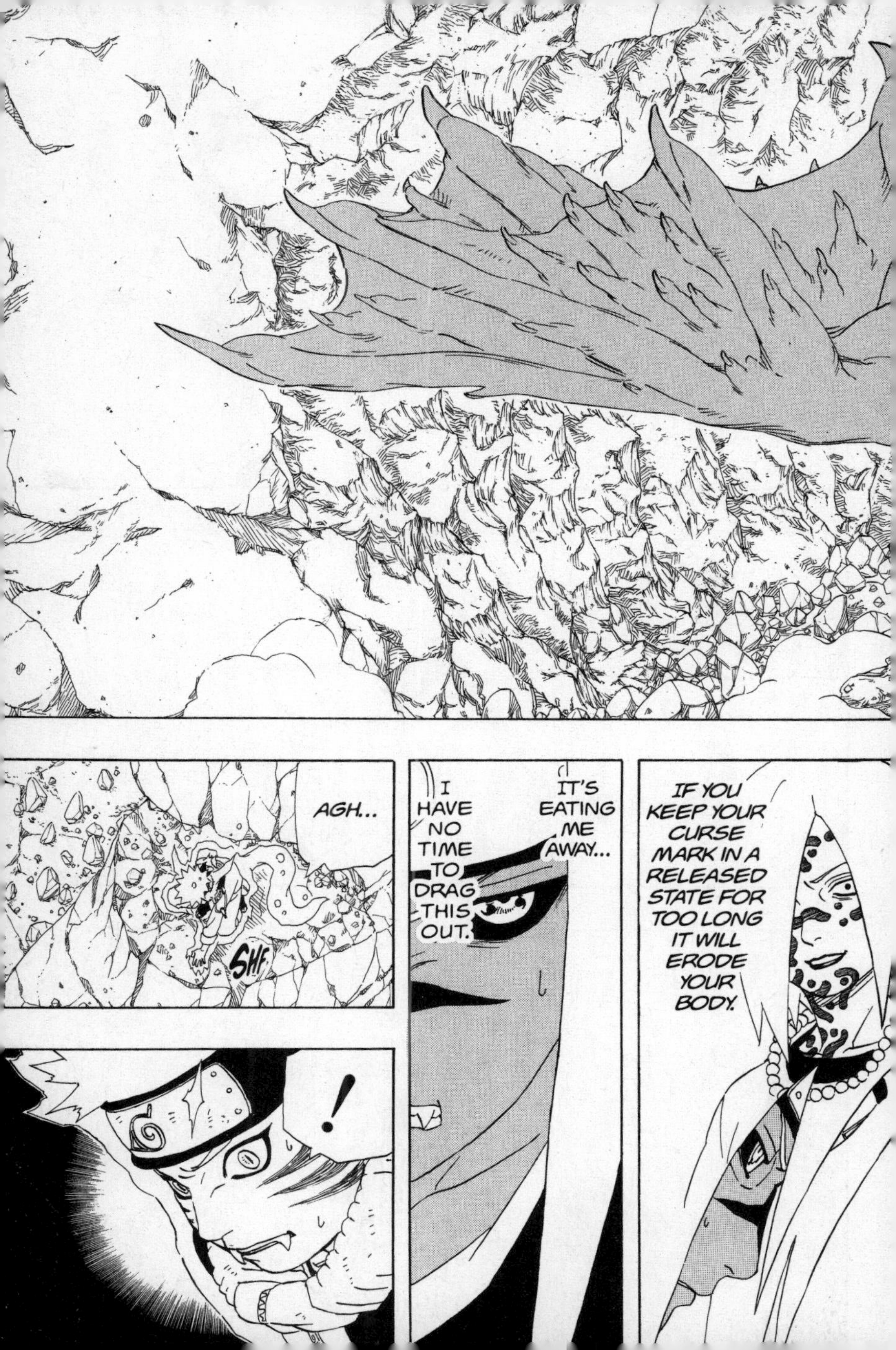
IF YOU KEEP YOUR CURSE MARK IN A RELEASED STATE FOR TOO LONG IT WILL ERODE YOUR BODY.
IT'S EATING ME AWAY...
I HAVE NO TIME TO DRAG THIS OUT.
AGH...
SHF
!

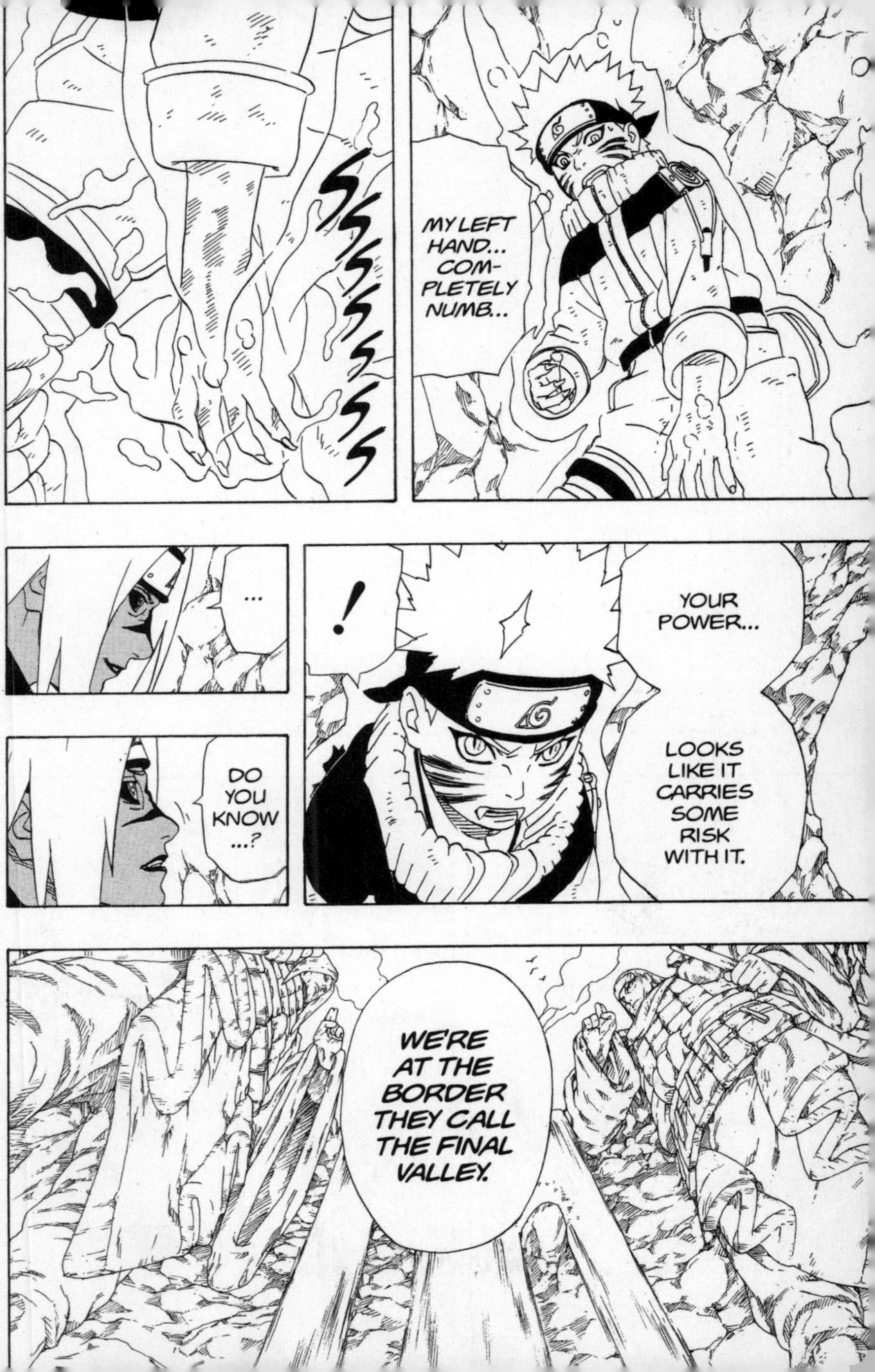
MY LEFT HAND... COM-PLETELY NUMB...
SSSSSSS
!
YOUR POWER...
LOOKS LIKE IT CARRIES SOME RISK WITH IT.
...
DO YOU KNOW ...?
WE'RE AT THE BORDER THEY CALL THE FINAL VALLEY.

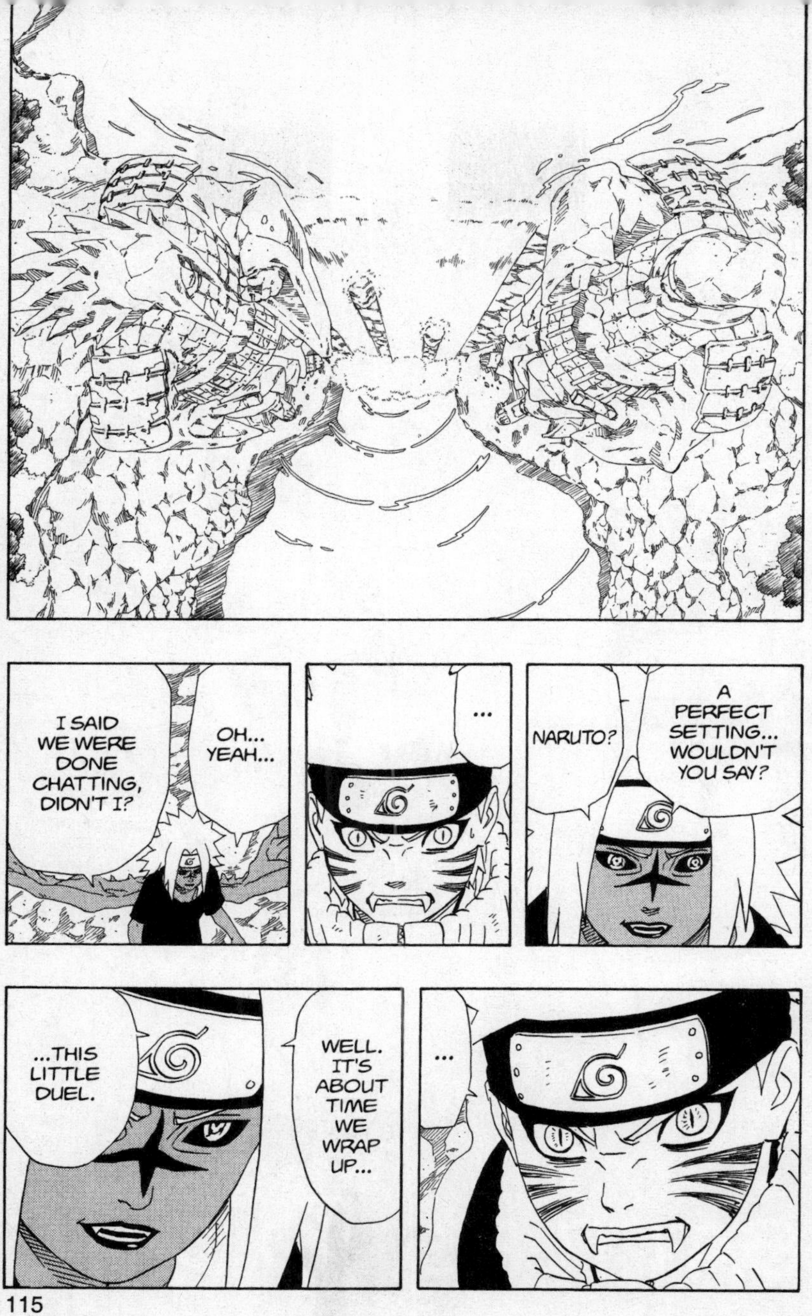
A PERFECT SETTING... WOULDN'T YOU SAY?
NARUTO?
...
OH... YEAH...
I SAID WE WERE DONE CHATTING, DIDN'T I?
...
WELL. IT'S ABOUT TIME WE WRAP UP...
...THIS LITTLE DUEL.

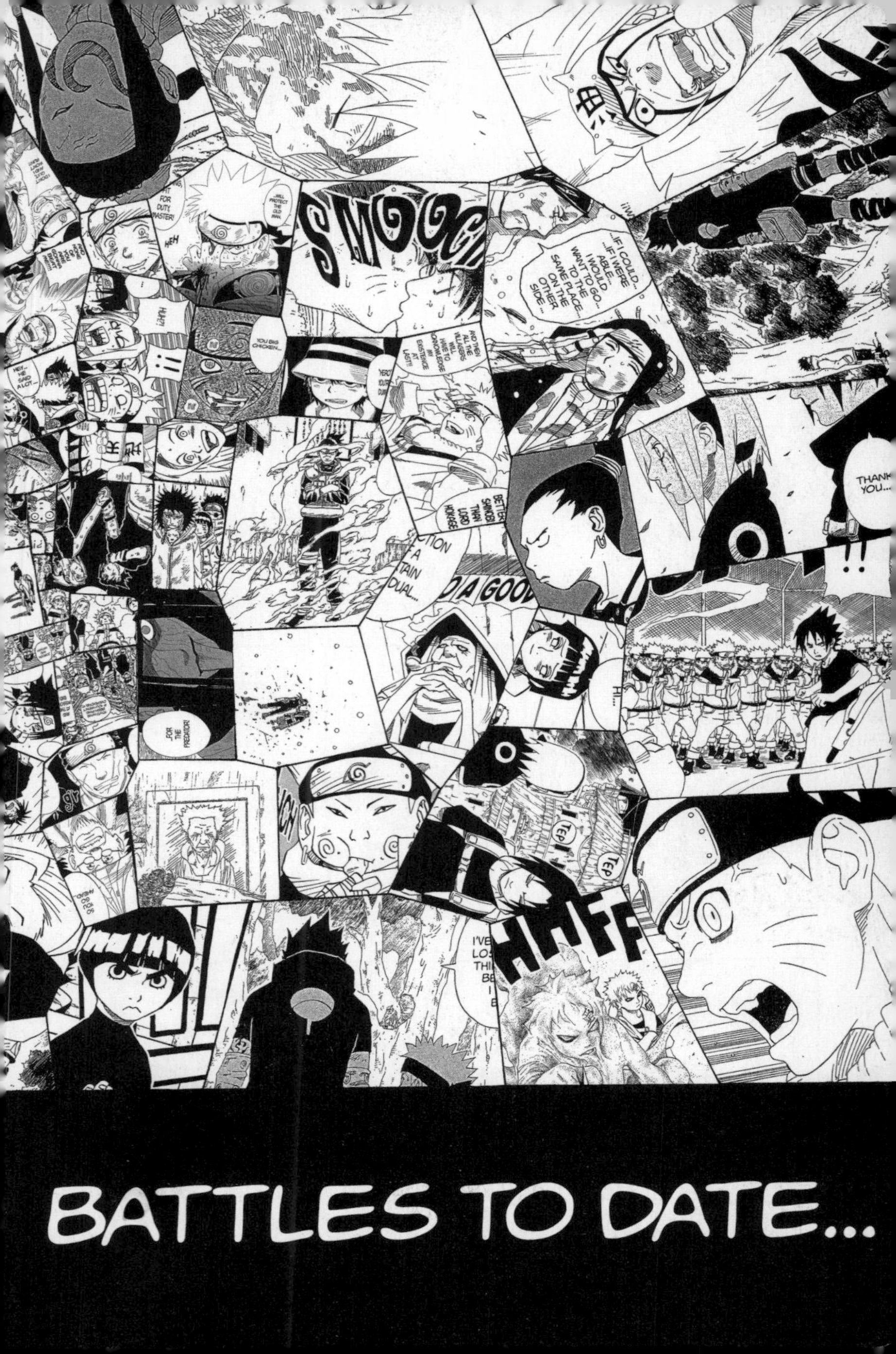
...IF I COULD... ...IF I WERE ...ABLE... I WOULD WANT TO GO... TO THE SAME PLACE... ON THE OTHER SIDE...
SMOOCH
I WILL PROTECT THE OLD MAN.
THANK YOU...
AND THEN ALL THE VILLAGERS WILL HAVE TO ACKNOWLEDGE MY EXISTENCE AT LAST!
YOU BIG CHICKEN...
HUH?!
BETTER SHINOBI THAN LORD HOKAGE
!!
...FOR THE PREDATOR!
TEP
TEP
HUFF

BATTLES TO DATE...

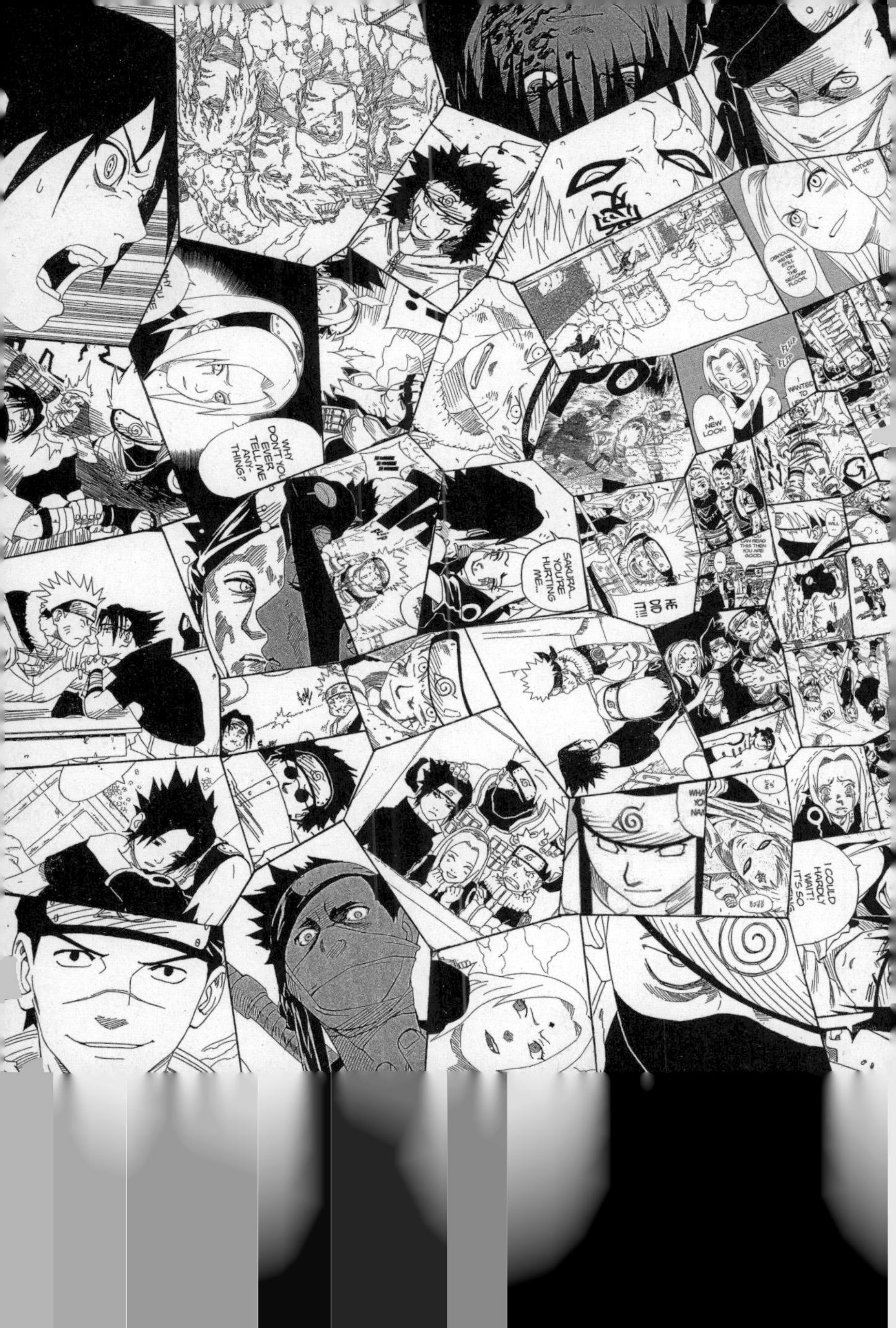
I NOTICED IT.
OBVIOUSLY WE'RE STILL ON THE SECOND FLOOR.
FLIP FLIP
I WANTED TO
A NEW LOOK!
I WILL...
YOU CAN READ THIS THEN YOU ARE GOOD.
...
SAKURA... YOU'RE HURTING ME...
WHY DON'T YOU EVER TELL ME ANY-THING?
I COULD HARDLY WAIT! IT'S SO

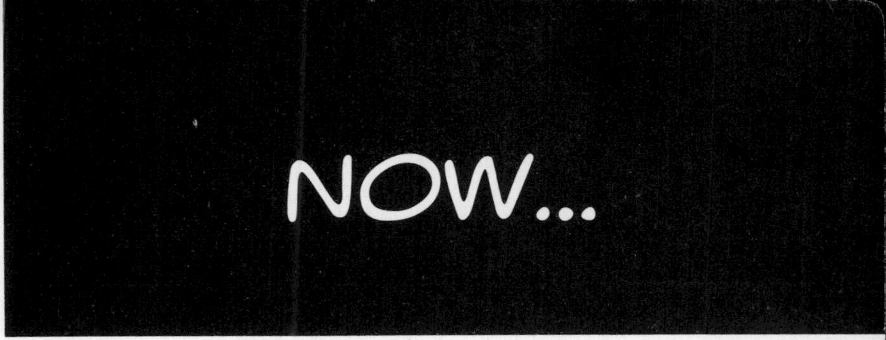
NOW...

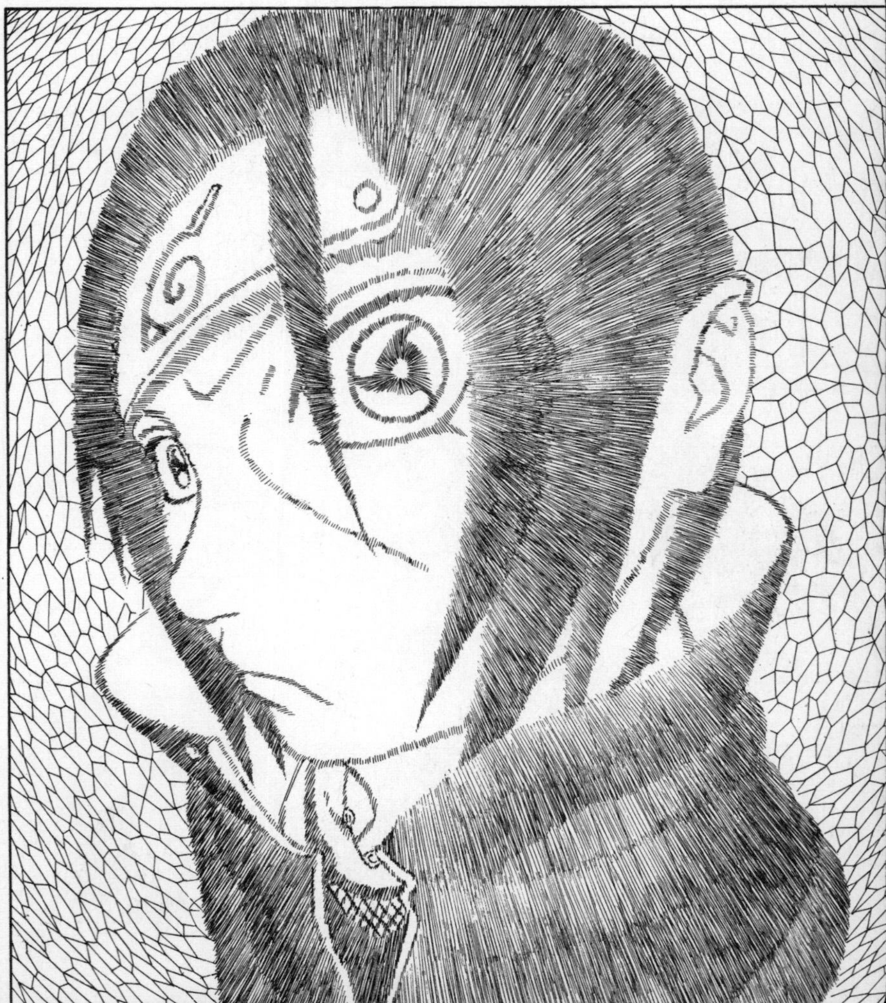

READ THIS WAY

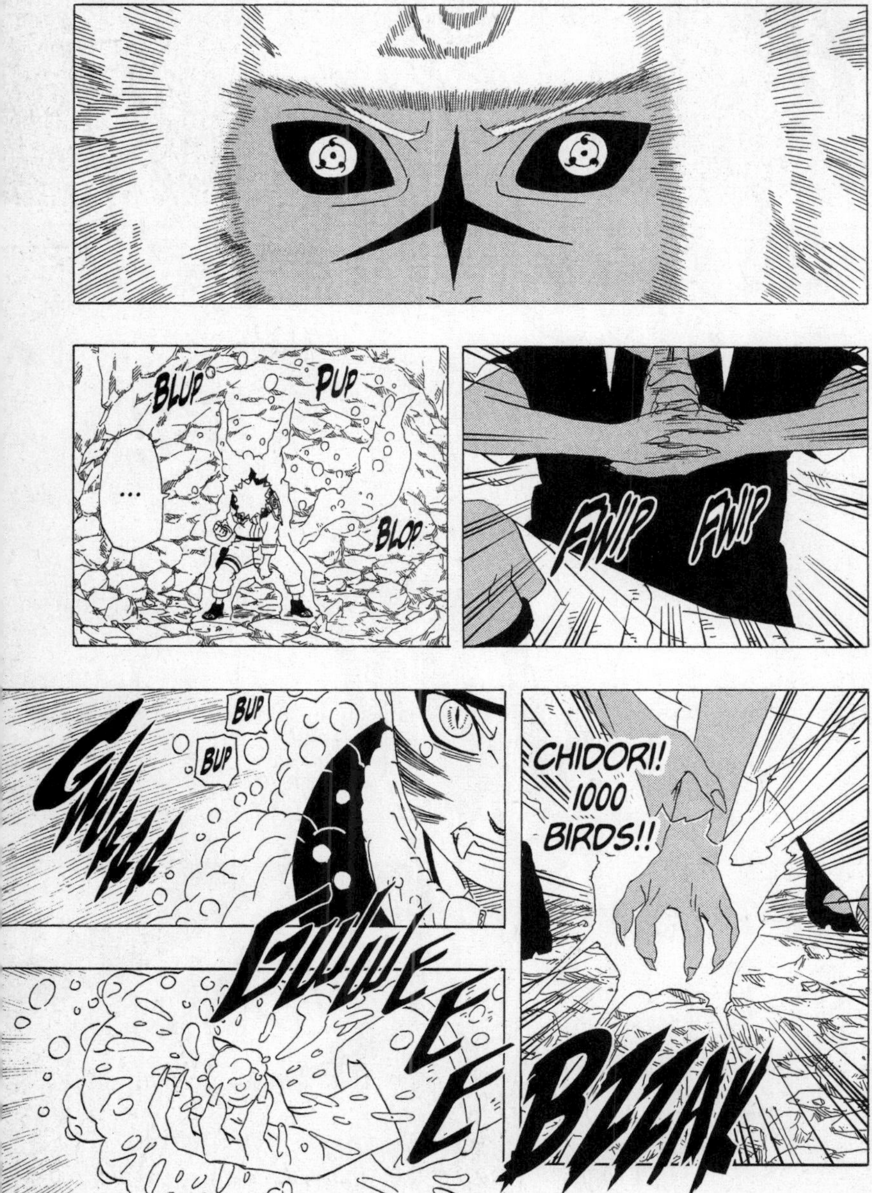
FWIP
FWIP
BLUP
PUP
...
BLOP
CHIDORI! 1000 BIRDS!!
BZZAK
BUP
BUP

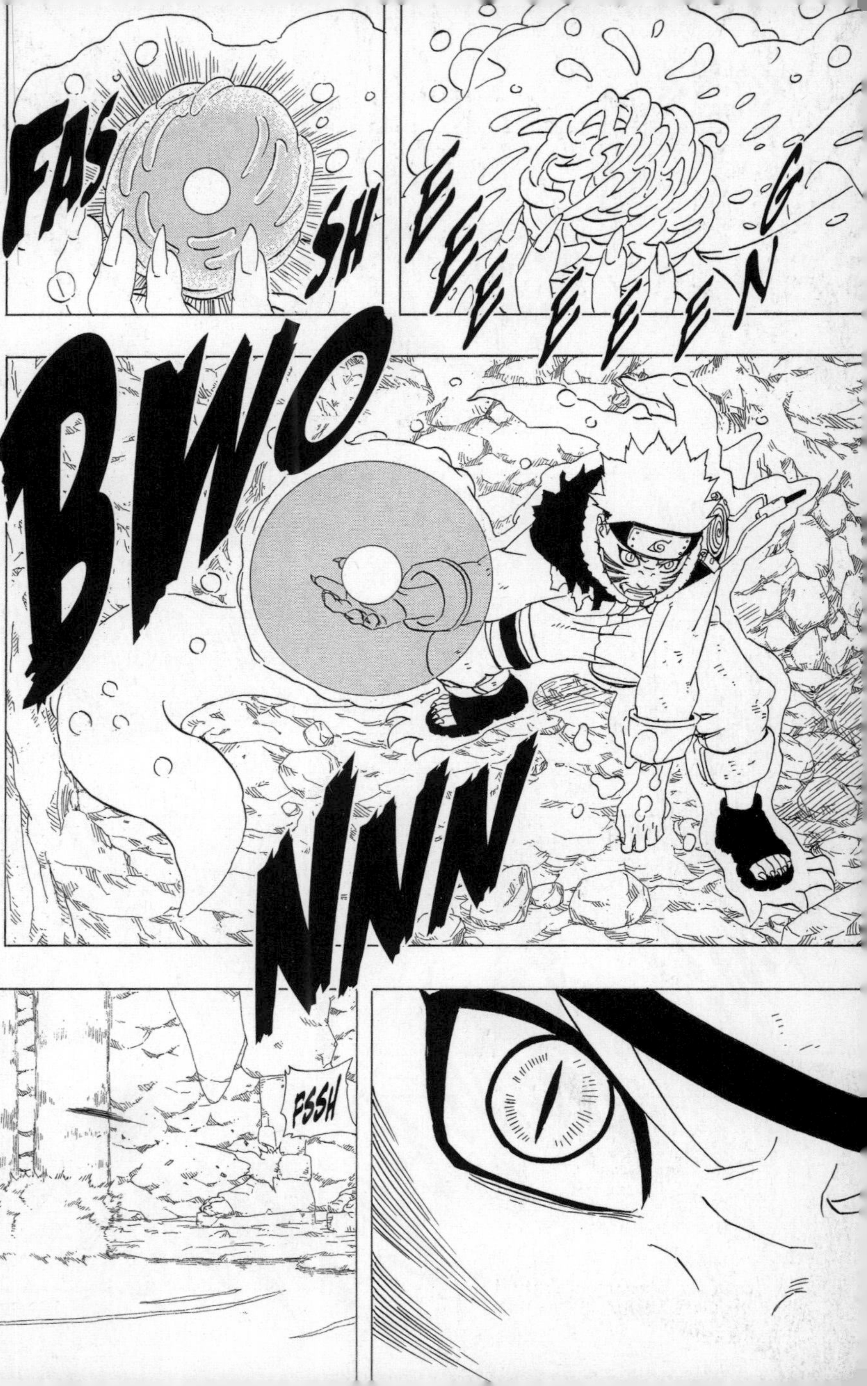
FAS
SHEEEEEEEEENG
BWONNNN
FSSH

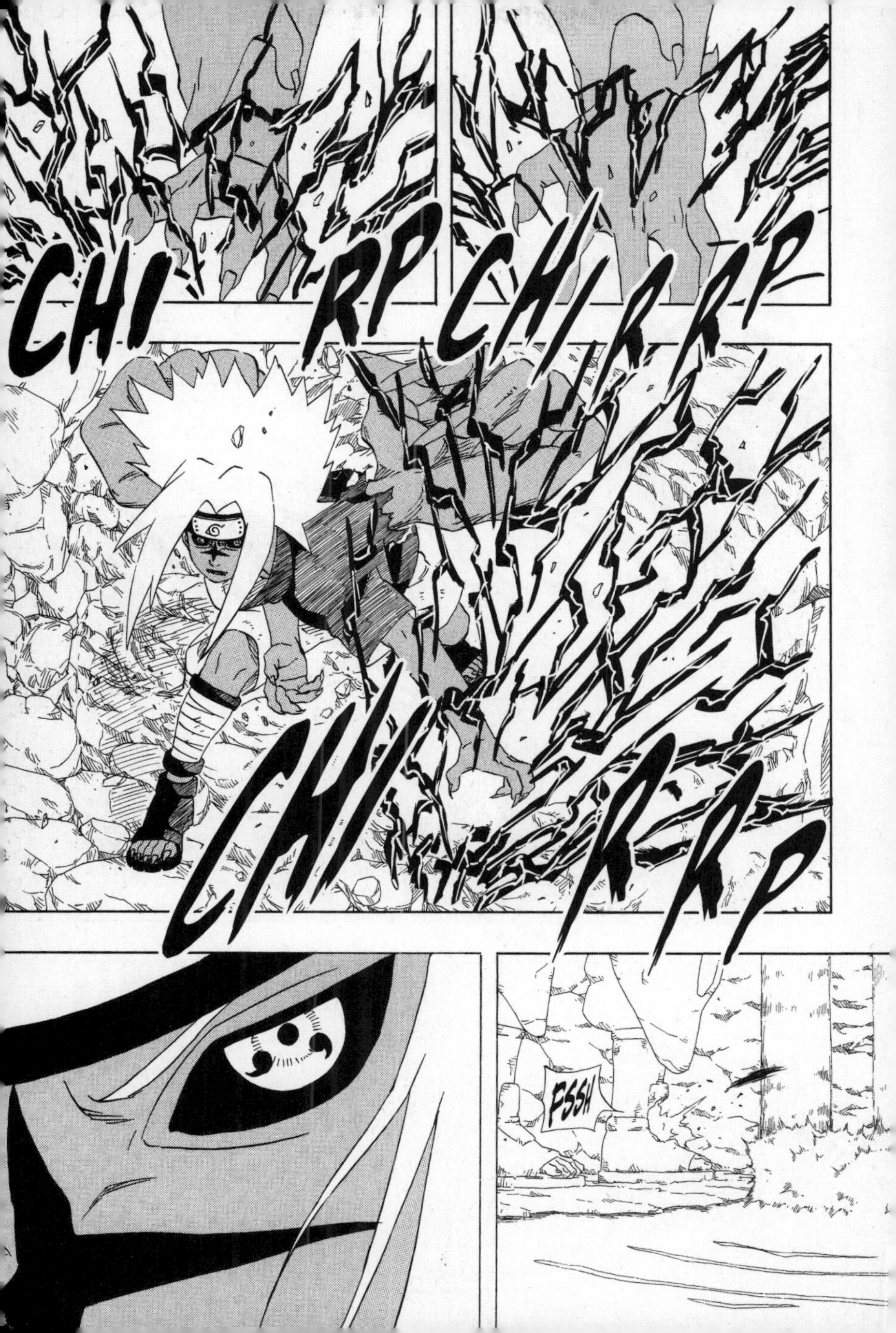

CHIRP
CHIRRP
CHIRRRP
FSSH

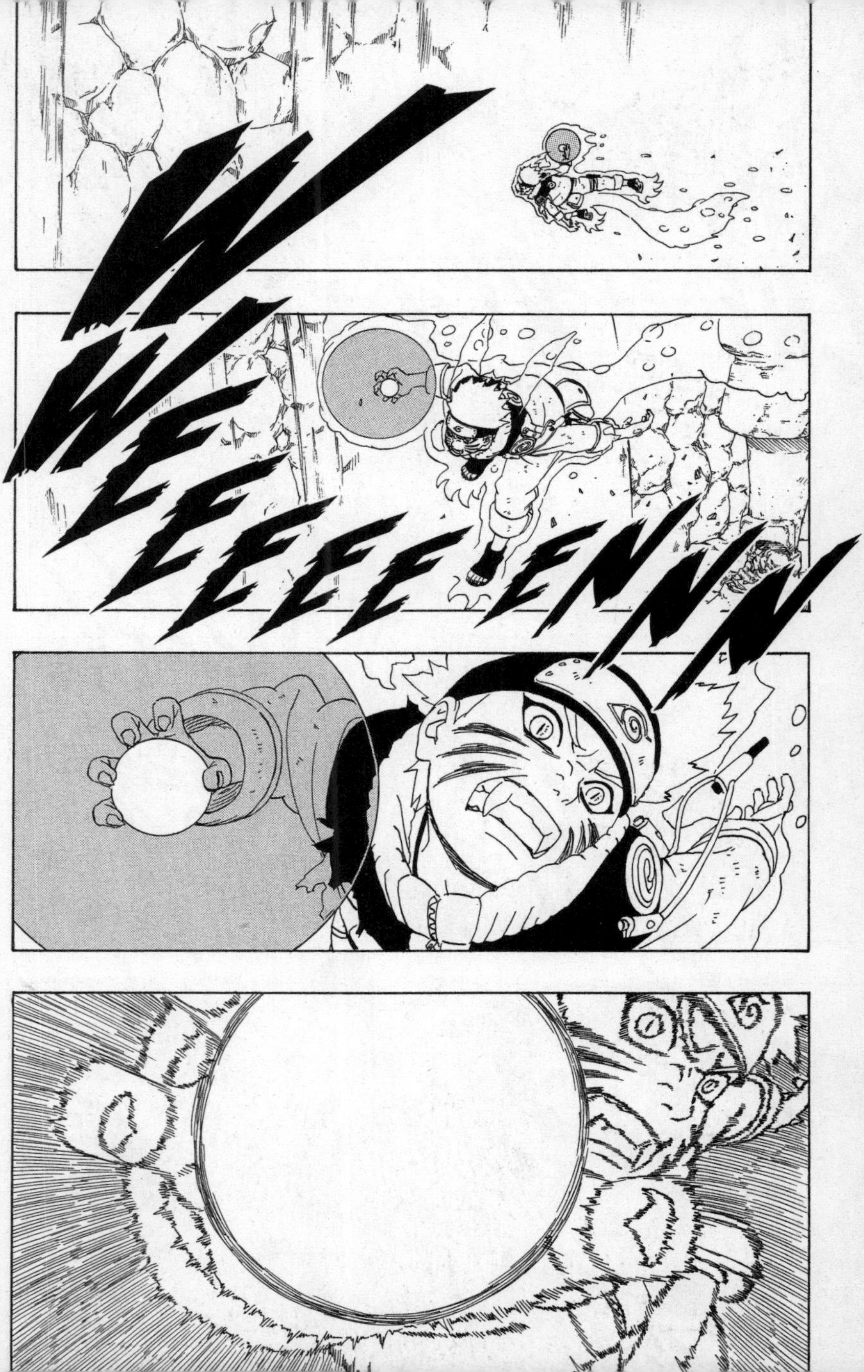
WWEEEEEENNN

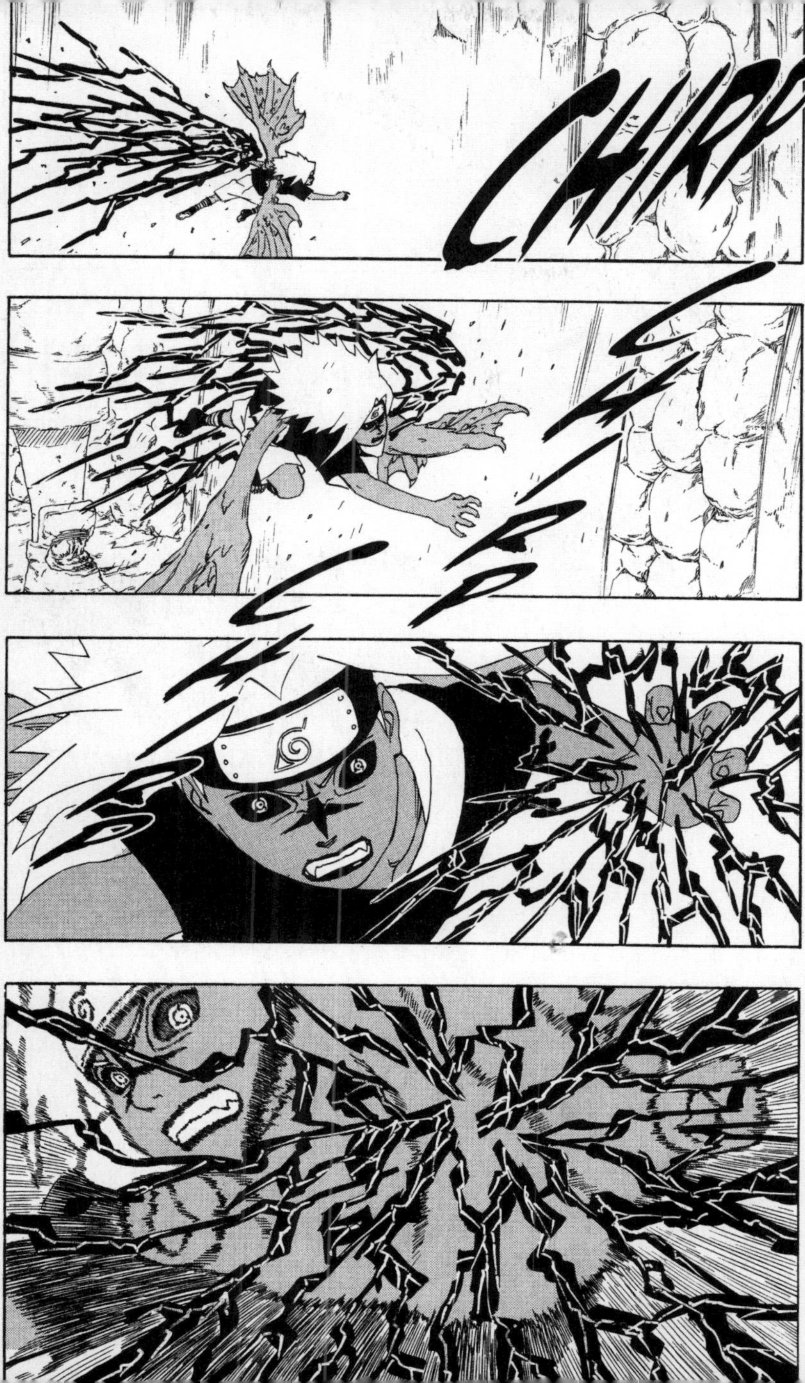
CHIRP
CHIRRP

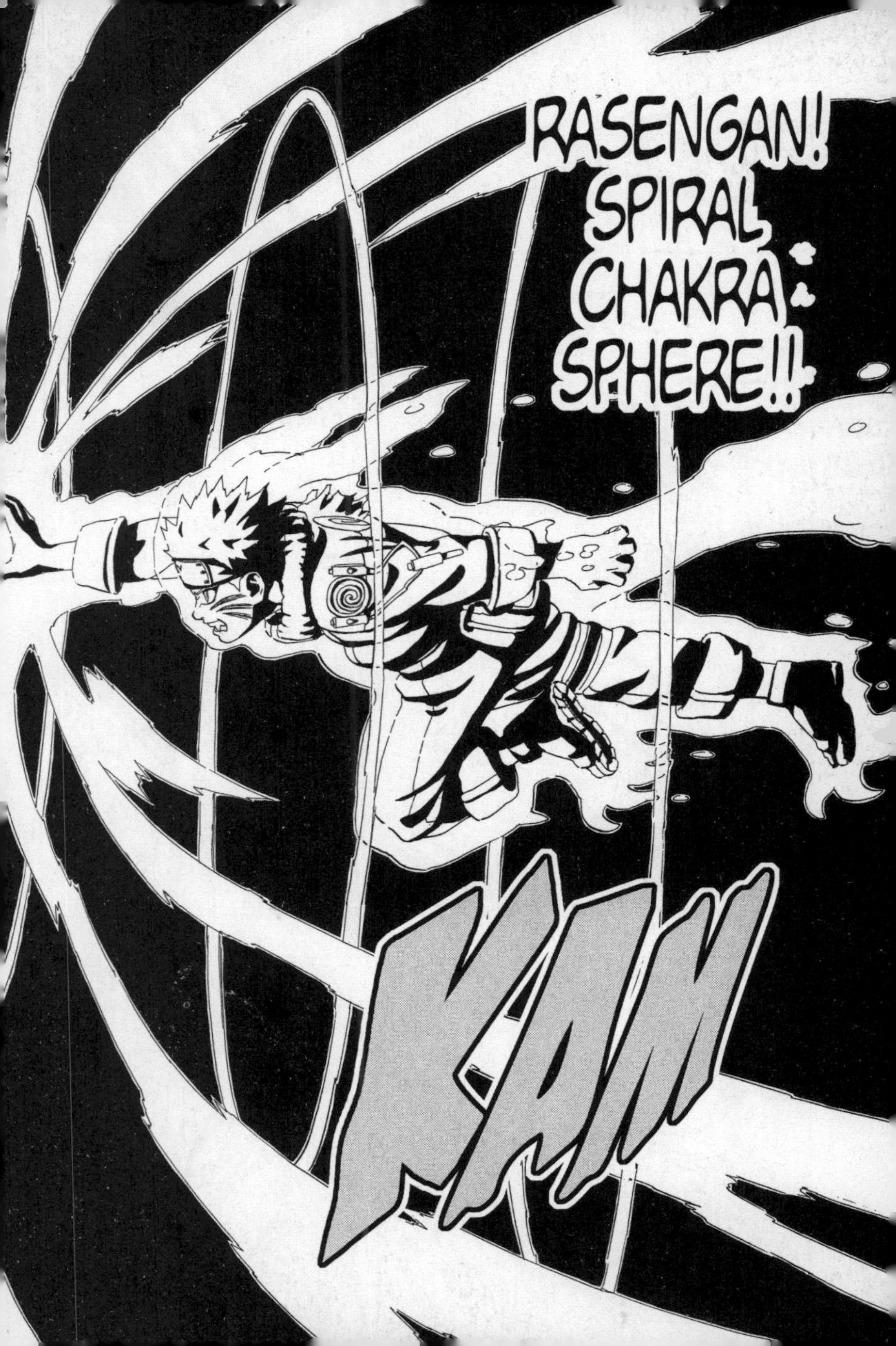
RASENGAN! SPIRAL CHAKRA SPHERE!!
VWAM

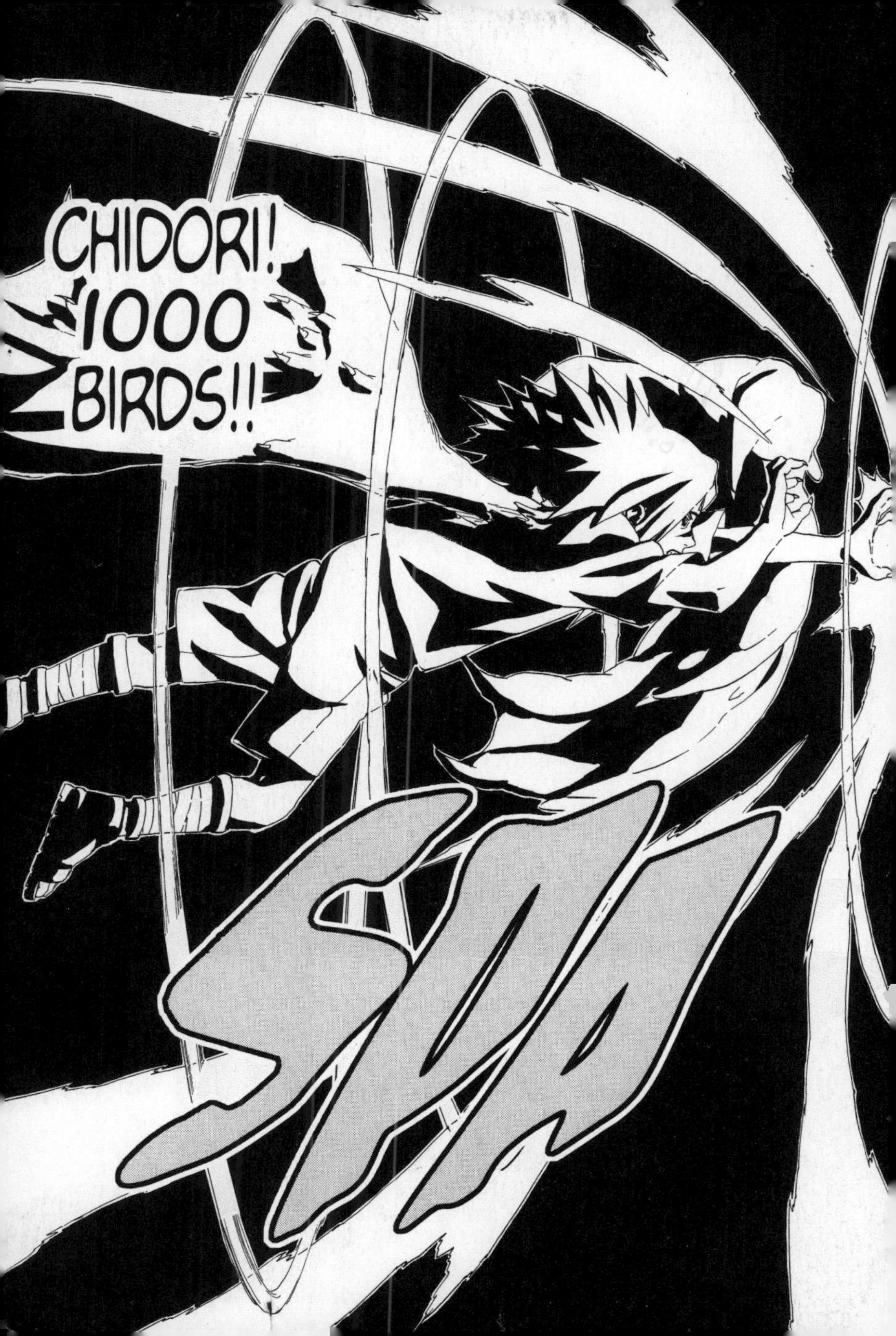
CHIDORI! 1000 BIRDS!!
SHA

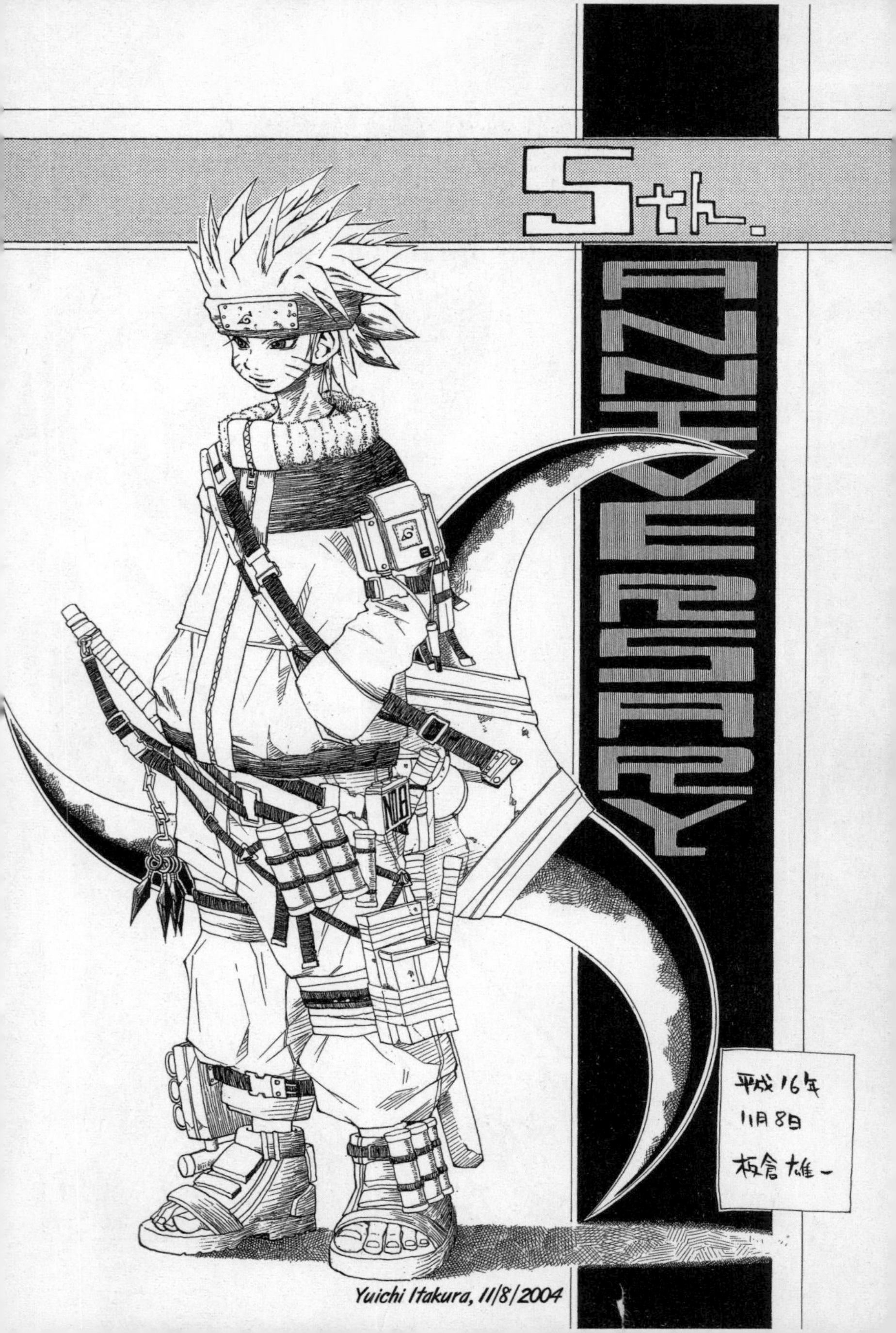
5th.
ANNIVERSARY
平成16年
11月8日
板倉雄一
Yuichi Itakura, 11/8/2004

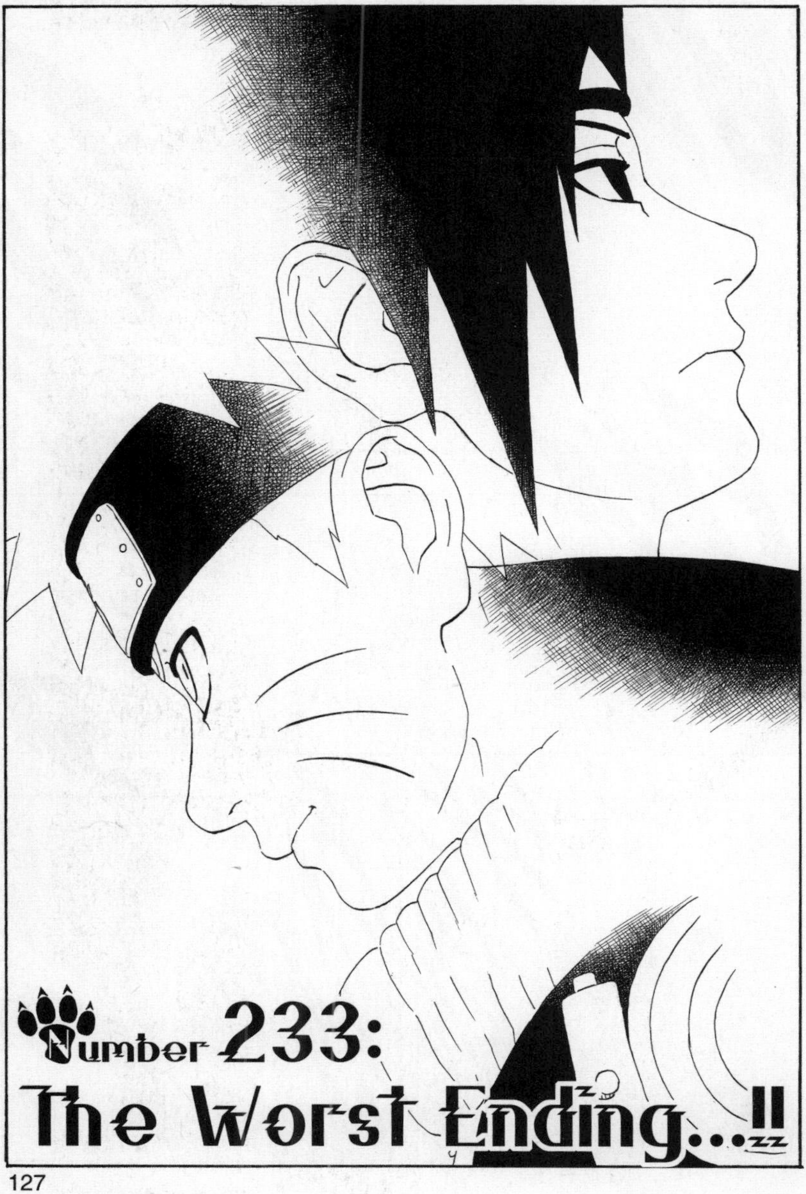
Number 233:
The Worst Ending...!!

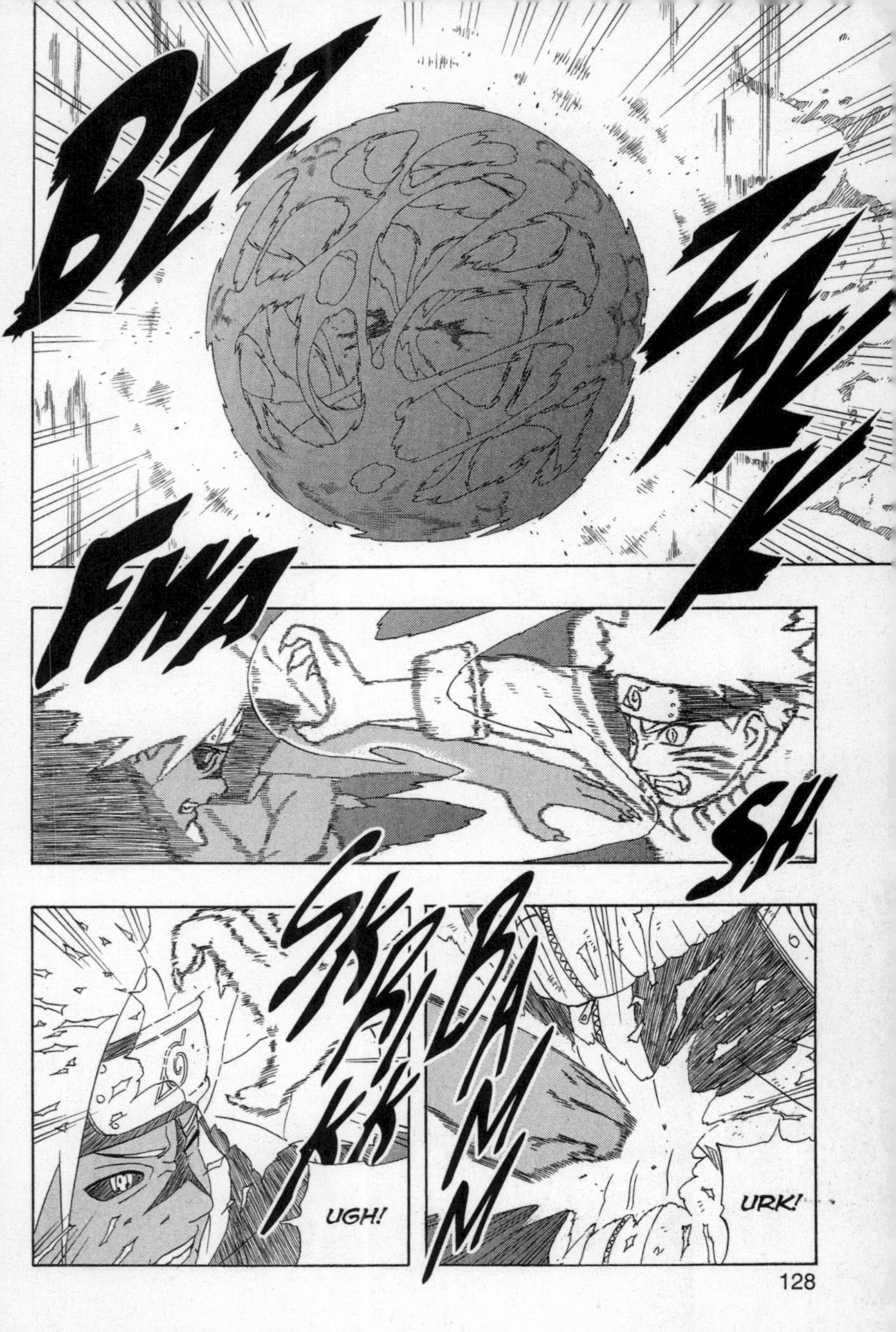
FWA
SH
URK!
UGH!

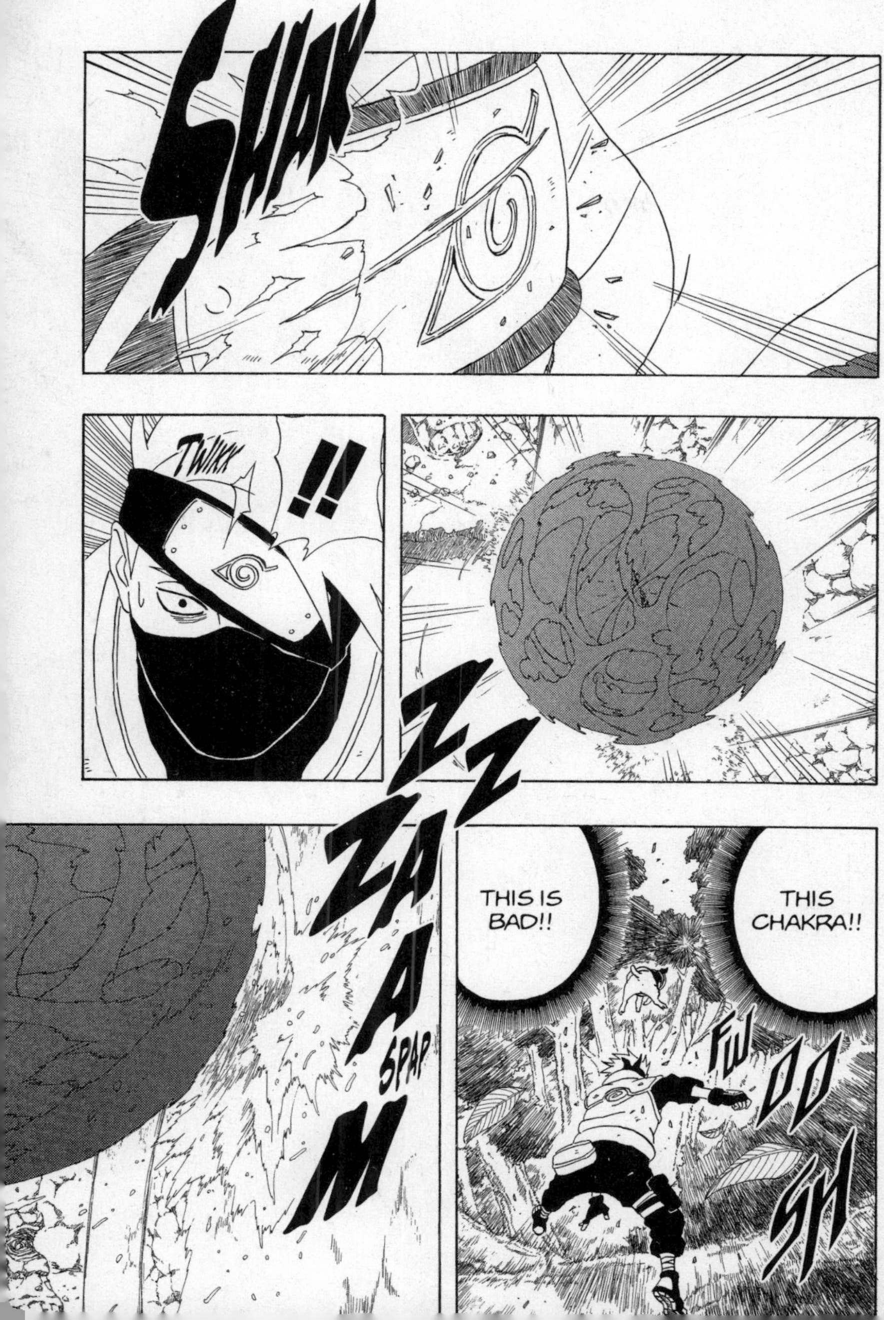
SHAK
!!
TWIKK
ZZZAAM
THIS CHAKRA!!
THIS IS BAD!!
FWOOSH
SPAP

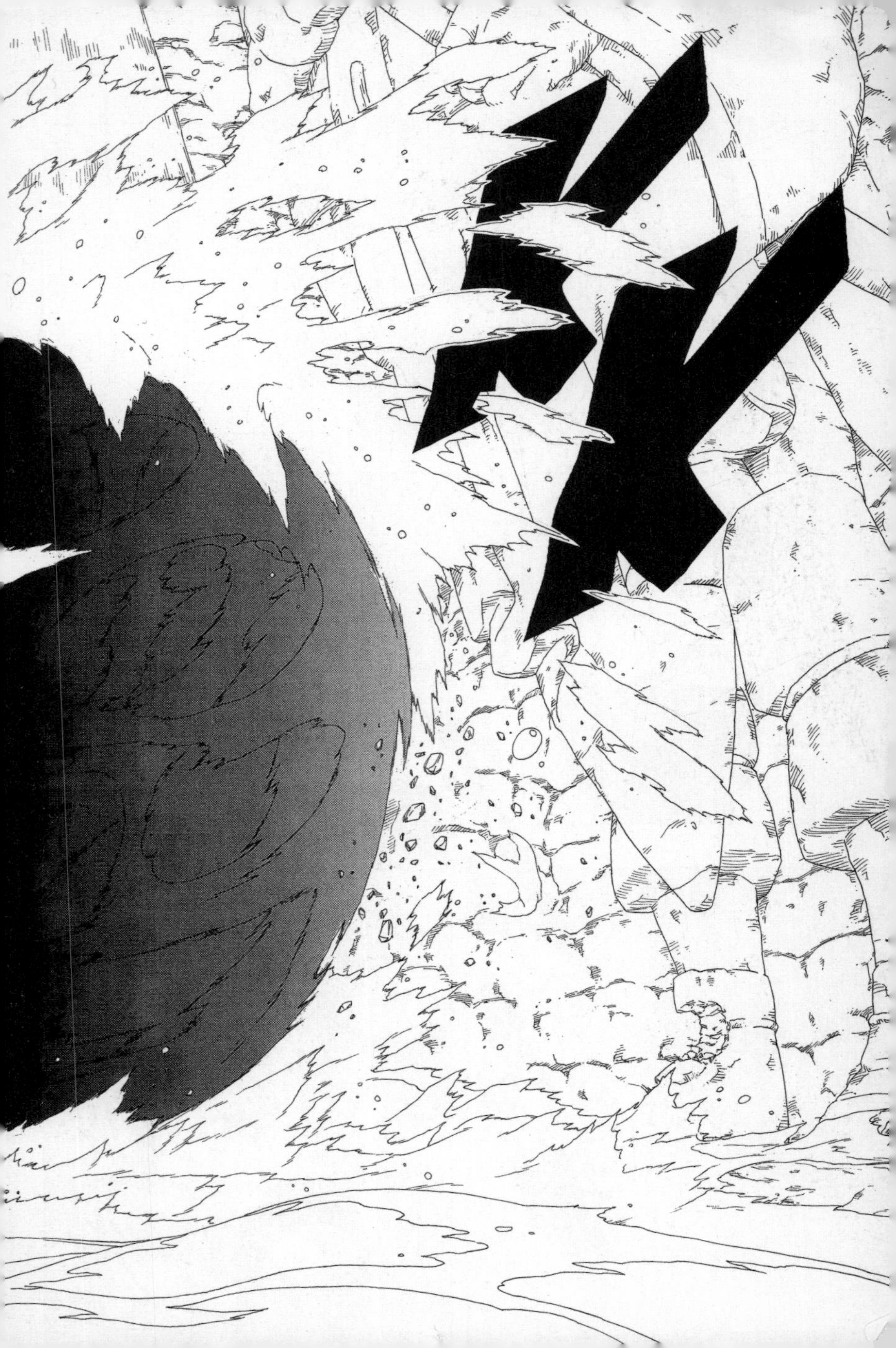

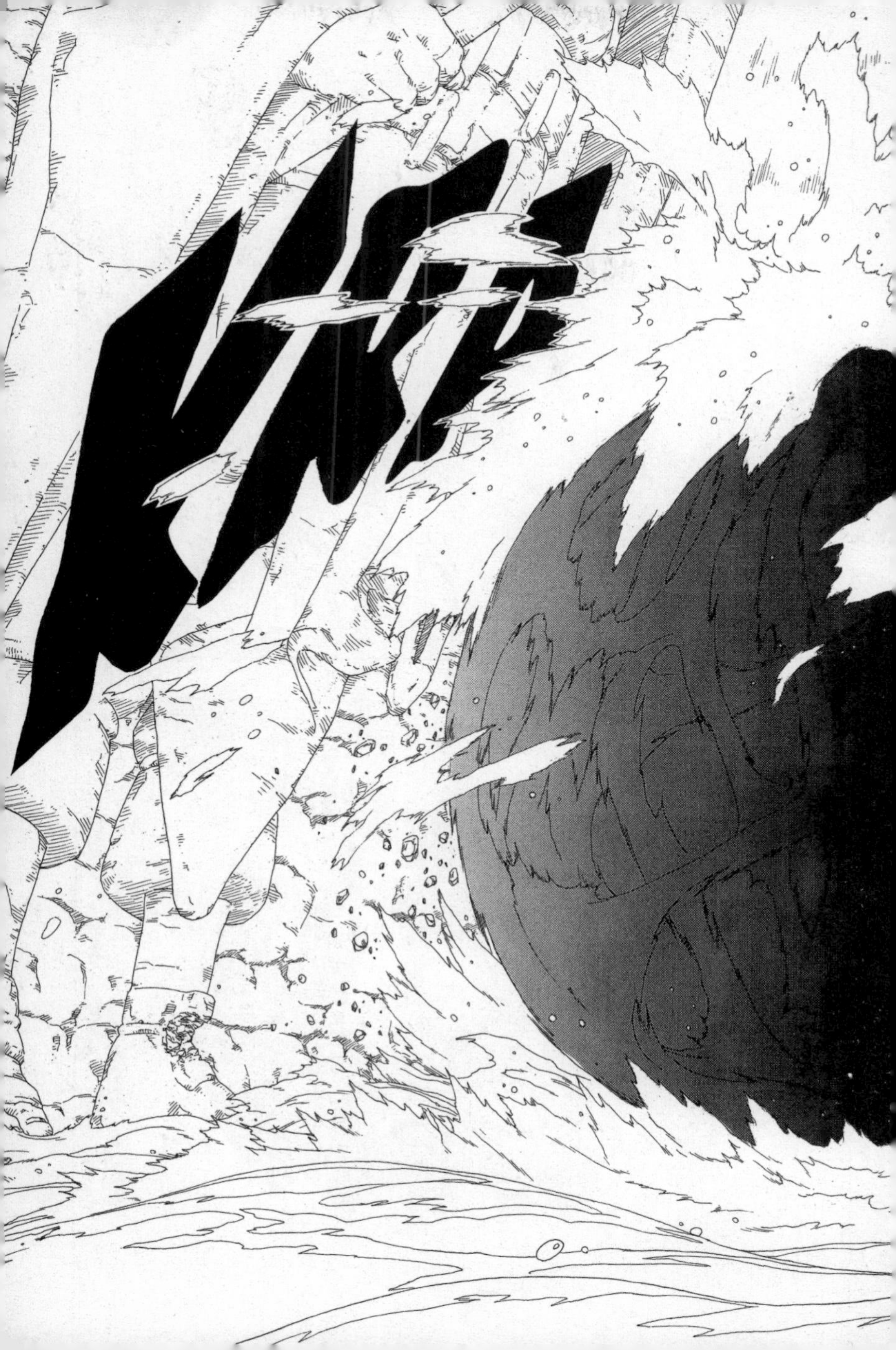

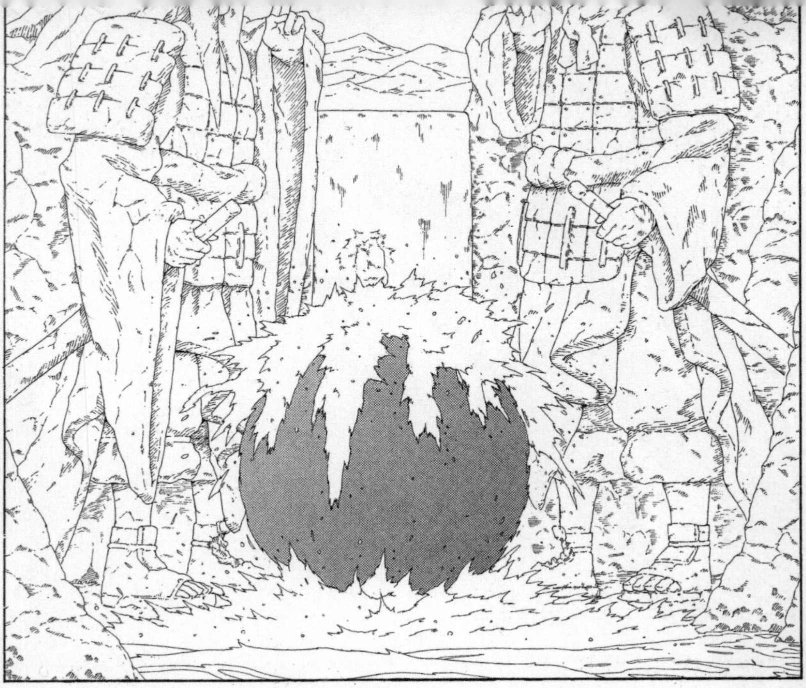

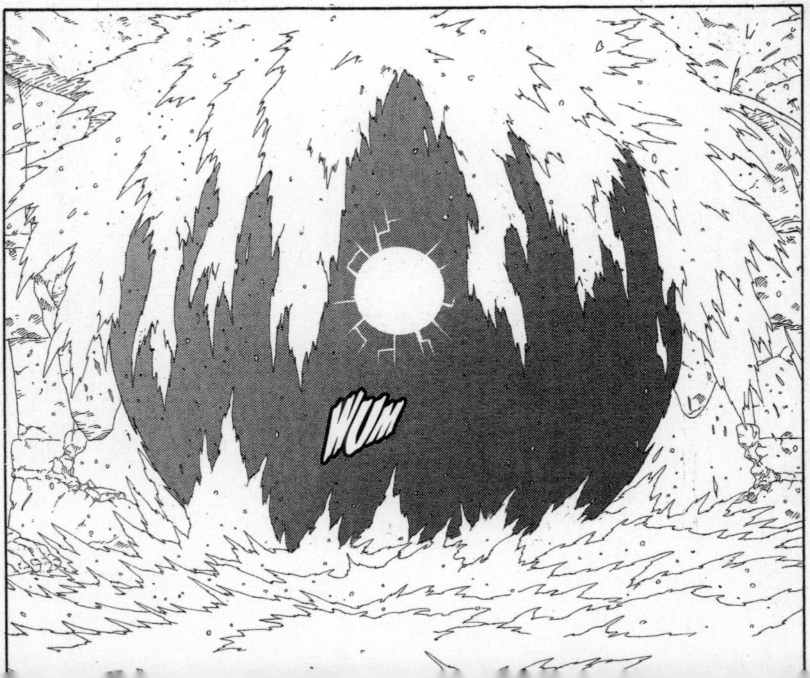
WUM

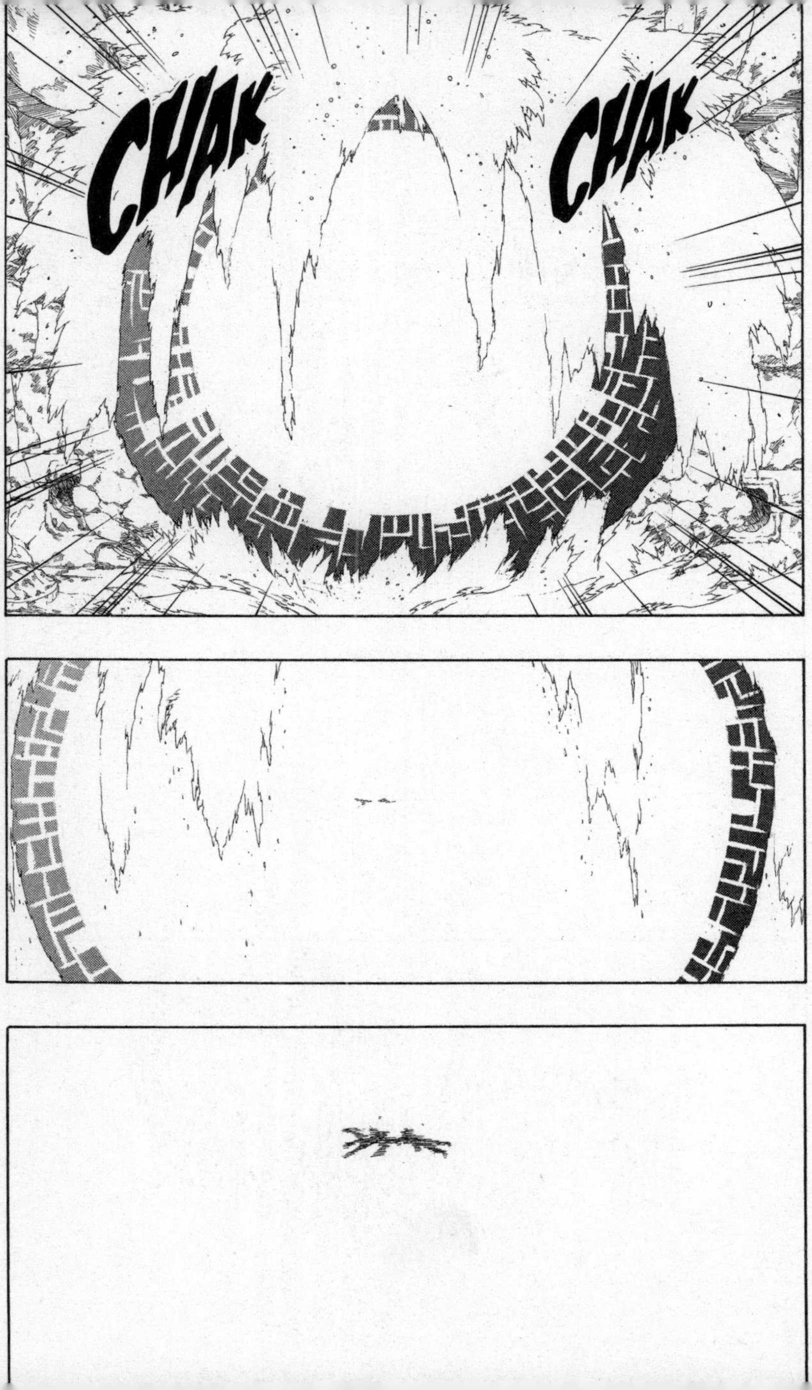
CHAK
CHAK

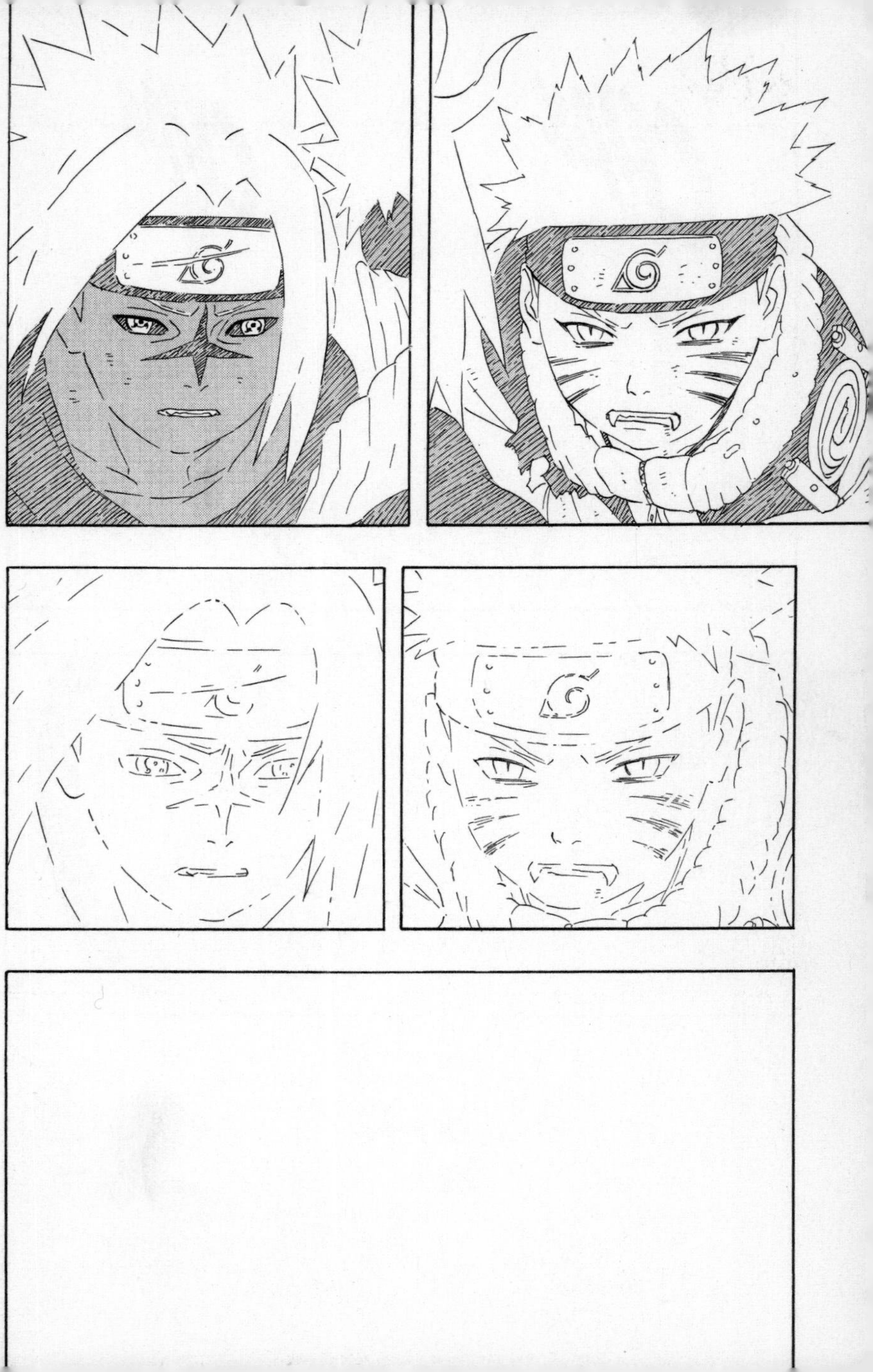

READ THIS WAY

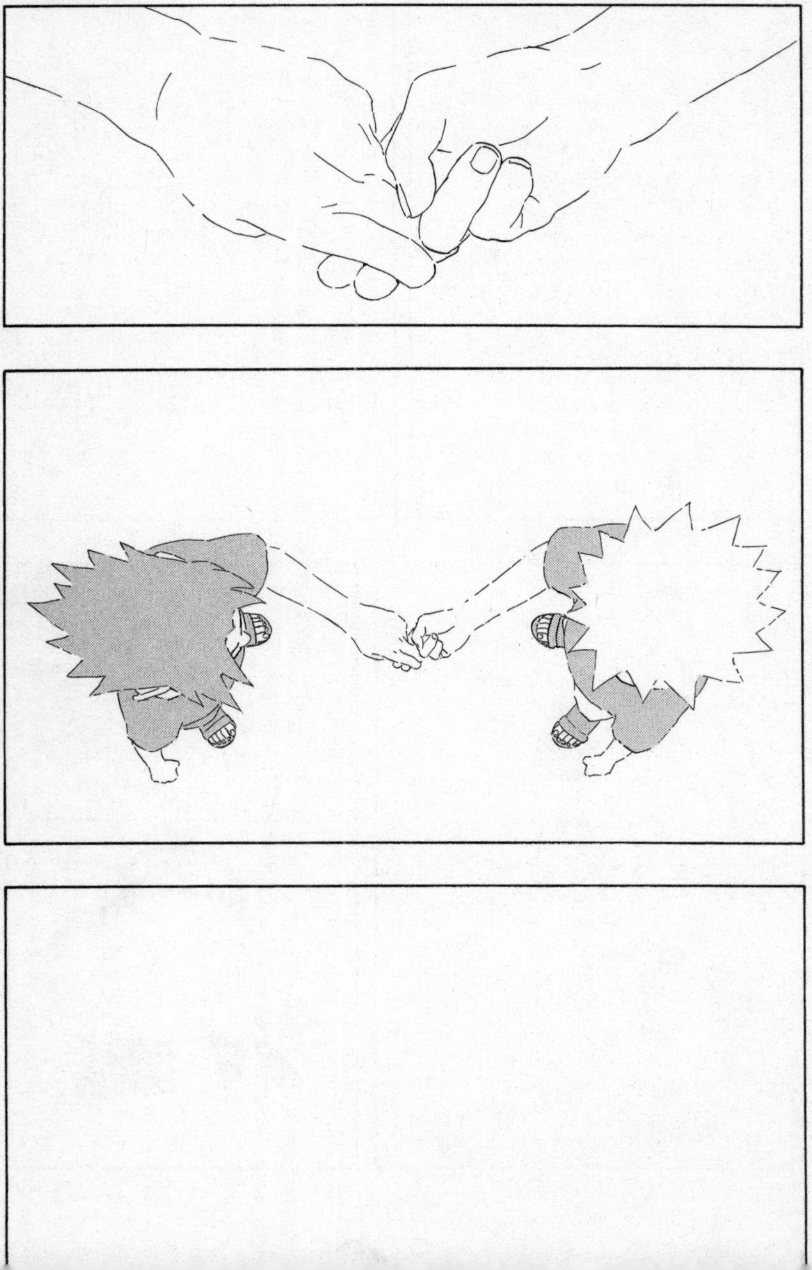

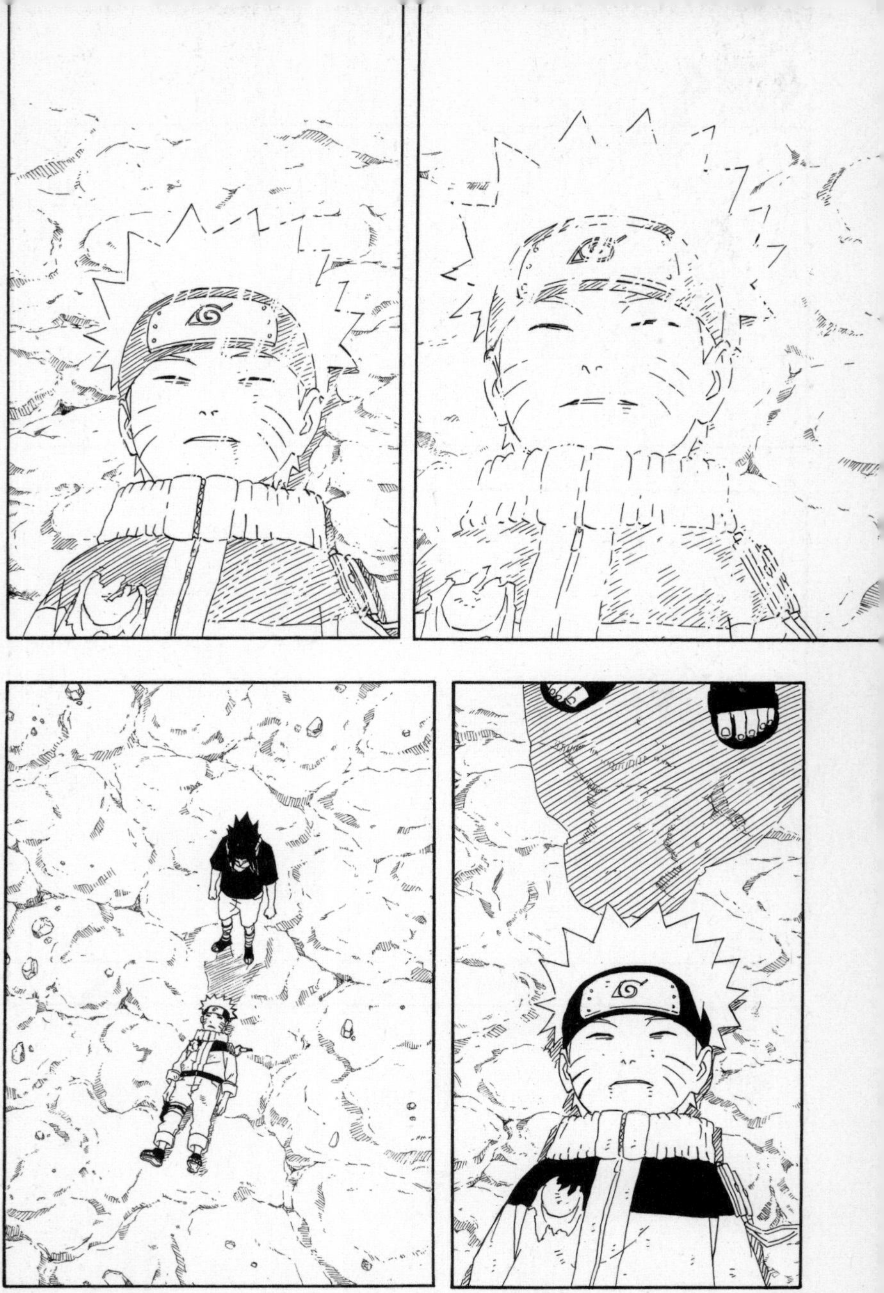

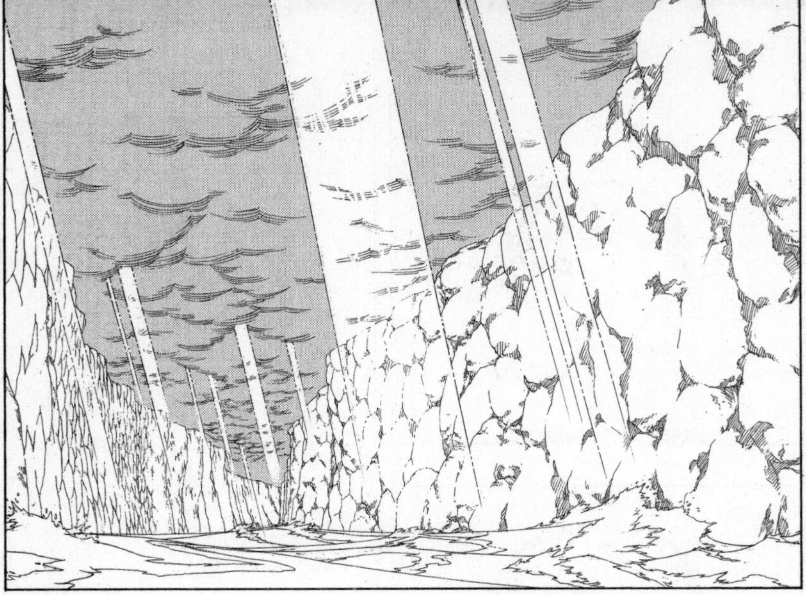
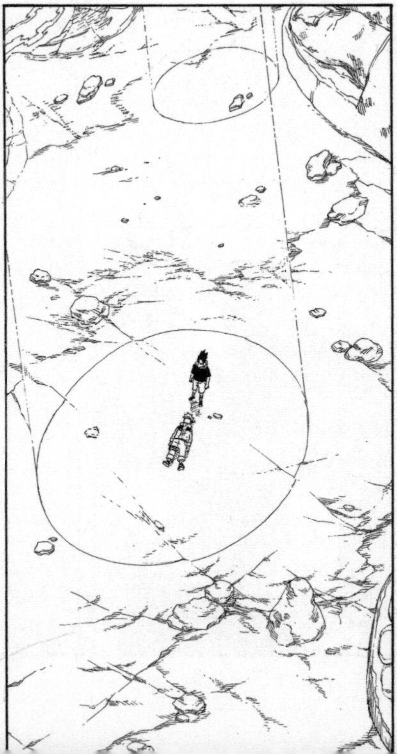
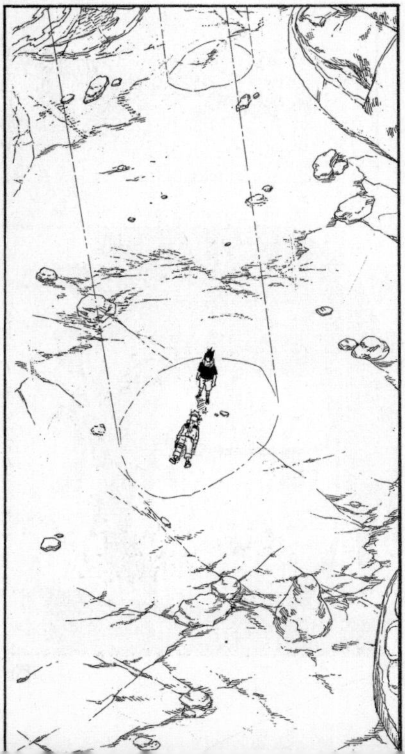

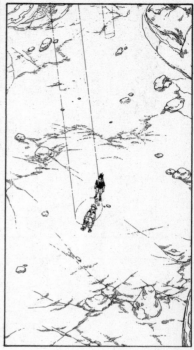

SHUF

READ THIS WAY

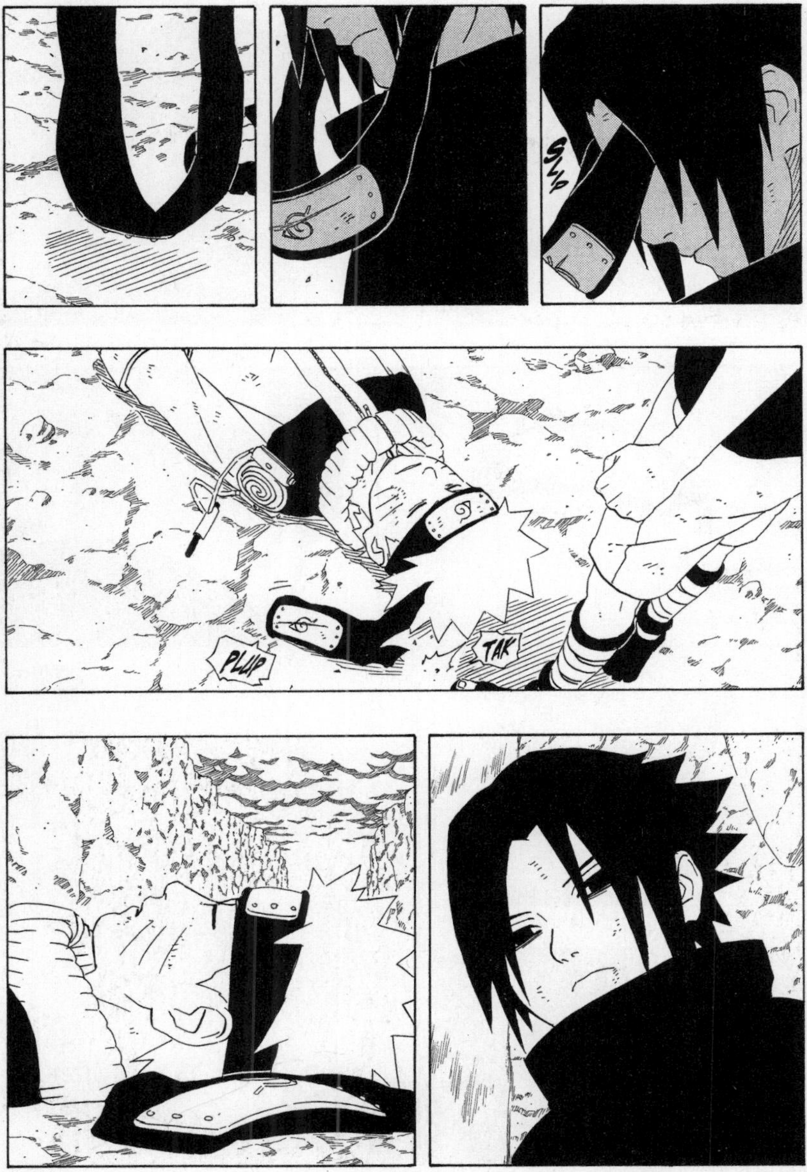
SLIP
TAK
PLUP

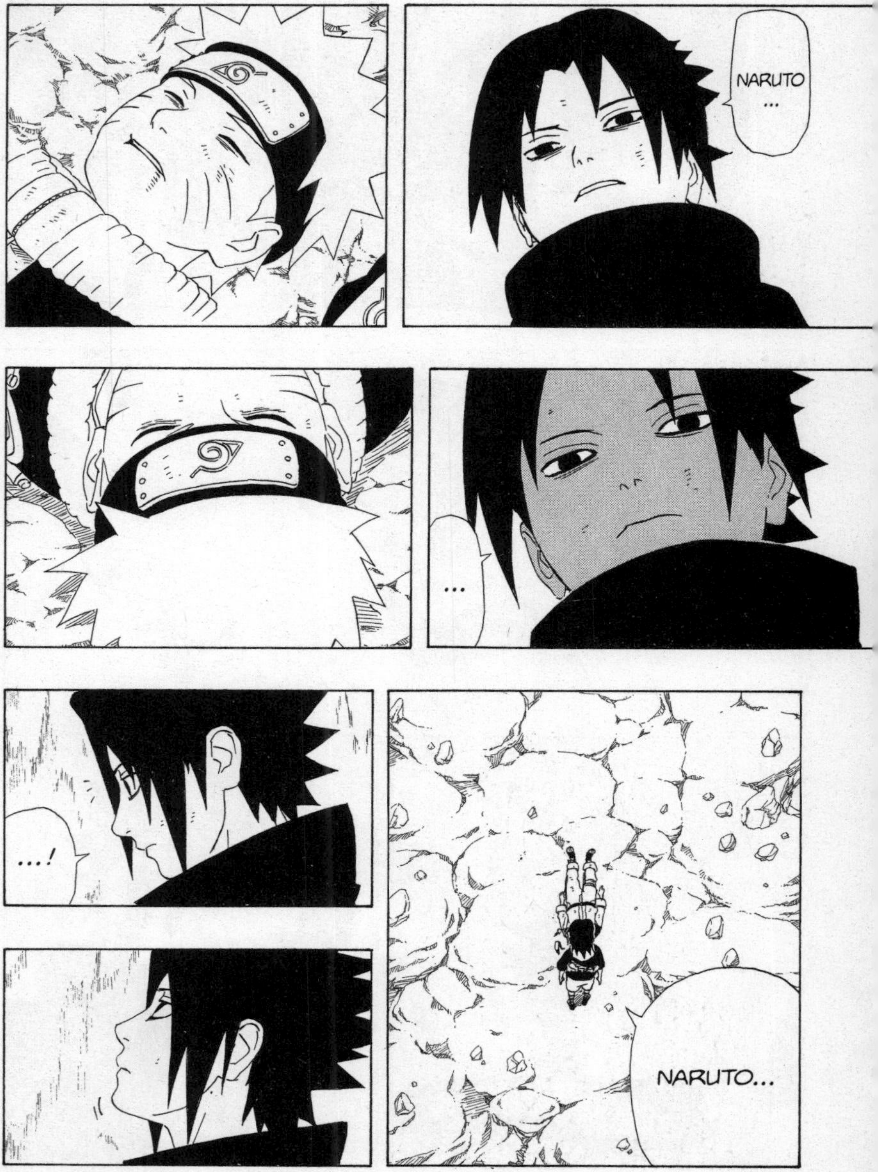
NARUTO ...
...
NARUTO...
...!

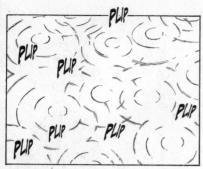

PLIP
PLIP
PLIP PLIP
PLIP
PLIP
PLIP PLIP
PLIP

PLIP
PLIP
PLIP

KSHSSHH HH

SHSSHHHH

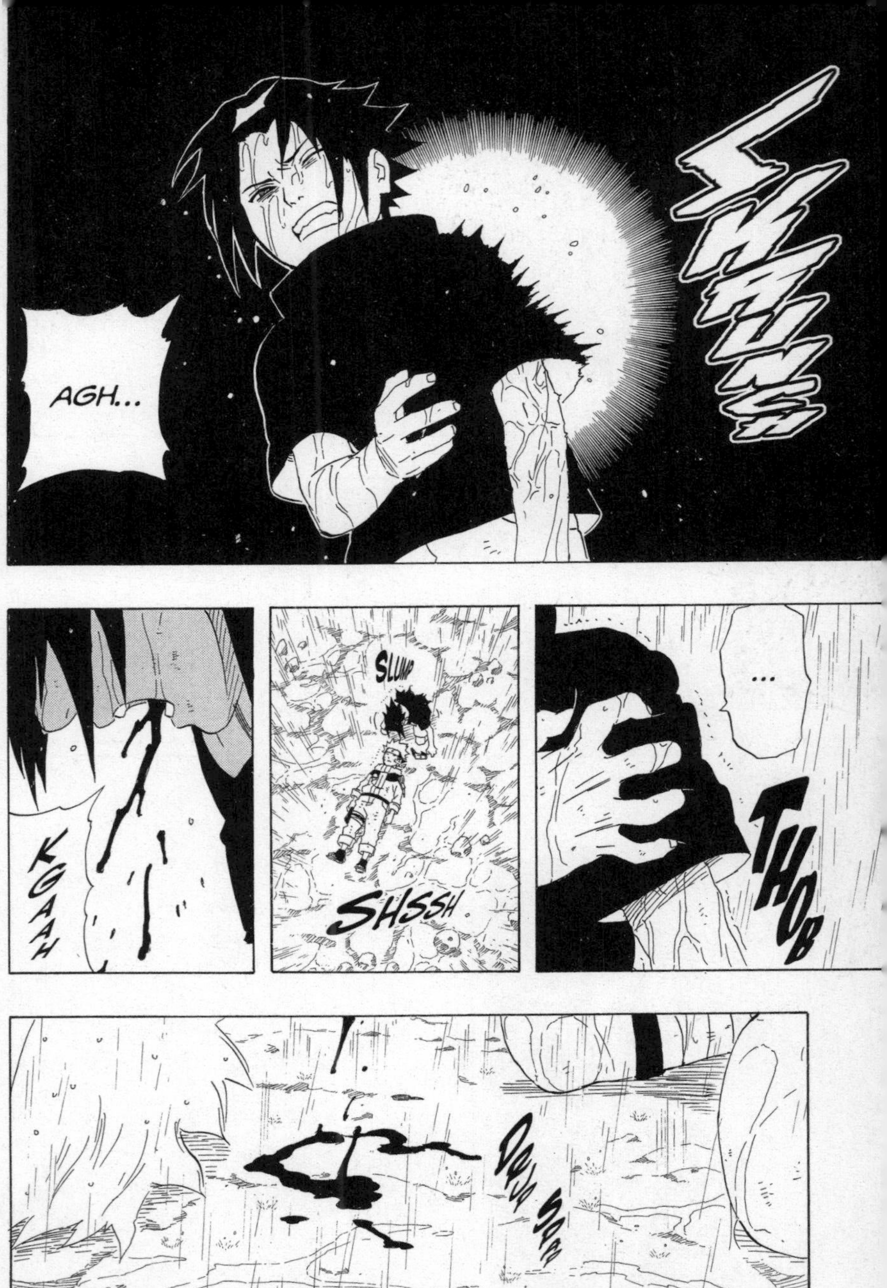
AGH...
...
THOB
SLUMP
SHSSH
KGAAH

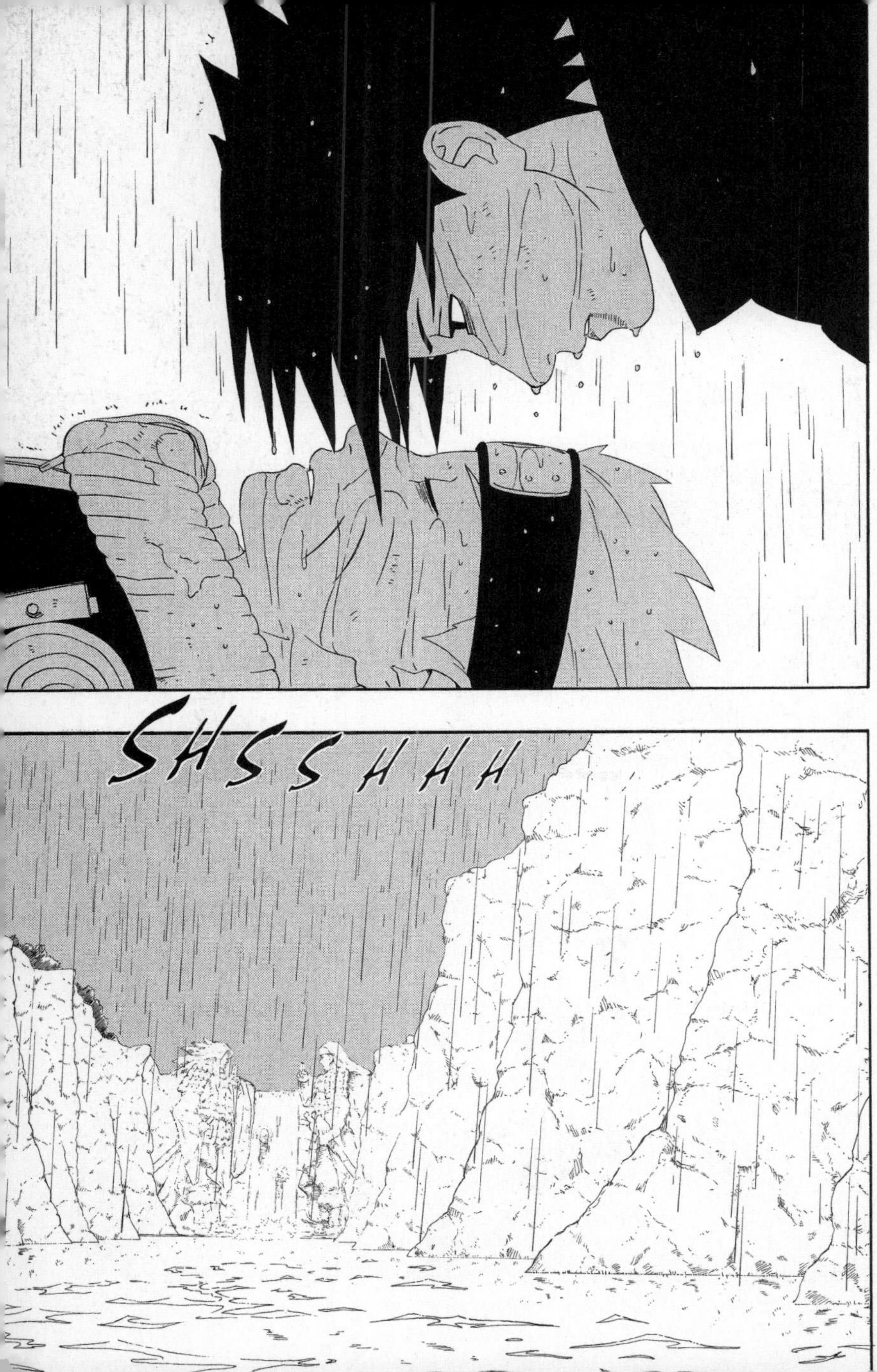
SHSSHHH

REALLY CLOSE...

WE'RE OKAY!

THIS WAY!!

CAN YOU STILL HOLD THE SCENT?!

IT'S RAIN- ING...

TUMP

TAK

SPLASH

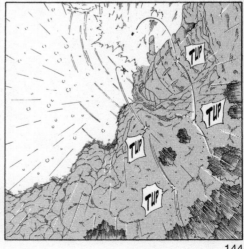

TUP

TUP

TUP

TUP

READ THIS WAY

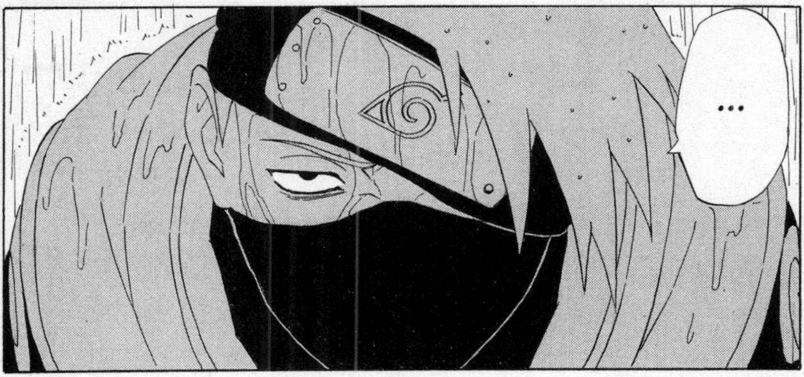
...

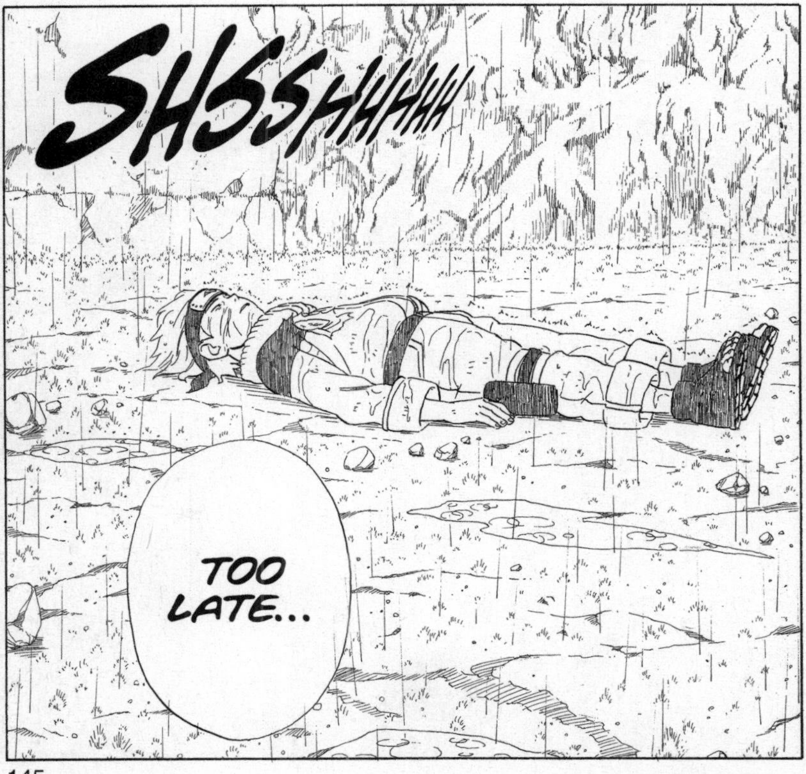
SHSSHHHH
TOO LATE...

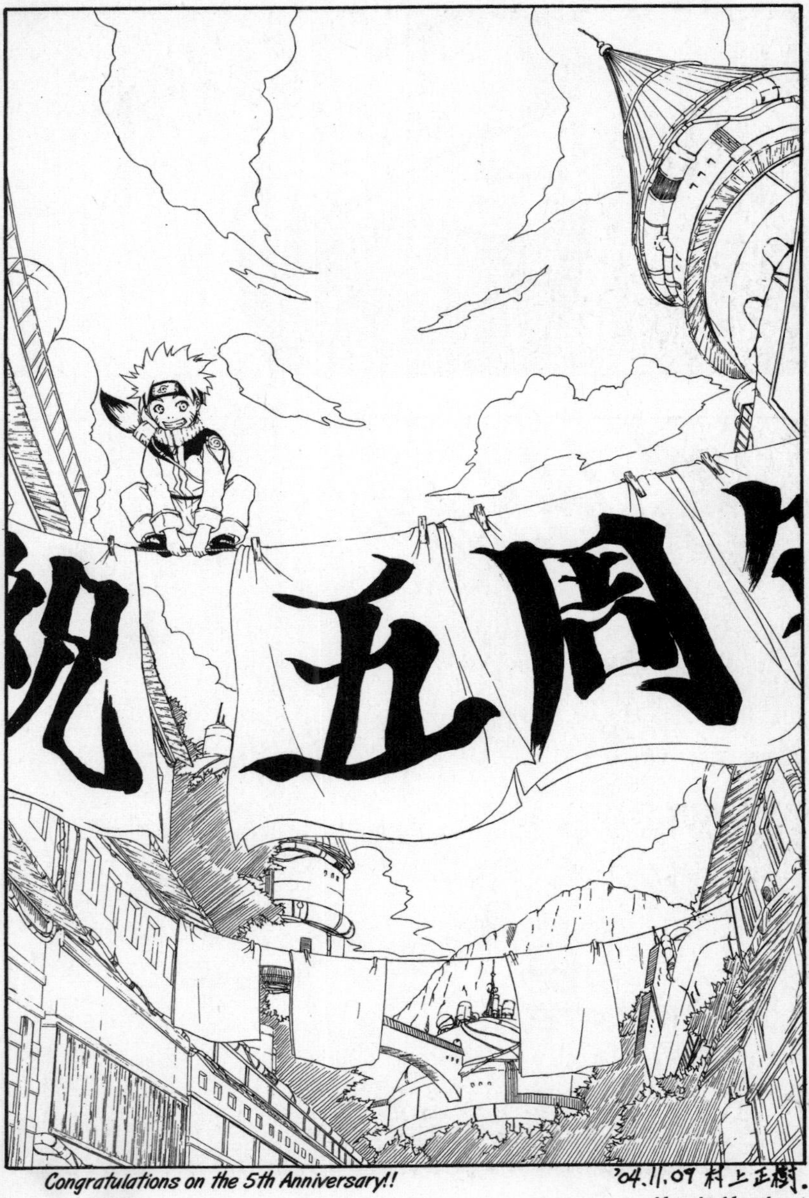
五周

Congratulations on the 5th Anniversary!!

'04.11.09 村上正樹.

Masaki Murakami

Number 234: Parting Ways...!!

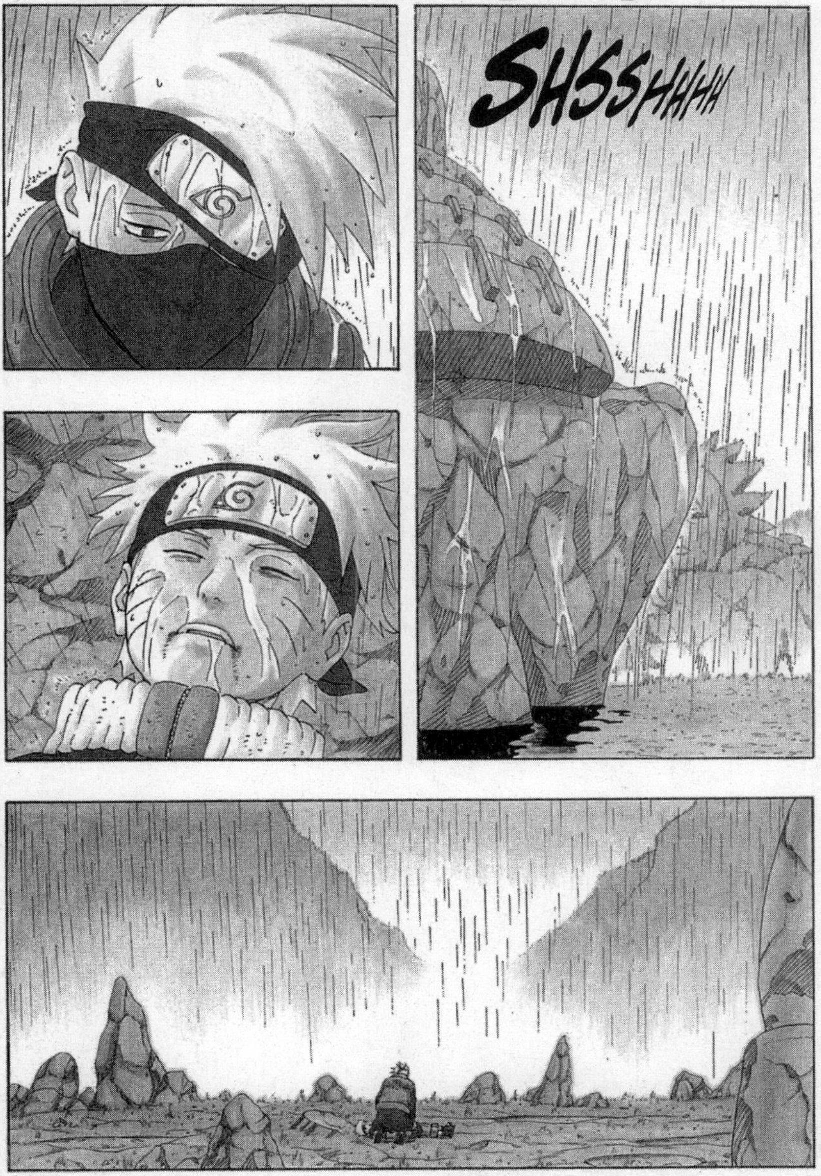
SHSSHHHH

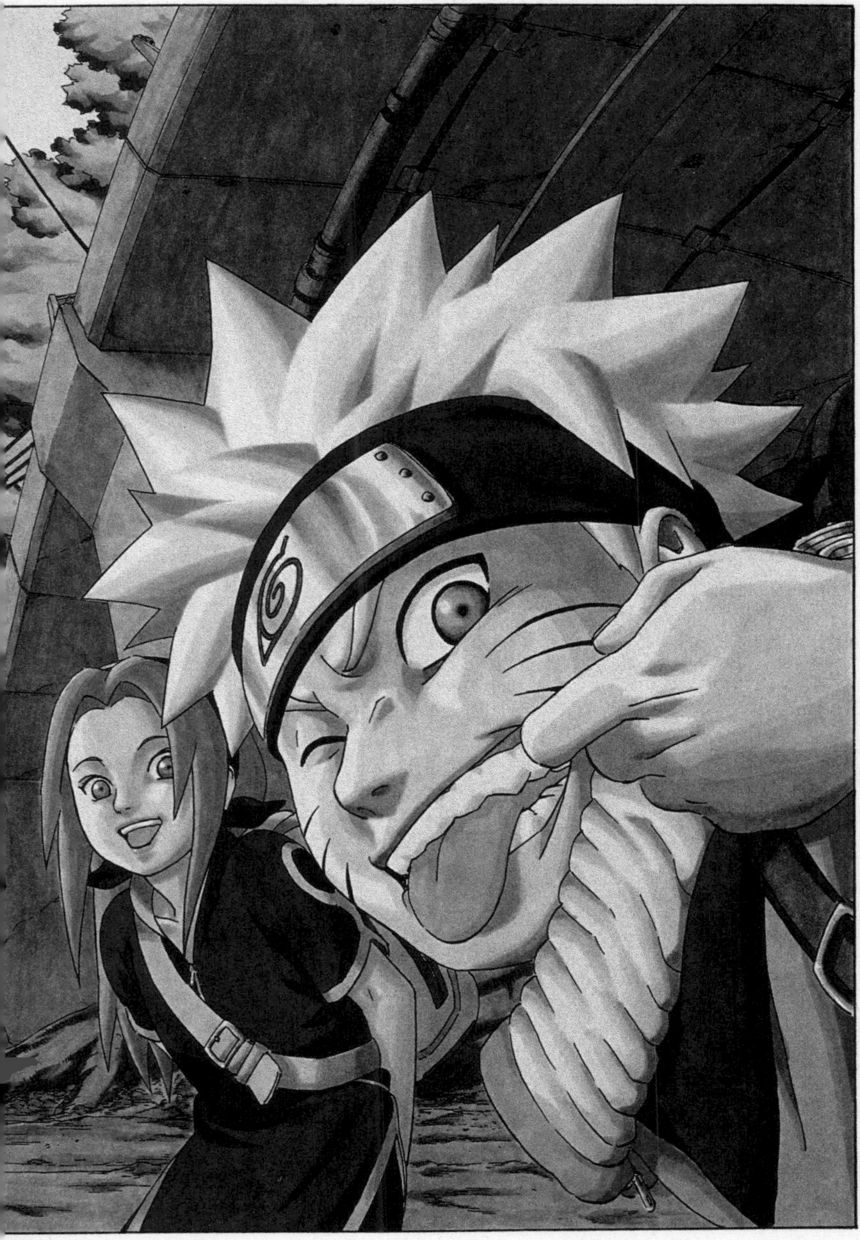

Number 234: Parting Ways...!!

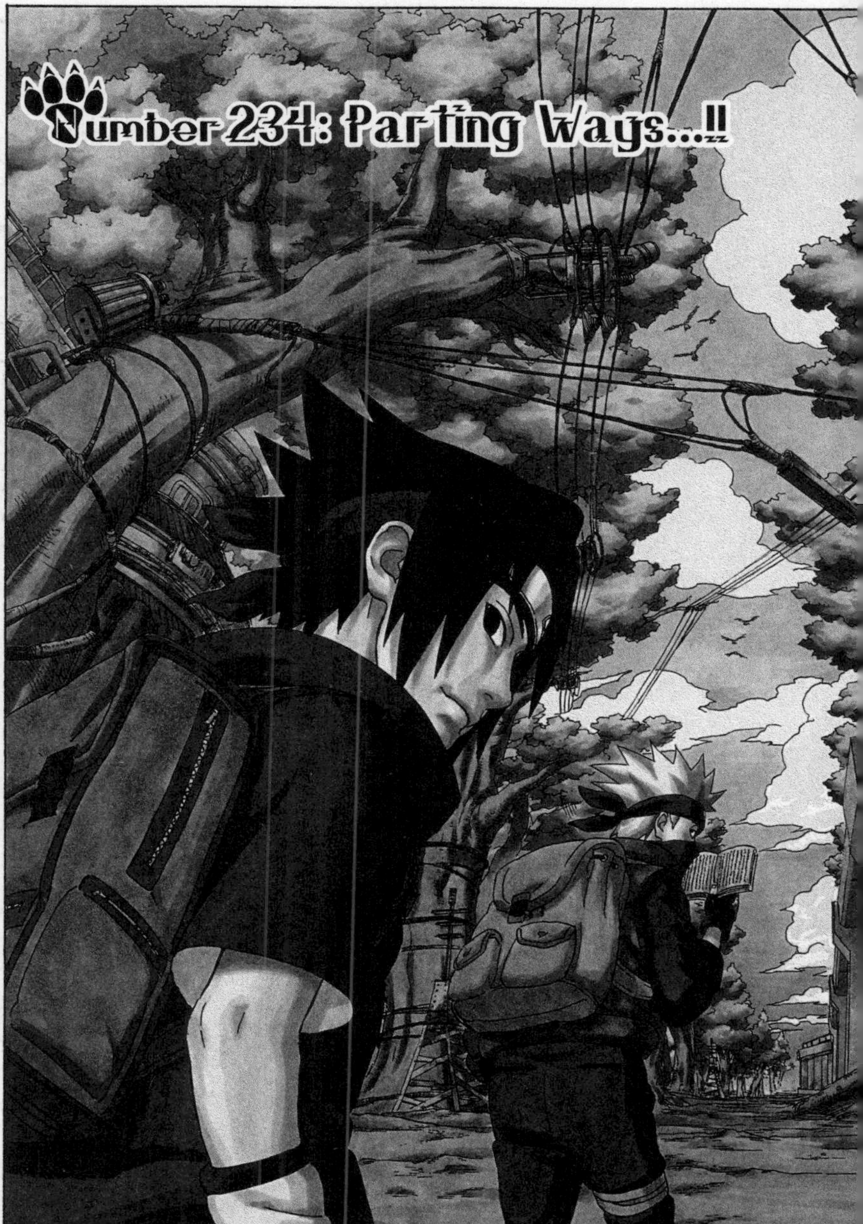

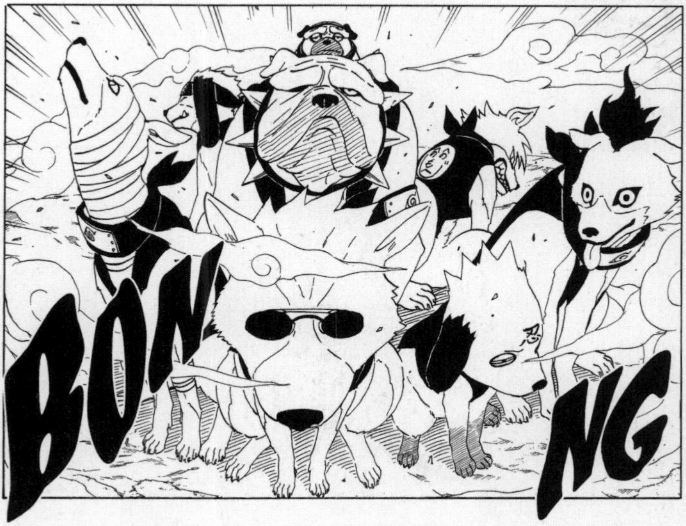
BOING

READ THIS WAY

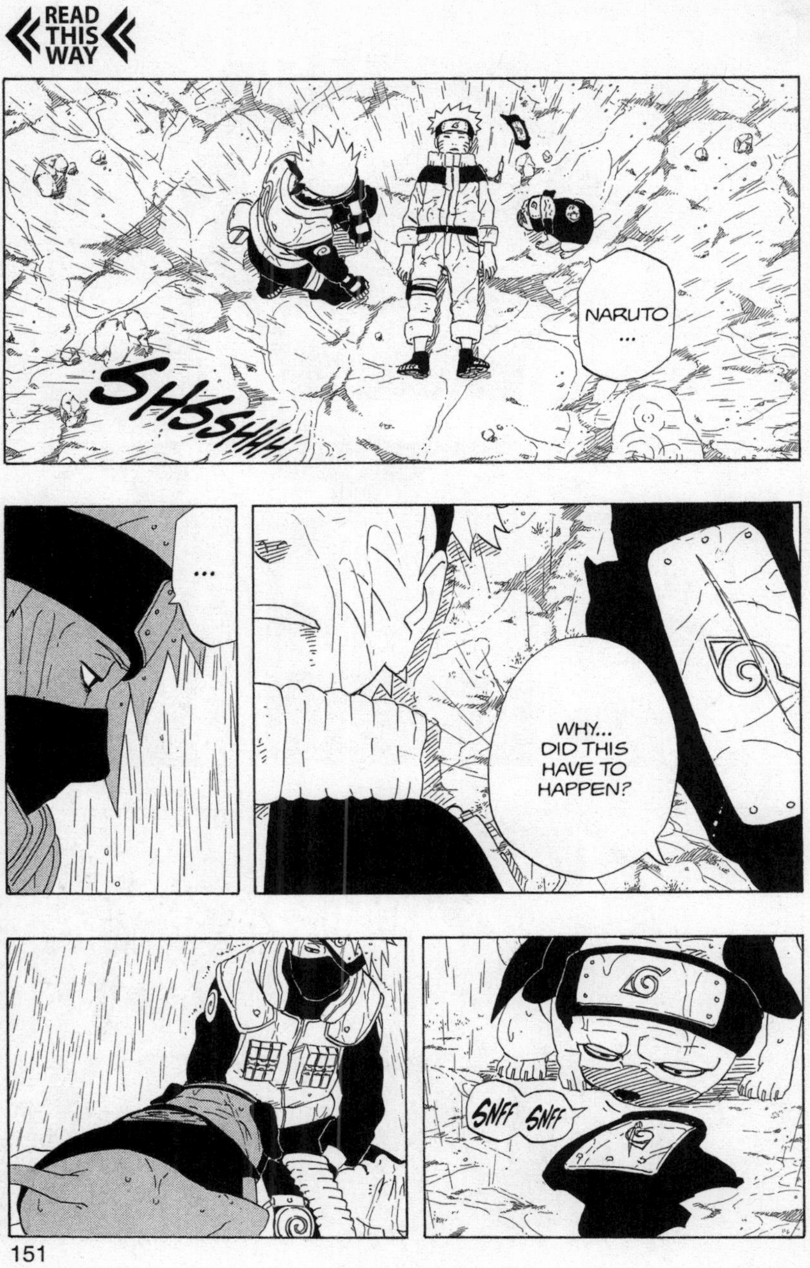
NARUTO ...
SHHSHHH
WHY... DID THIS HAVE TO HAPPEN?
...
SNFF SNFF

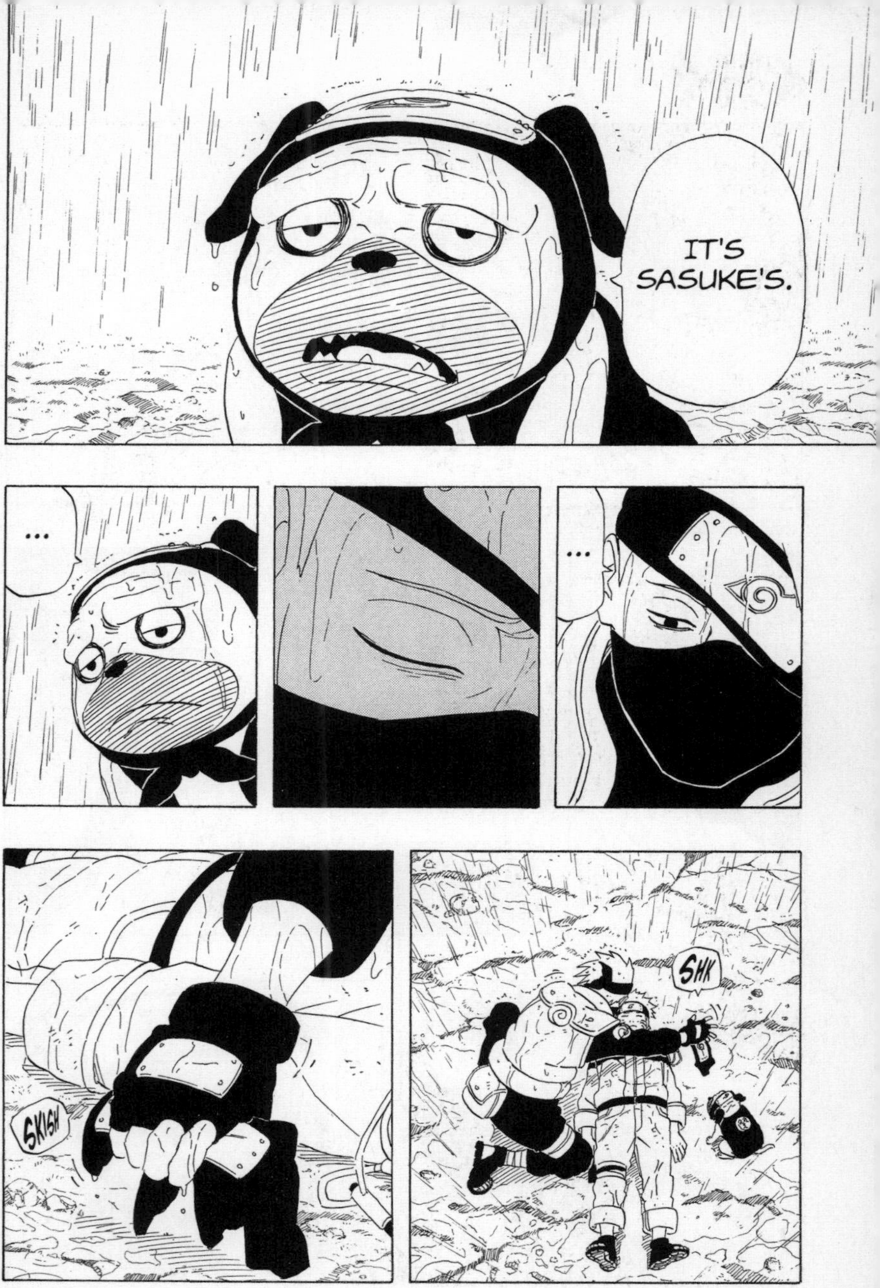
IT'S SASUKE'S.
...
...
SHK
SKISH

READ THIS WAY

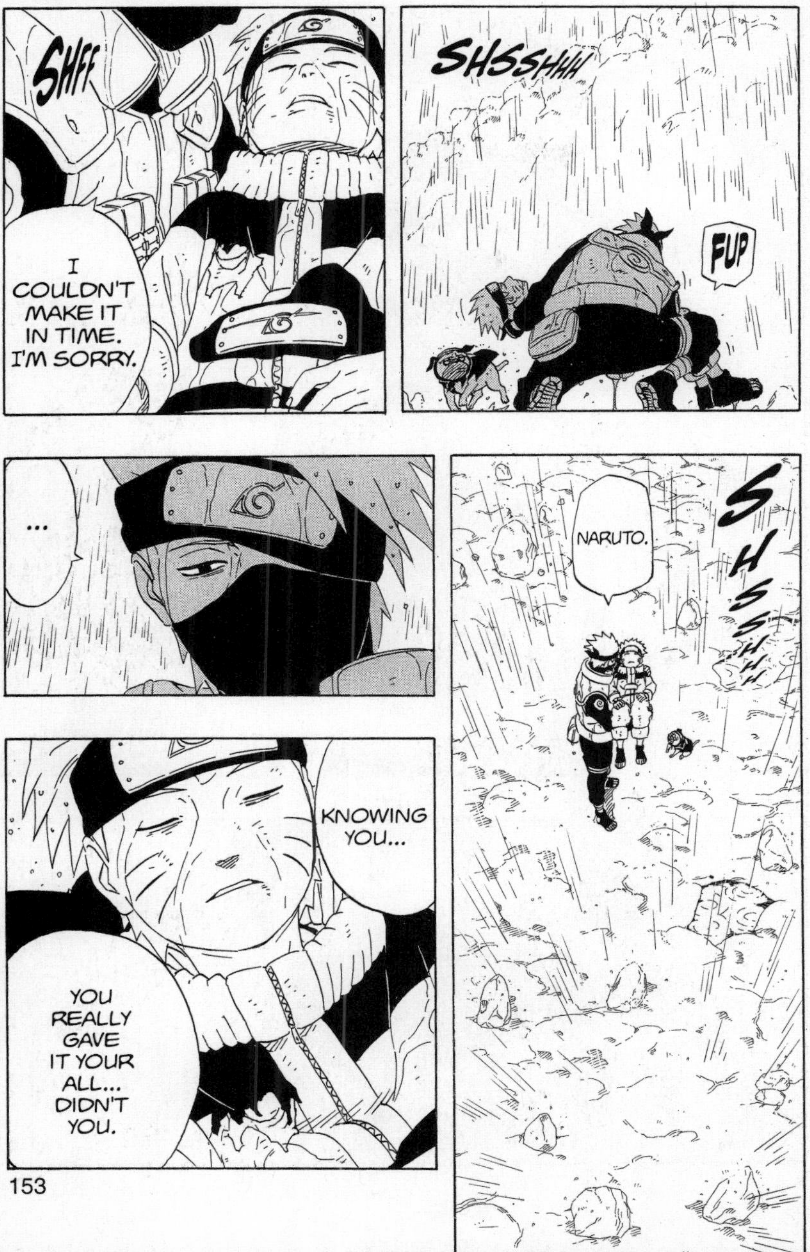
SHSSHHH
FUP
SHFF
I COULDN'T MAKE IT IN TIME. I'M SORRY.
NARUTO.
SHSSHHH
...
KNOWING YOU...
YOU REALLY GAVE IT YOUR ALL... DIDN'T YOU.

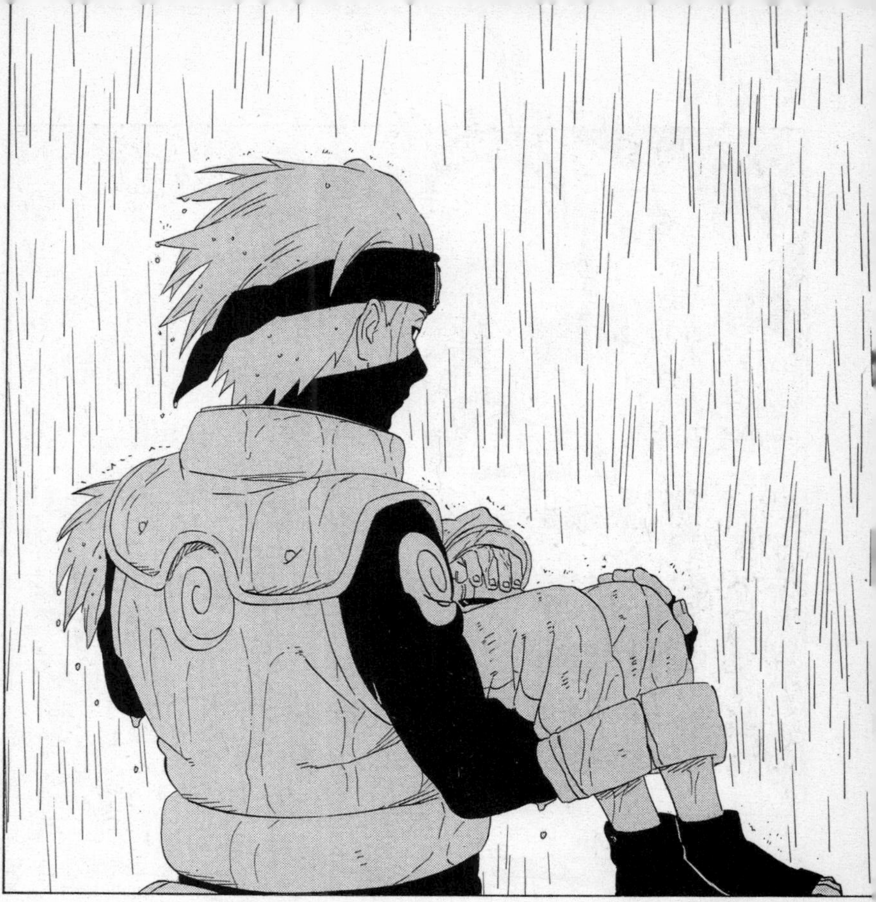
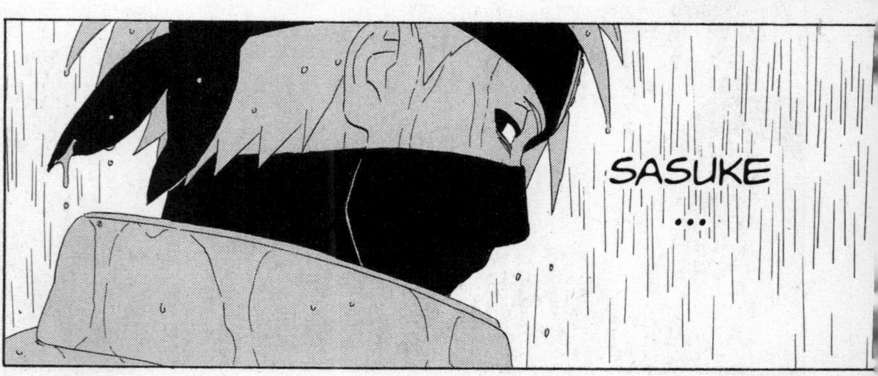
SASUKE
...

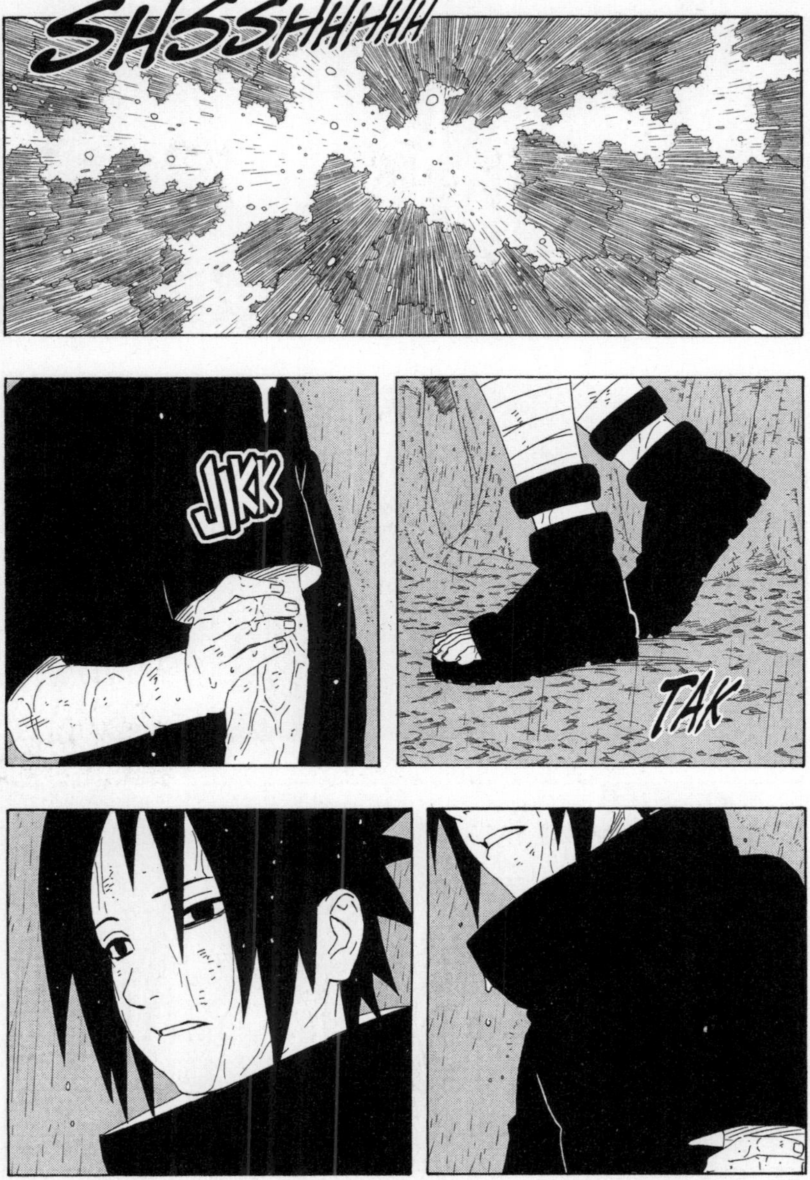
SHSSHHHH
TAK
JIKK

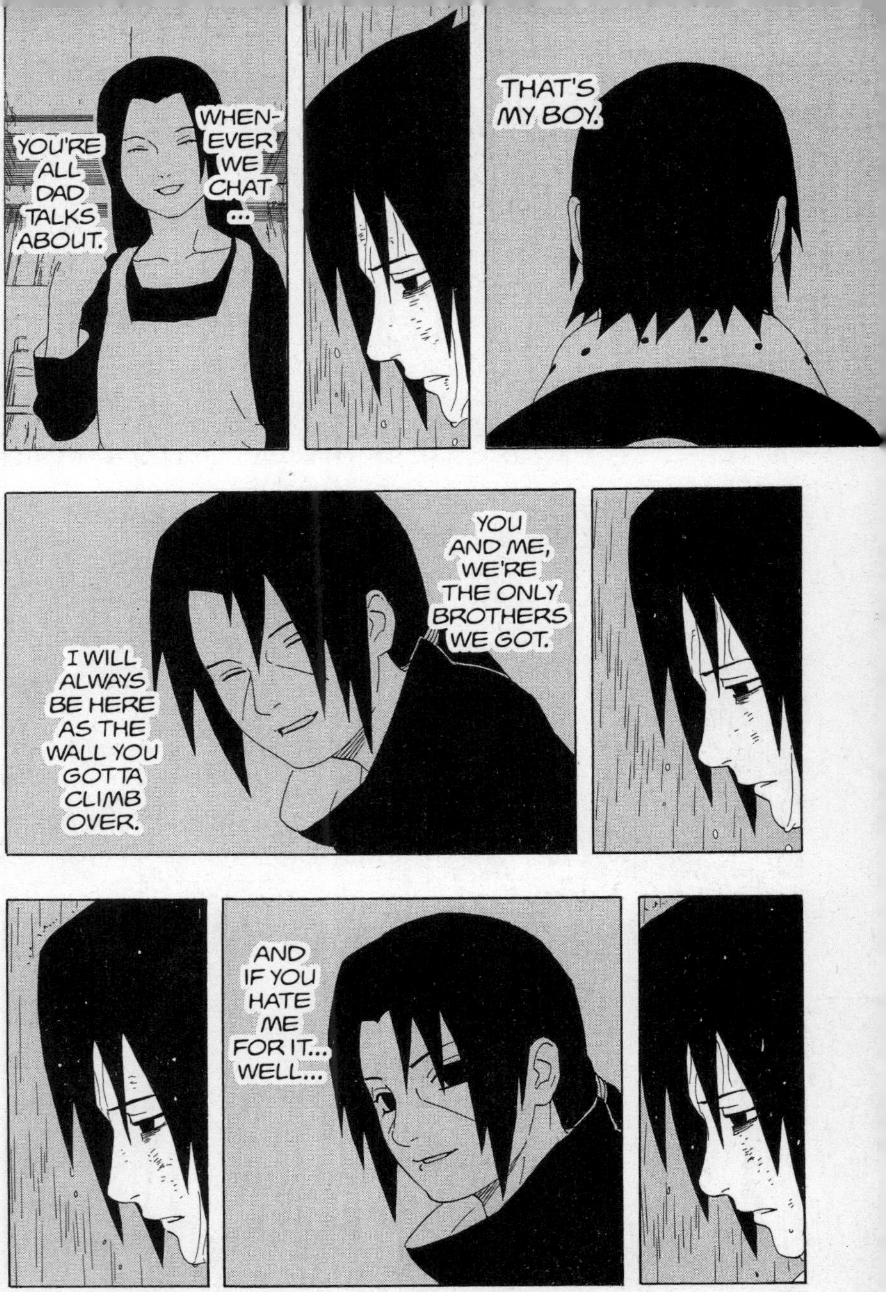
THAT'S MY BOY.
WHEN-EVER WE CHAT...
YOU'RE ALL DAD TALKS ABOUT.
YOU AND ME, WE'RE THE ONLY BROTHERS WE GOT.
I WILL ALWAYS BE HERE AS THE WALL YOU GOTTA CLIMB OVER.
AND IF YOU HATE ME FOR IT... WELL...

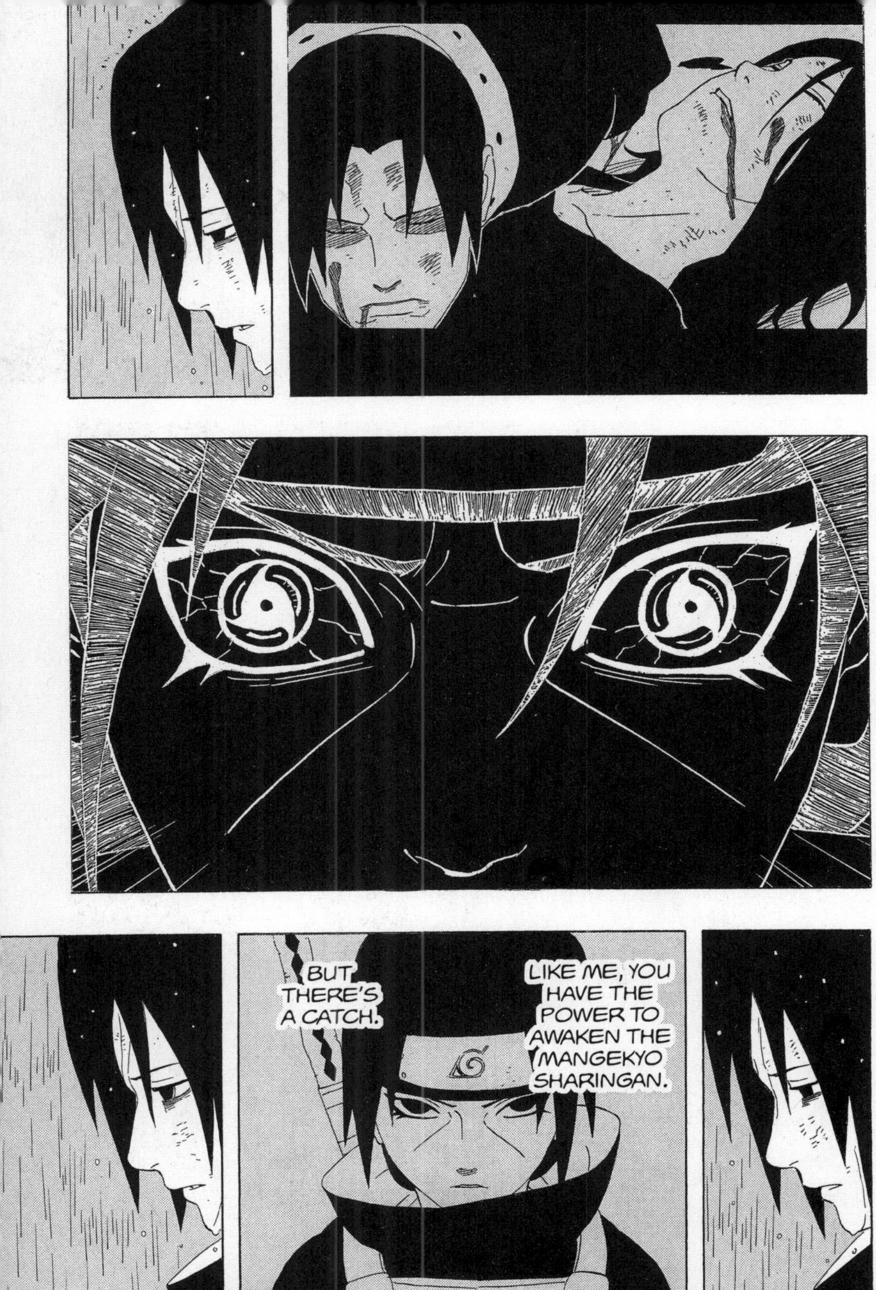
LIKE ME, YOU HAVE THE POWER TO AWAKEN THE MANGEKYO SHARINGAN.
BUT THERE'S A CATCH.

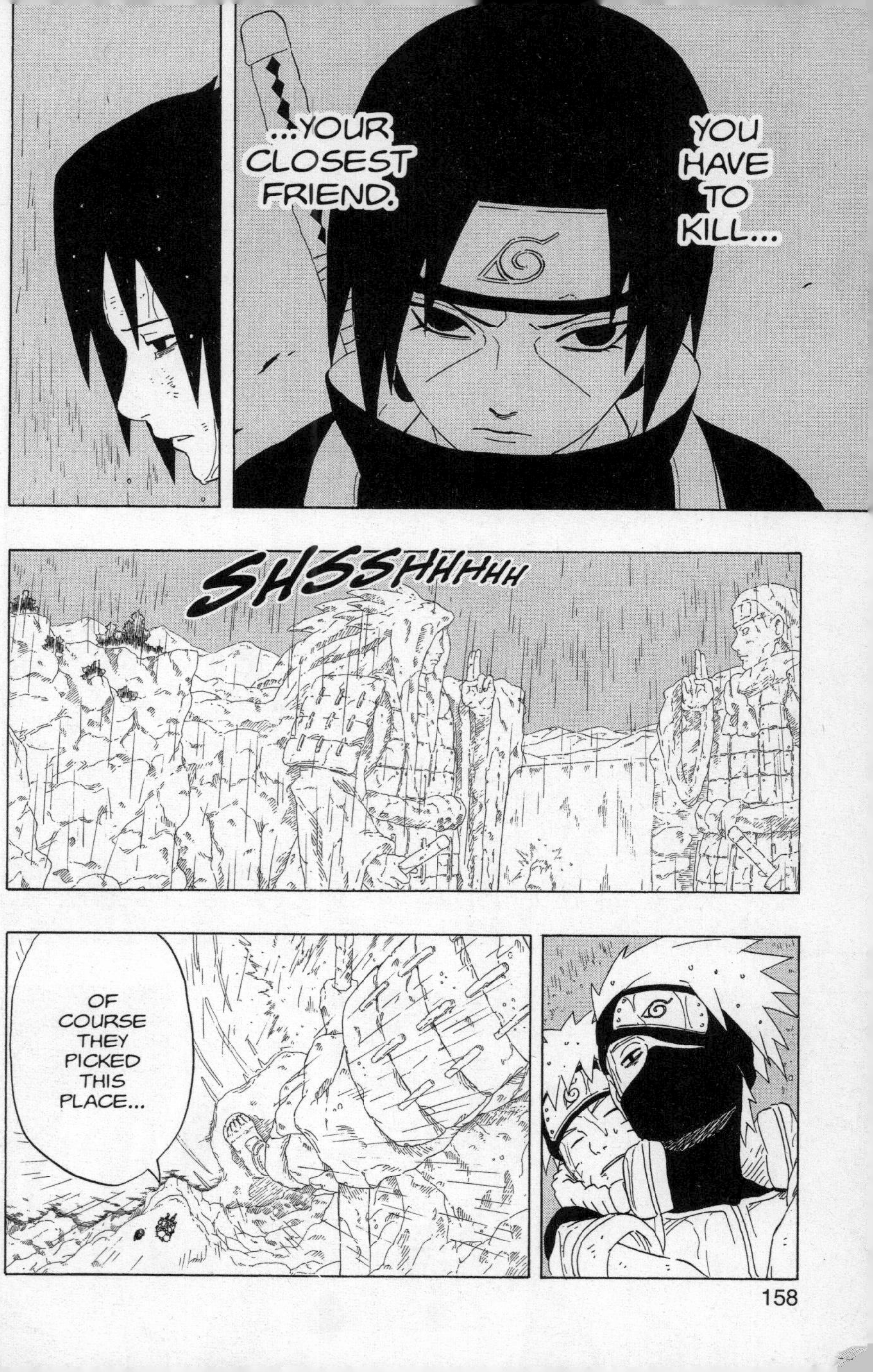
YOU HAVE TO KILL...
...YOUR CLOSEST FRIEND.
SHSSHHHH
OF COURSE THEY PICKED THIS PLACE...

READ THIS WAY

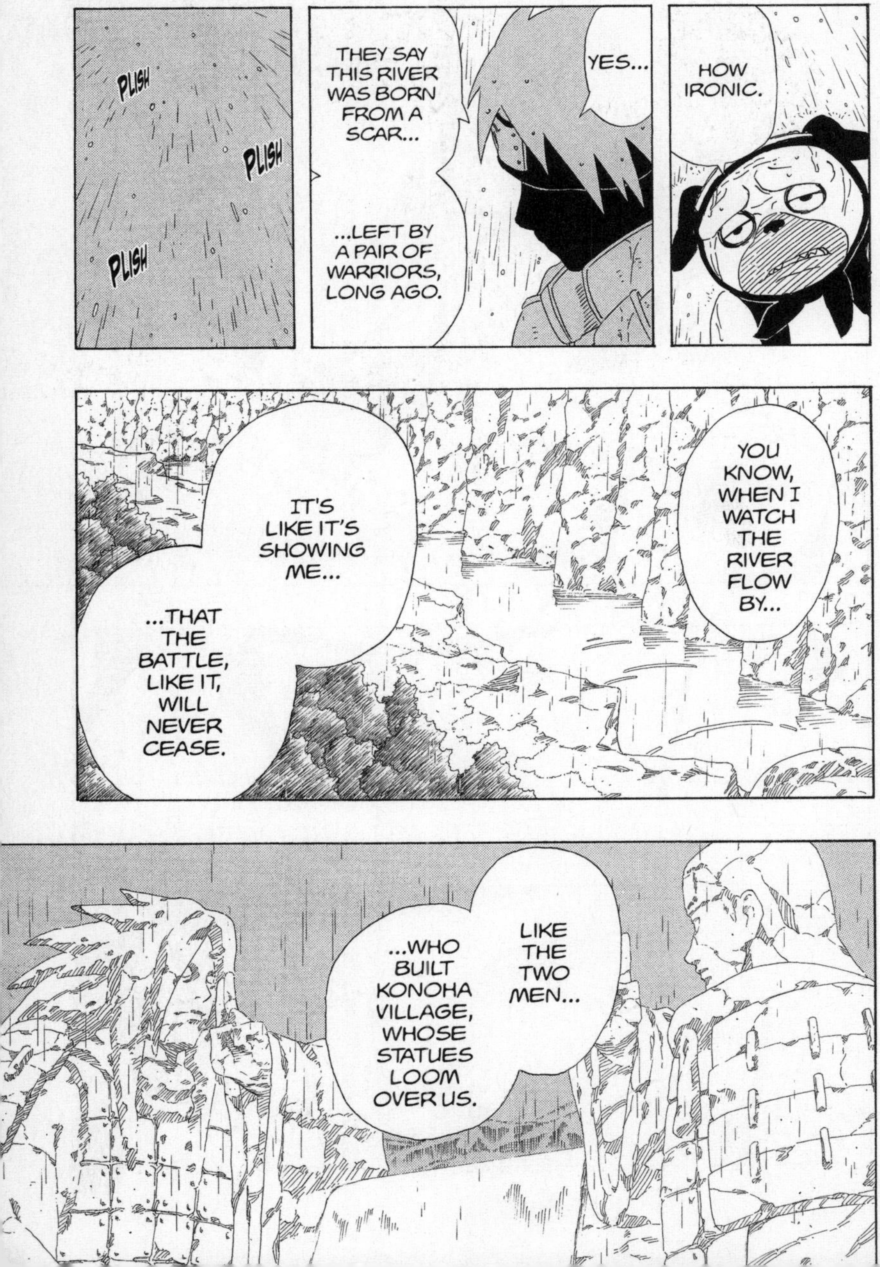
HOW IRONIC.
YES...
THEY SAY THIS RIVER WAS BORN FROM A SCAR...
...LEFT BY A PAIR OF WARRIORS, LONG AGO.
PLISH
PLISH
PLISH
YOU KNOW, WHEN I WATCH THE RIVER FLOW BY...
IT'S LIKE IT'S SHOWING ME...
...THAT THE BATTLE, LIKE IT, WILL NEVER CEASE.
LIKE THE TWO MEN...
...WHO BUILT KONOHA VILLAGE, WHOSE STATUES LOOM OVER US.

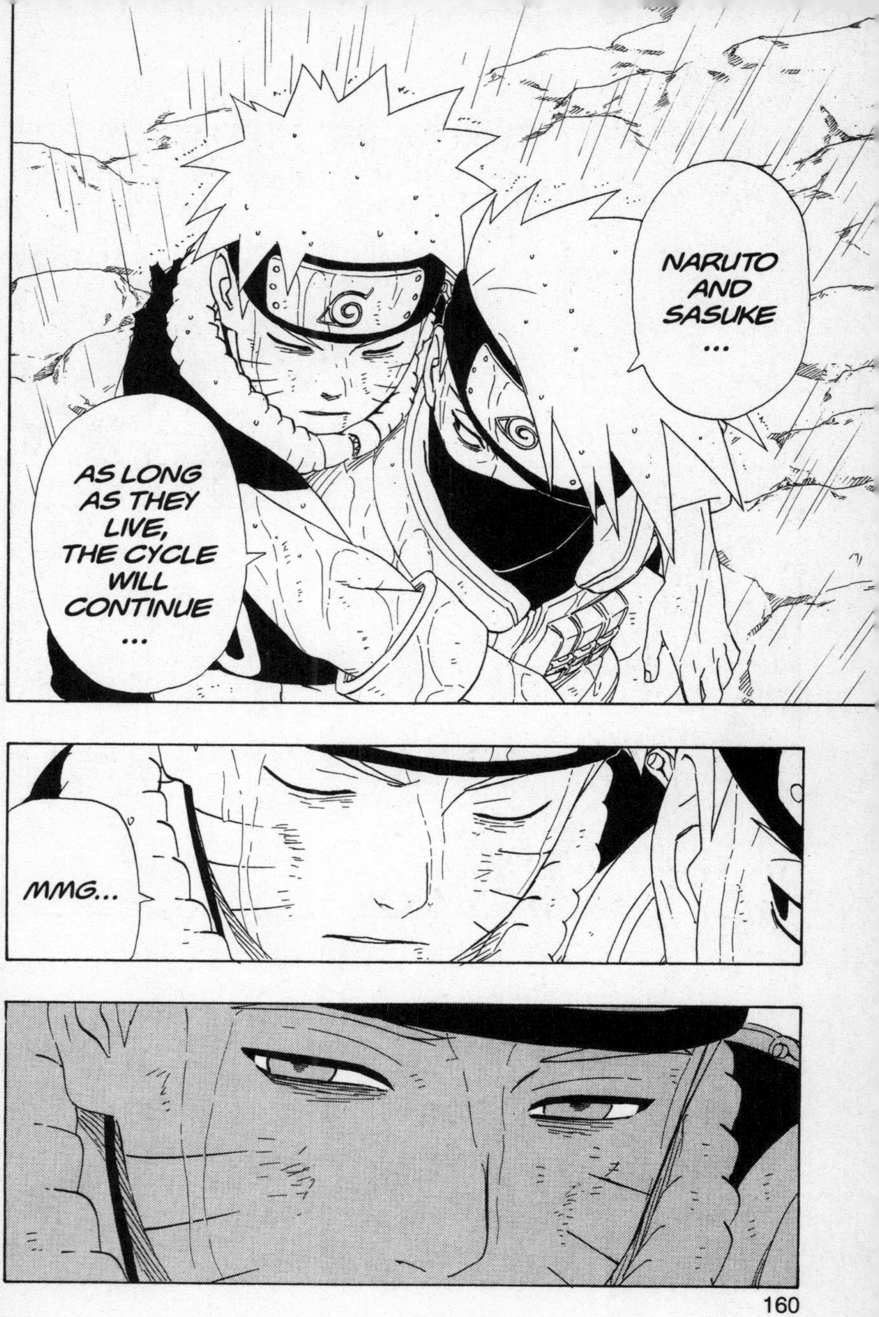
NARUTO AND SASUKE ...
AS LONG AS THEY LIVE, THE CYCLE WILL CONTINUE ...
MMG...

READ THIS WAY

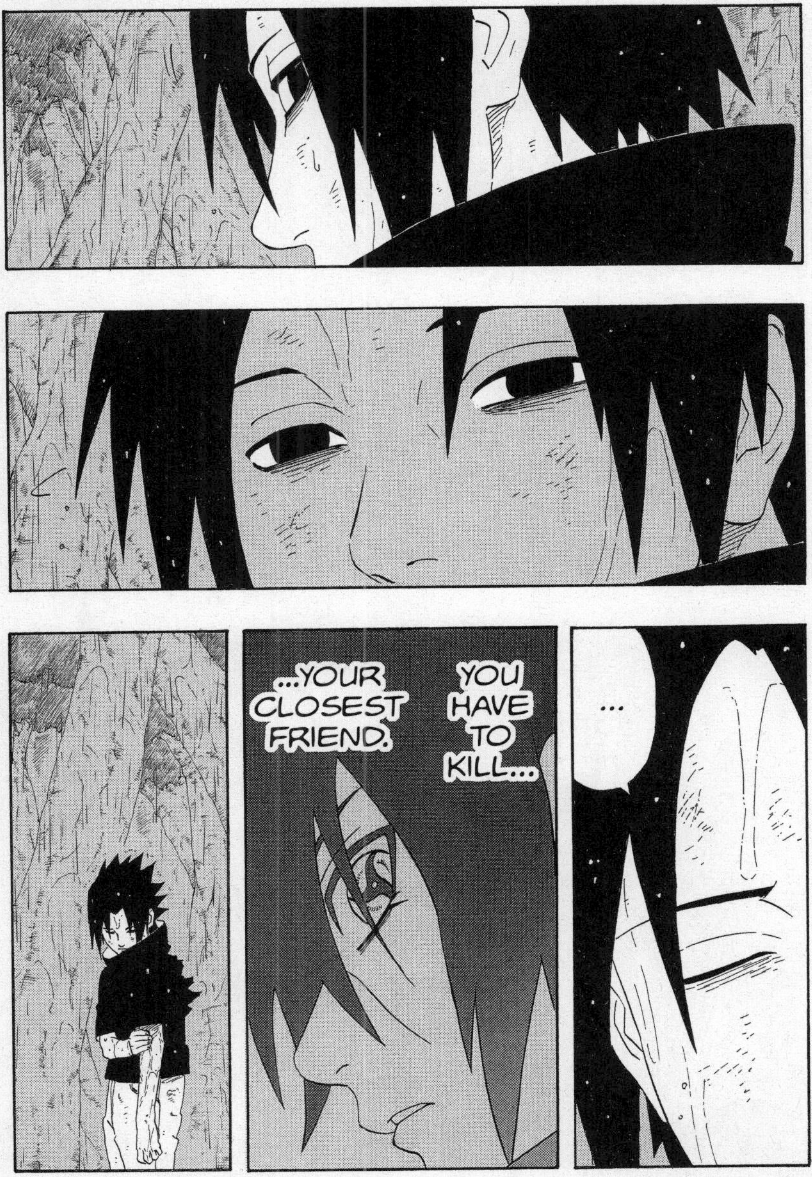
...
YOU HAVE TO KILL...
...YOUR CLOSEST FRIEND.

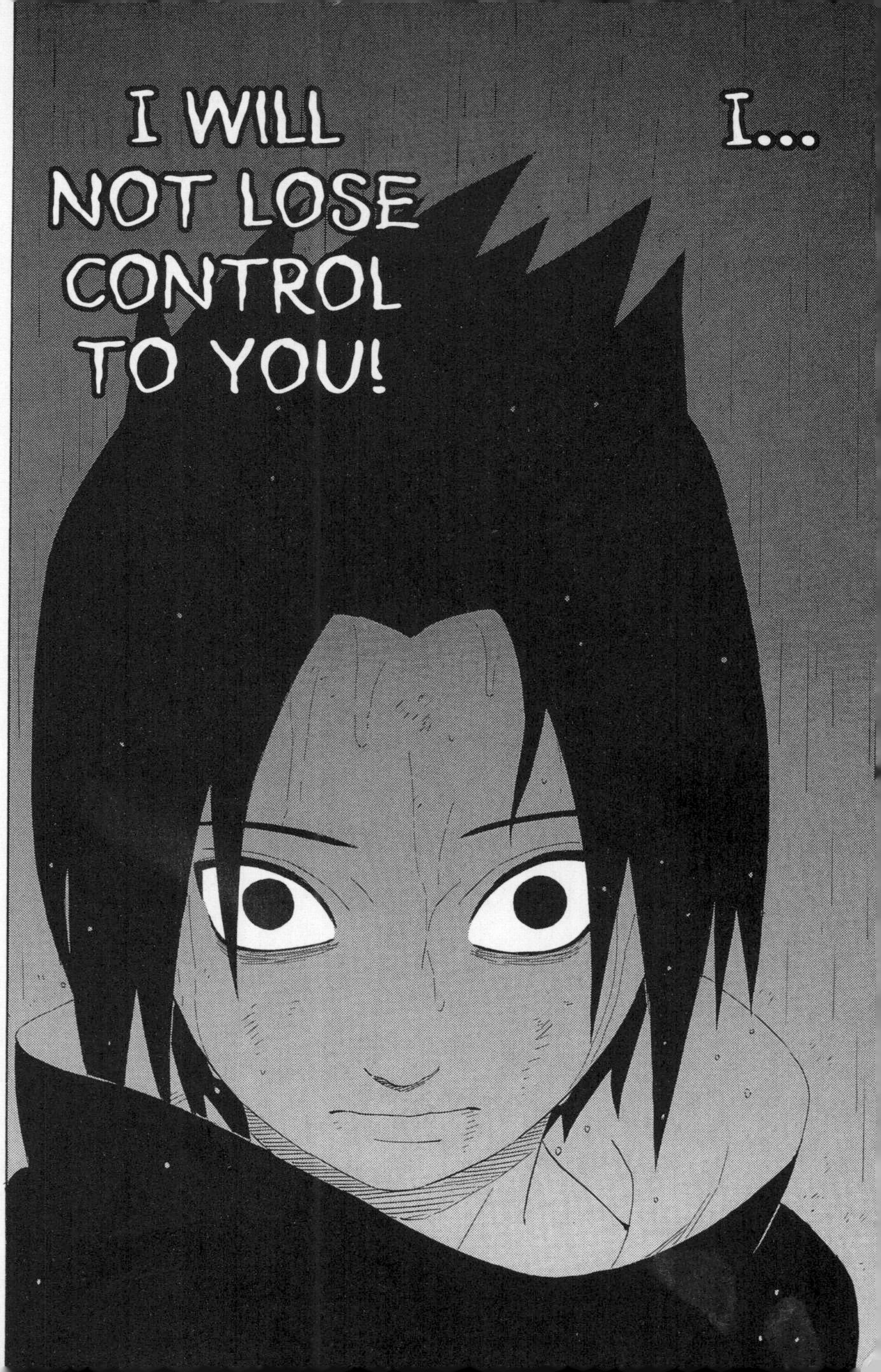
I...
I WILL NOT LOSE CONTROL TO YOU!

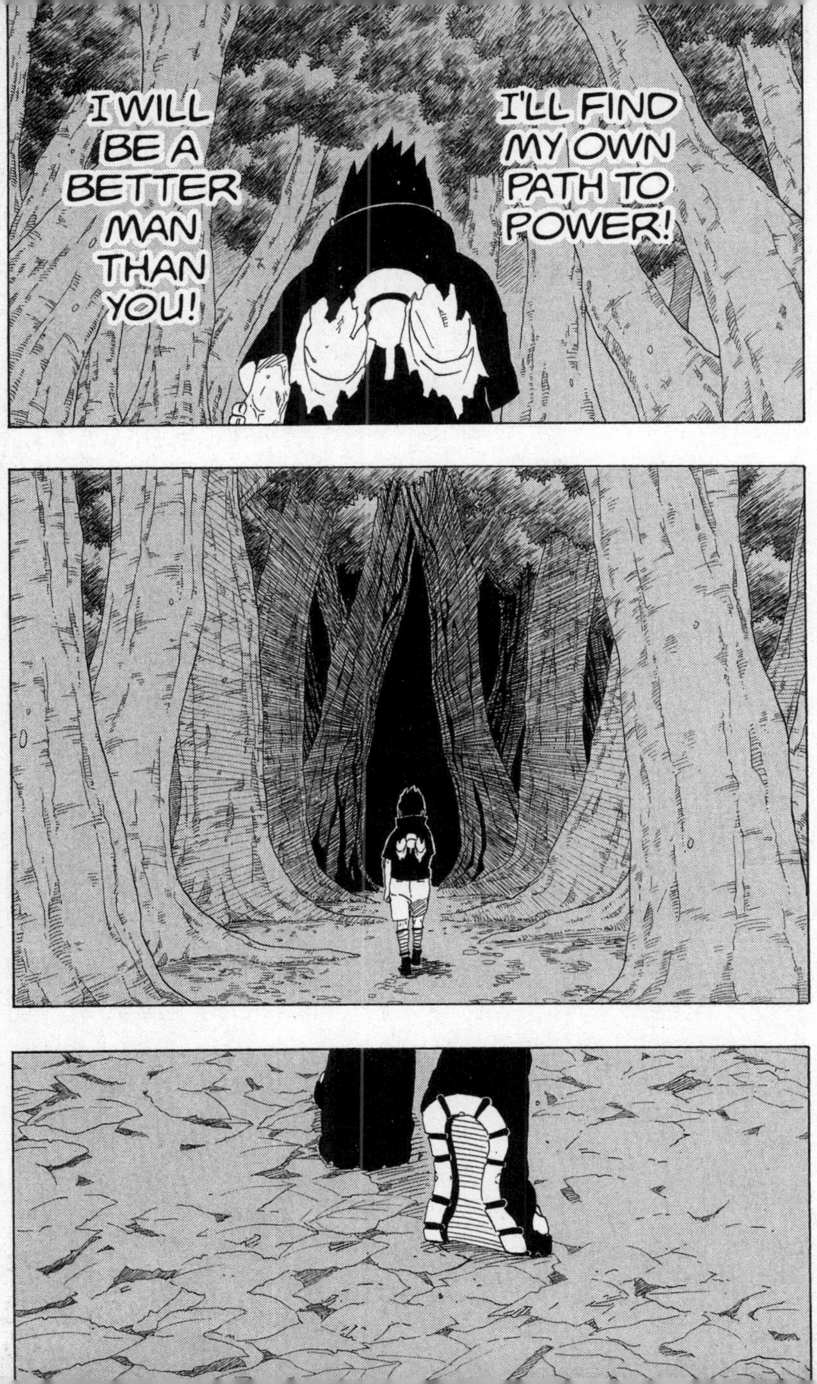
I'LL FIND MY OWN PATH TO POWER!
I WILL BE A BETTER MAN THAN YOU!

I WILL!!

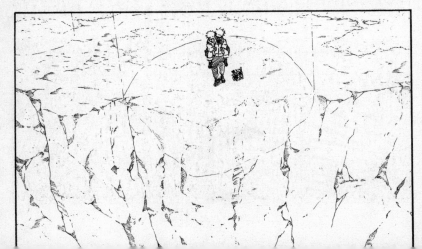

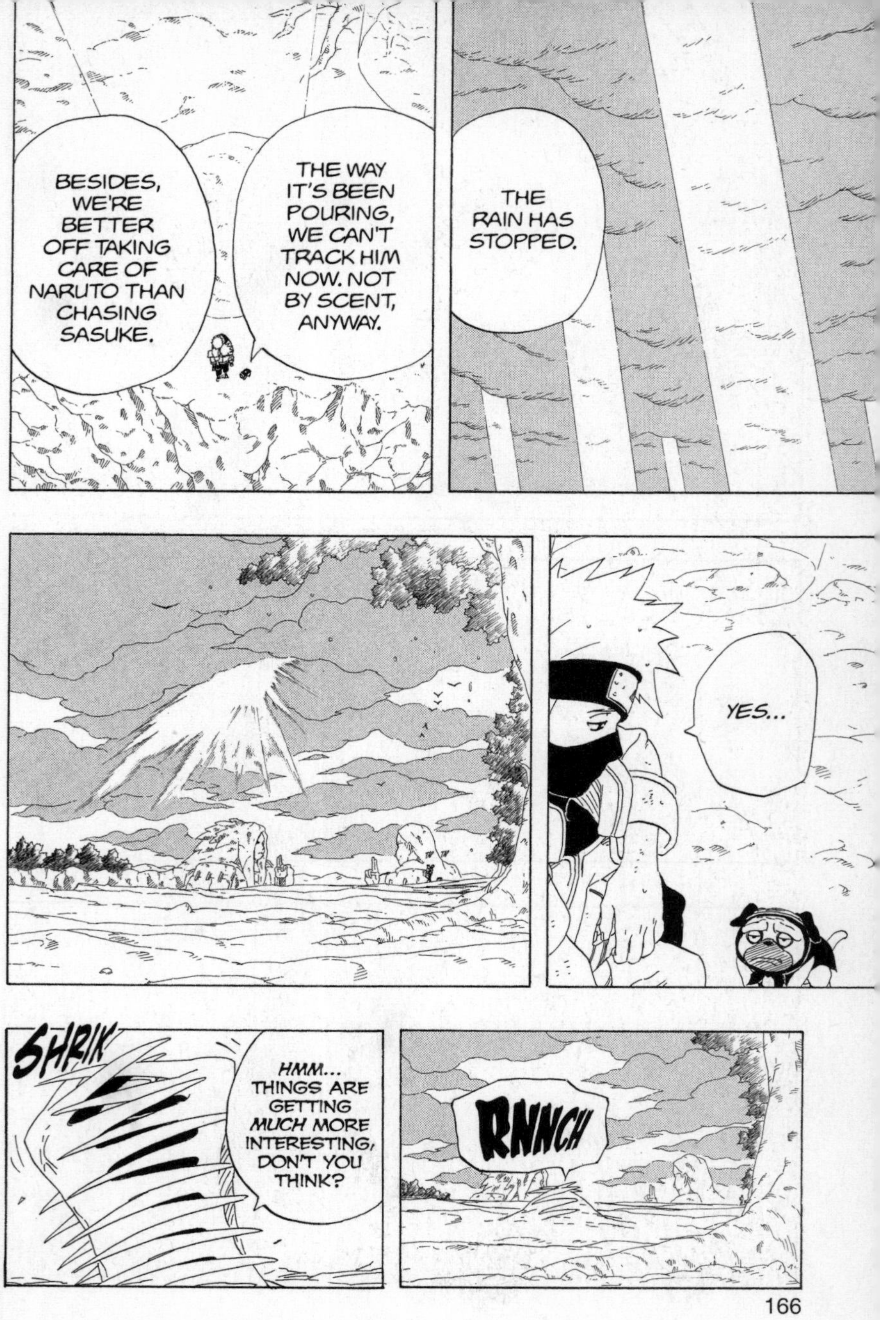
THE RAIN HAS STOPPED.
THE WAY IT'S BEEN POURING, WE CAN'T TRACK HIM NOW. NOT BY SCENT, ANYWAY.
BESIDES, WE'RE BETTER OFF TAKING CARE OF NARUTO THAN CHASING SASUKE.
YES...
RNNCH
HMM... THINGS ARE GETTING *MUCH* MORE INTERESTING, DON'T YOU THINK?
SHRIK

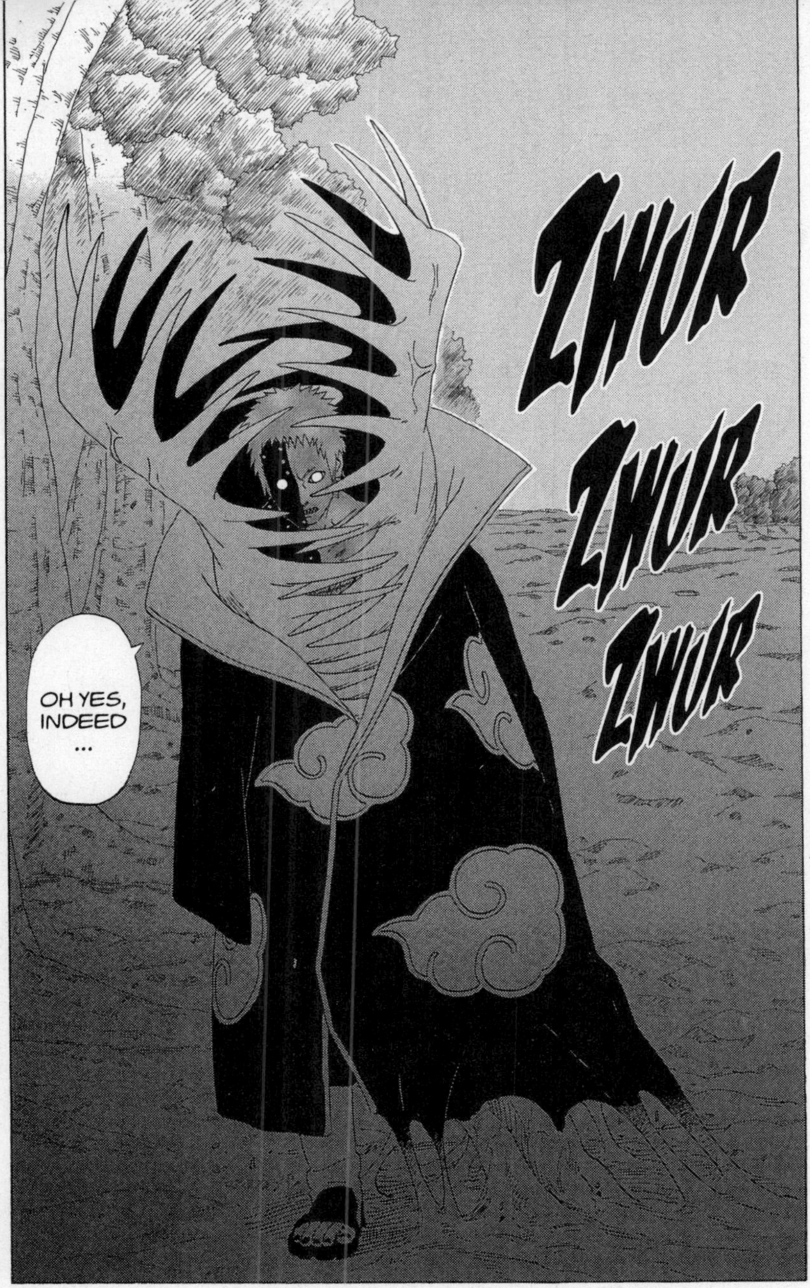
ZWUR
ZWUR
ZWUR
OH YES, INDEED ...

NARUTO™

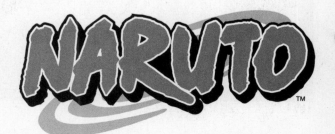

Number 235: Mission Failed...!!

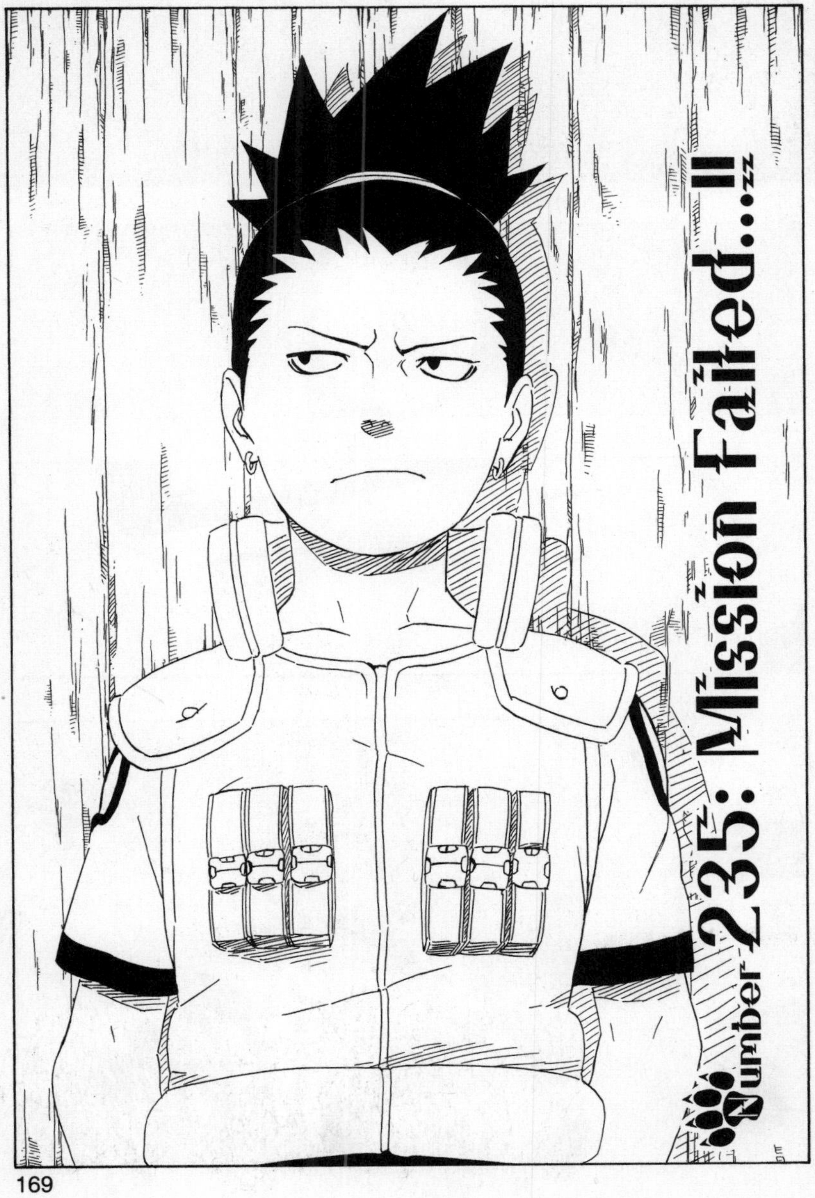

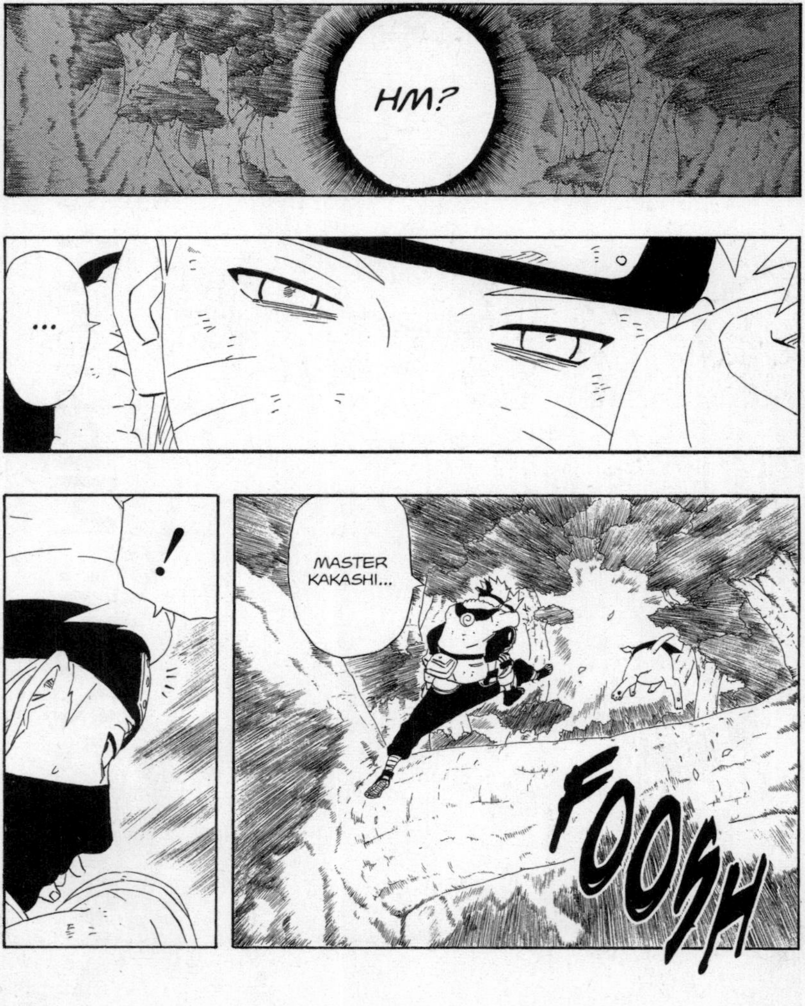
HM?
...
MASTER KAKASHI...
FOOSH
!

READ THIS WAY

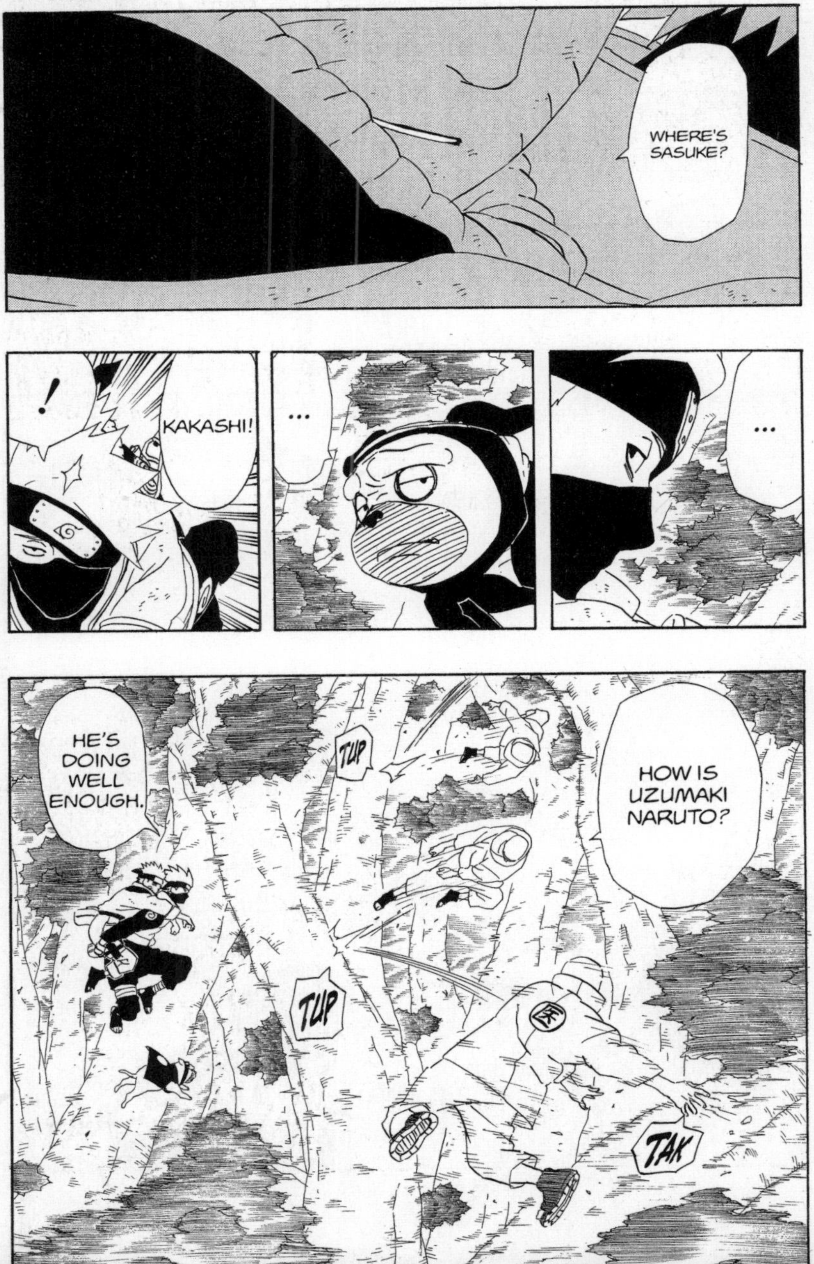
WHERE'S SASUKE?
...
...
!
KAKASHI!
HOW IS UZUMAKI NARUTO?
TUP
HE'S DOING WELL ENOUGH.
TUP
TAK

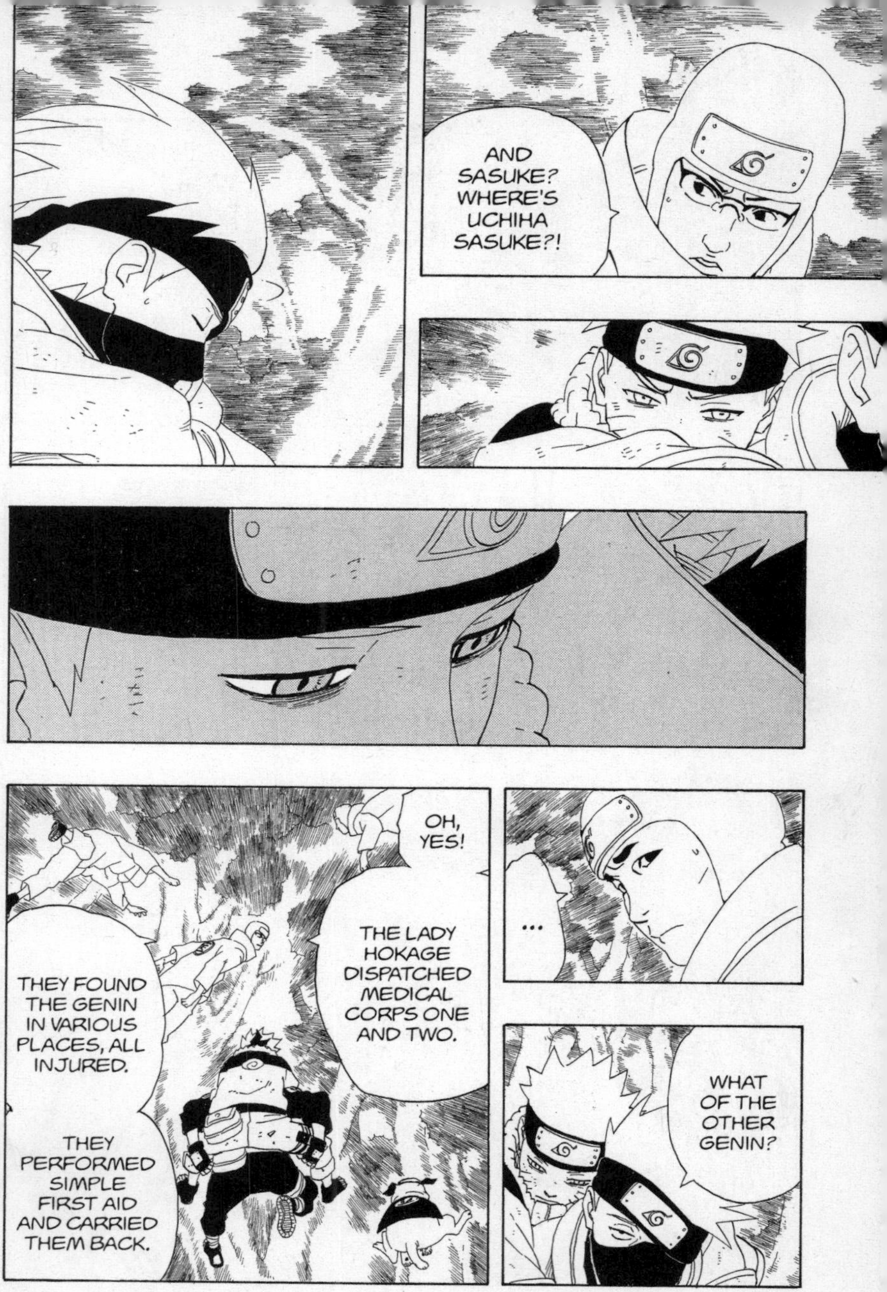
AND SASUKE? WHERE'S UCHIHA SASUKE?!
...
WHAT OF THE OTHER GENIN?
OH, YES!
THE LADY HOKAGE DISPATCHED MEDICAL CORPS ONE AND TWO.
THEY FOUND THE GENIN IN VARIOUS PLACES, ALL INJURED.
THEY PERFORMED SIMPLE FIRST AID AND CARRIED THEM BACK.

READ THIS WAY

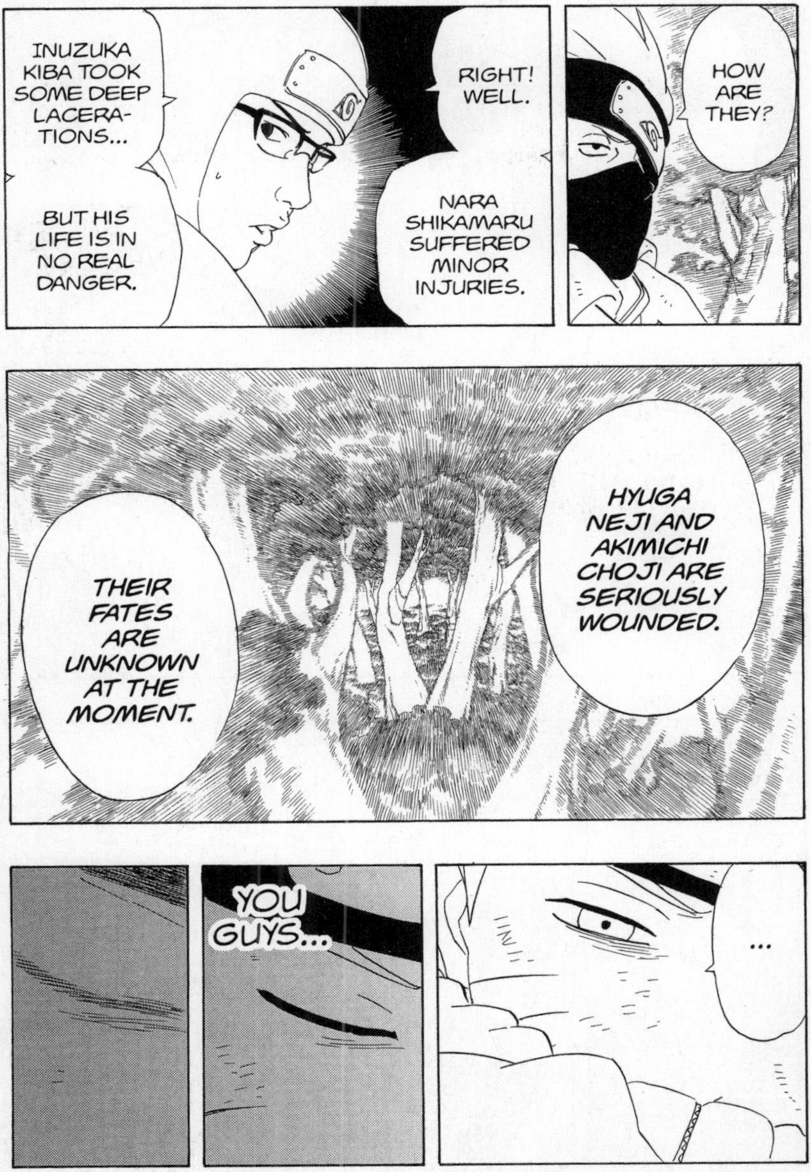
HOW ARE THEY?
RIGHT! WELL.
NARA SHIKAMARU SUFFERED MINOR INJURIES.
INUZUKA KIBA TOOK SOME DEEP LACERA-TIONS...
BUT HIS LIFE IS IN NO REAL DANGER.
HYUGA NEJI AND AKIMICHI CHOJI ARE SERIOUSLY WOUNDED.
THEIR FATES ARE UNKNOWN AT THE MOMENT.
...
YOU GUYS...

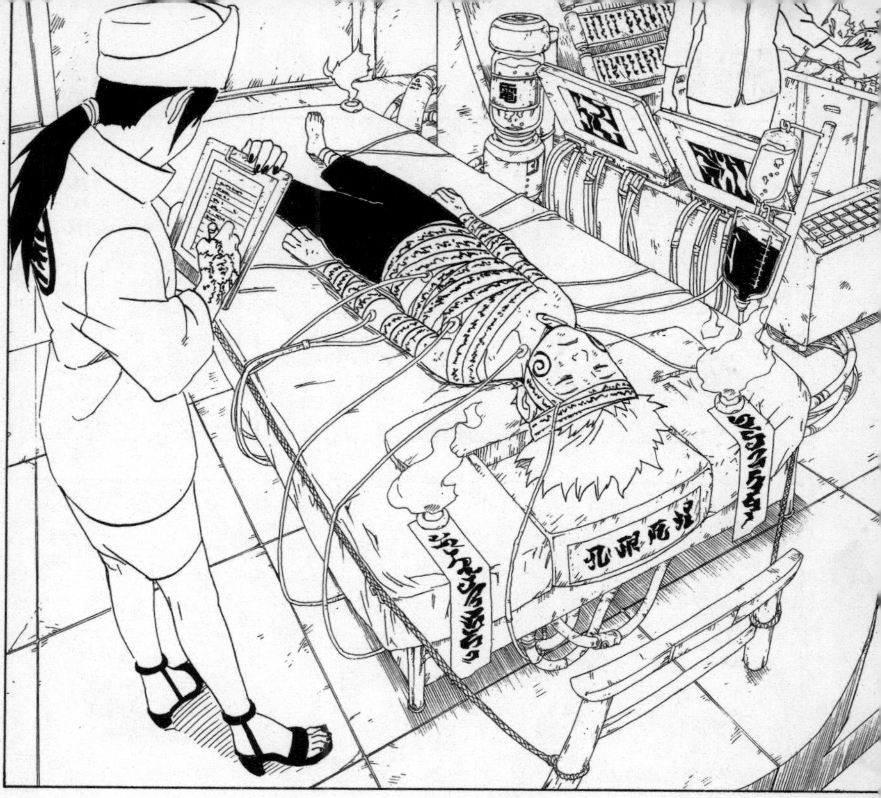

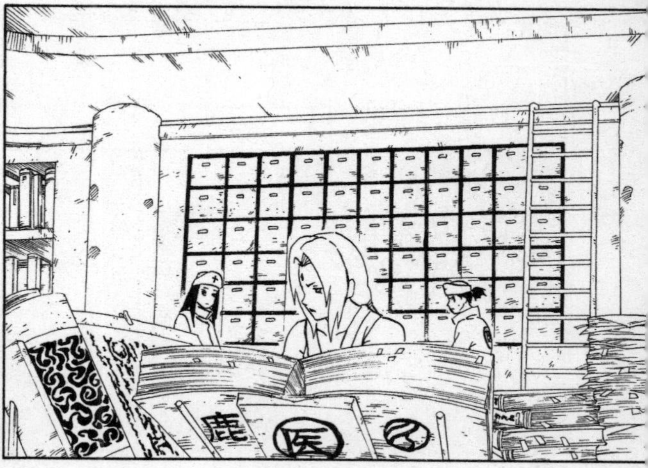

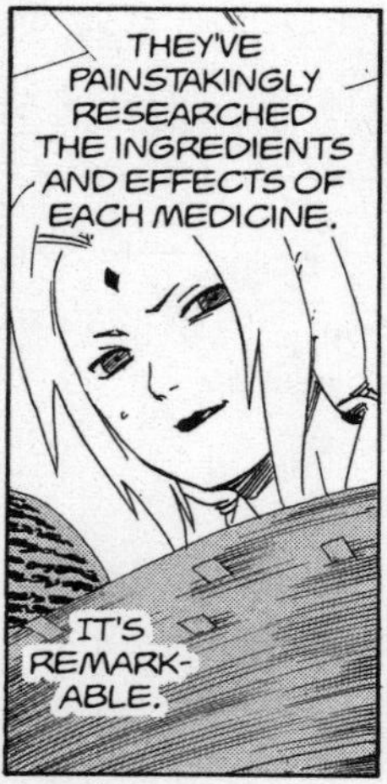
THEY'VE PAINSTAKINGLY RESEARCHED THE INGREDIENTS AND EFFECTS OF EACH MEDICINE.
IT'S REMARK-ABLE.

READ THIS WAY

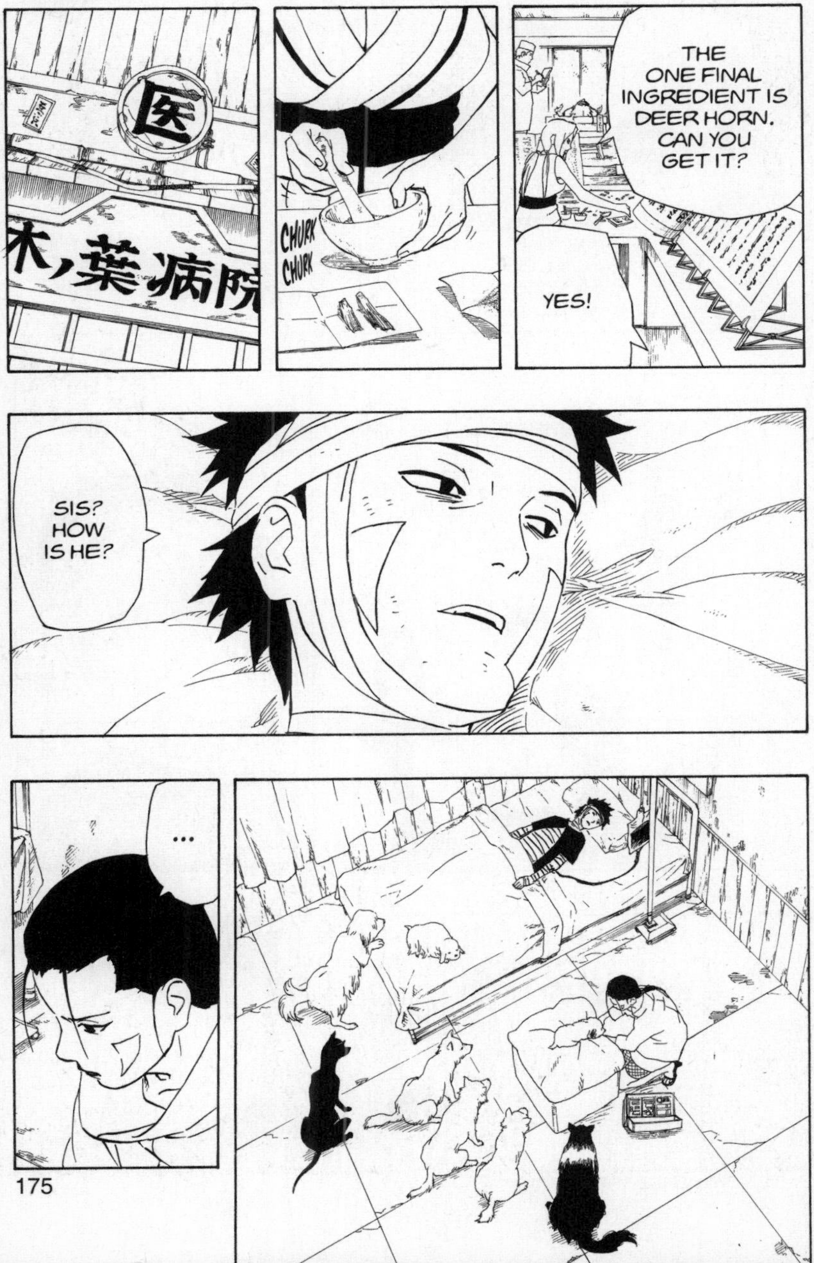
THE ONE FINAL INGREDIENT IS DEER HORN. CAN YOU GET IT?
YES!
CHURK CHURK
医
木ノ葉病院
SIS? HOW IS HE?
...

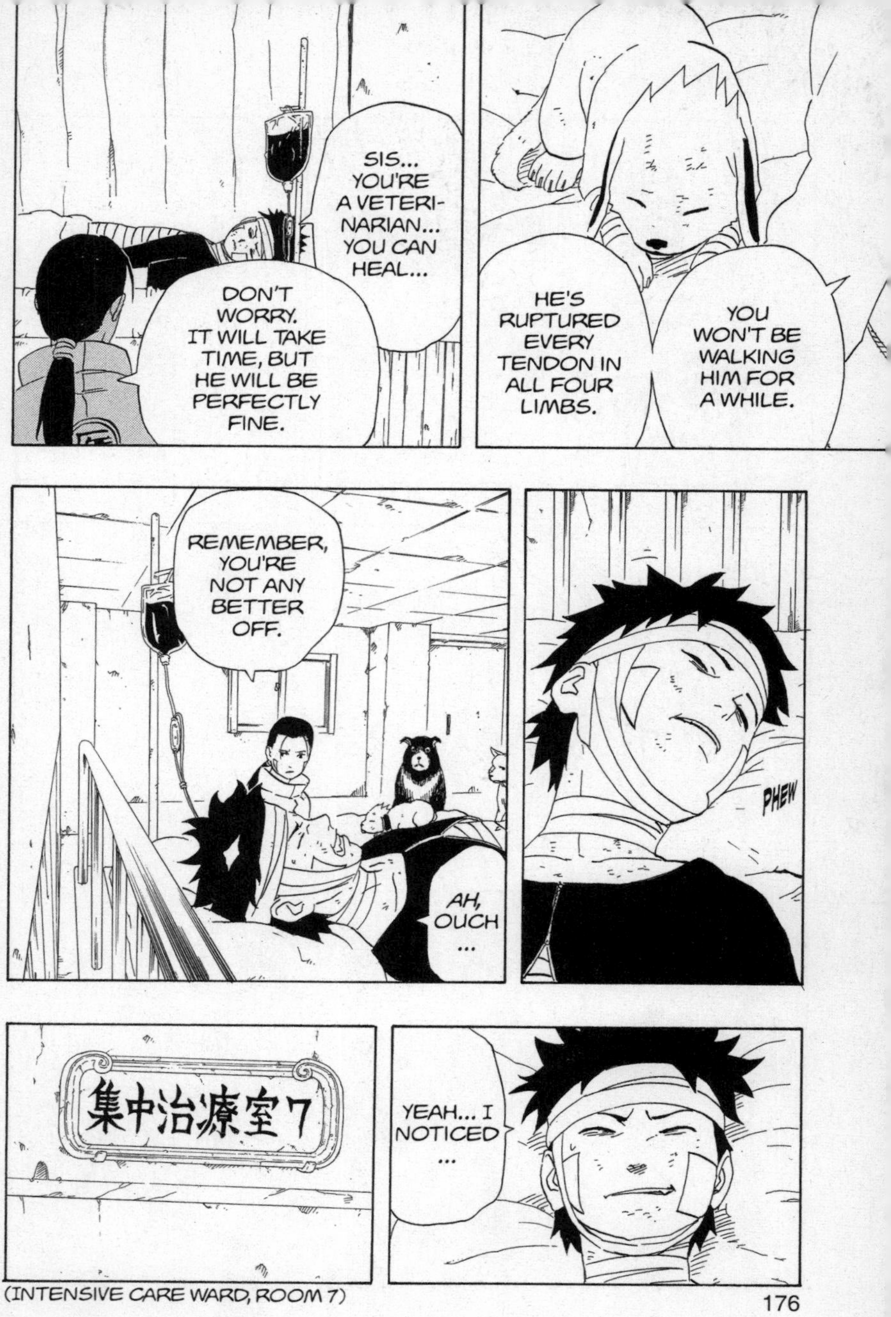

YOU WON'T BE WALKING HIM FOR A WHILE.
HE'S RUPTURED EVERY TENDON IN ALL FOUR LIMBS.
SIS... YOU'RE A VETERINARIAN... YOU CAN HEAL...
DON'T WORRY. IT WILL TAKE TIME, BUT HE WILL BE PERFECTLY FINE.
PHEW
REMEMBER, YOU'RE NOT ANY BETTER OFF.
AH, OUCH ...
YEAH... I NOTICED ...
集中治療室7

(INTENSIVE CARE WARD, ROOM 7)

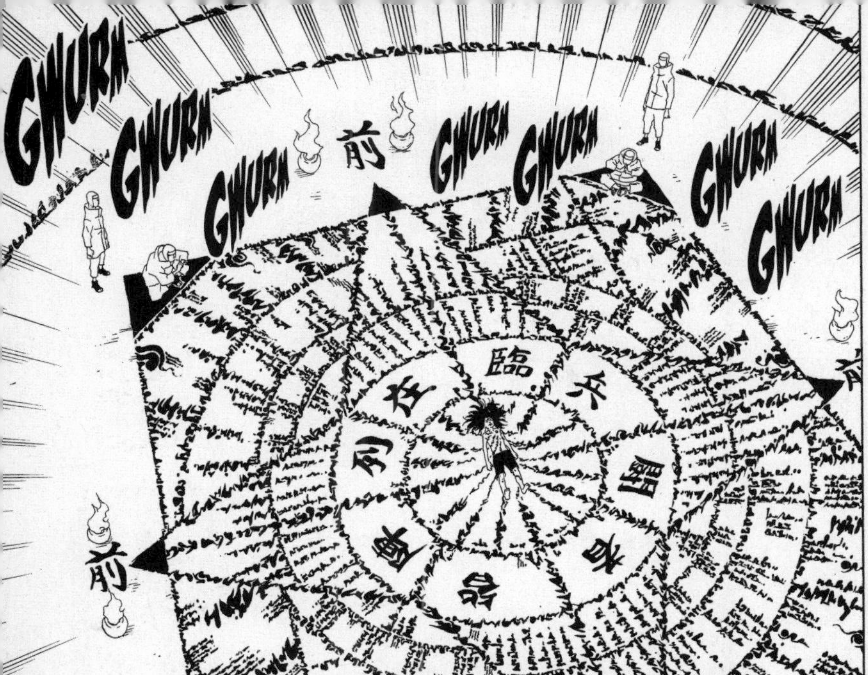
GWURH
GWURH
GWURH
前
GWURH
GWURH
GWURH
GWURH
臨
兵
在
列
前
前
前

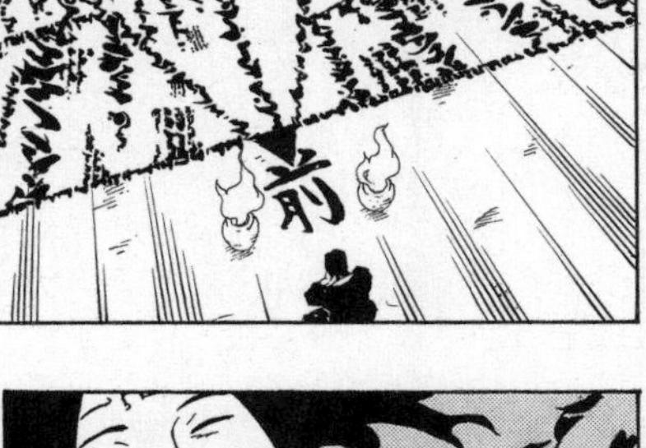
FLIT FLIT

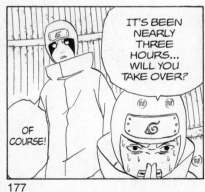

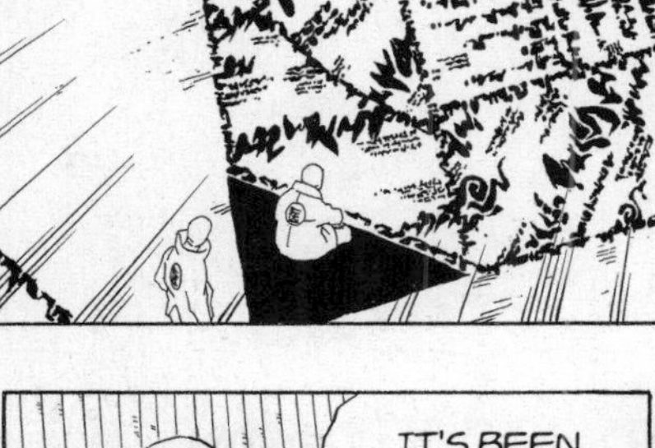
IT'S BEEN NEARLY THREE HOURS... WILL YOU TAKE OVER?
HUF HUF
HUF
OF COURSE!

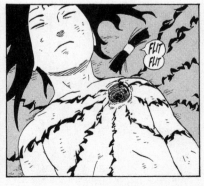

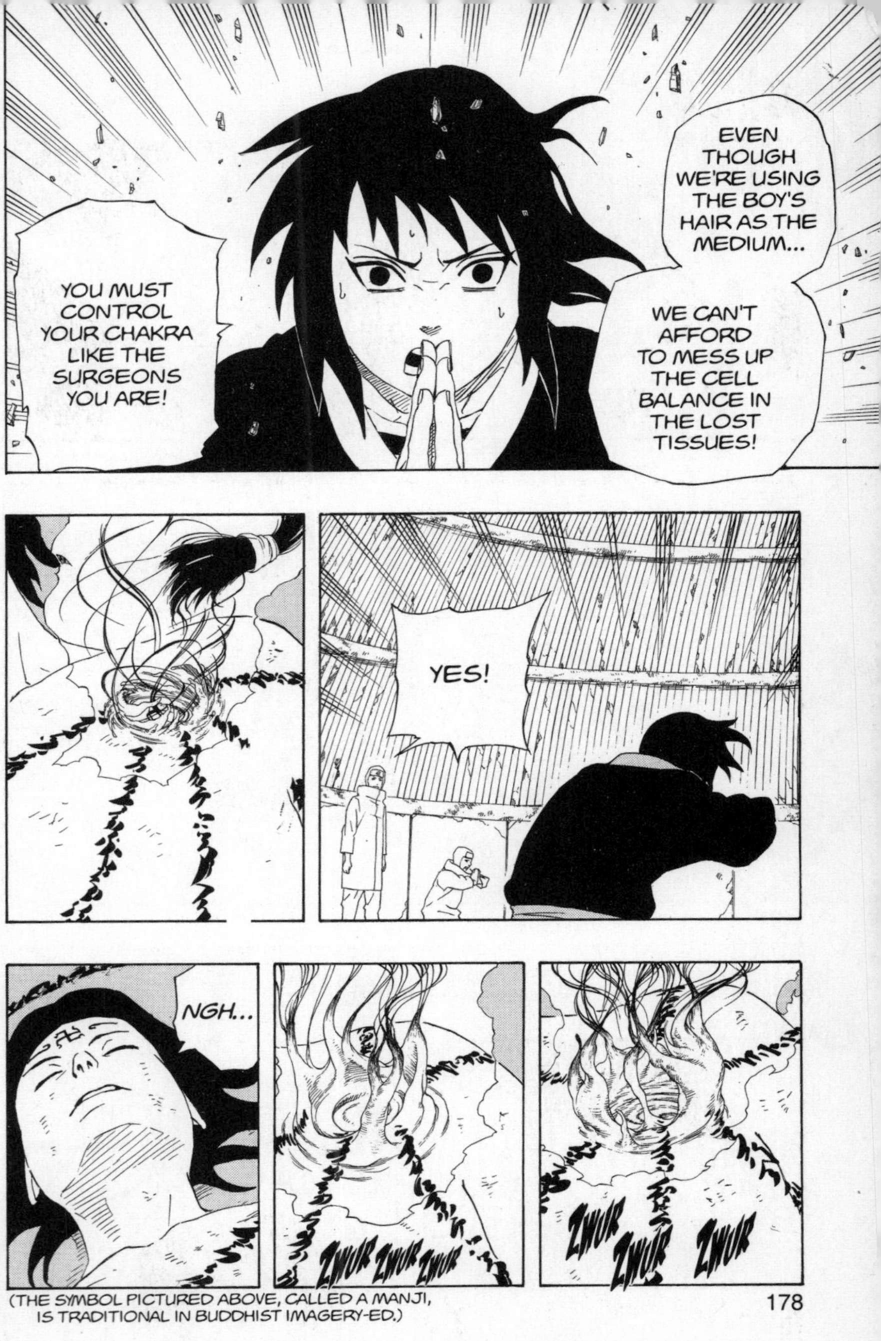
EVEN THOUGH WE'RE USING THE BOY'S HAIR AS THE MEDIUM...
WE CAN'T AFFORD TO MESS UP THE CELL BALANCE IN THE LOST TISSUES!
YOU MUST CONTROL YOUR CHAKRA LIKE THE SURGEONS YOU ARE!
YES!
ZWUR
ZWUR
ZWUR
ZWUR
ZWUR
ZWUR
NGH...

(THE SYMBOL PICTURED ABOVE, CALLED A MANJI, IS TRADITIONAL IN BUDDHIST IMAGERY-ED.)

READ THIS WAY

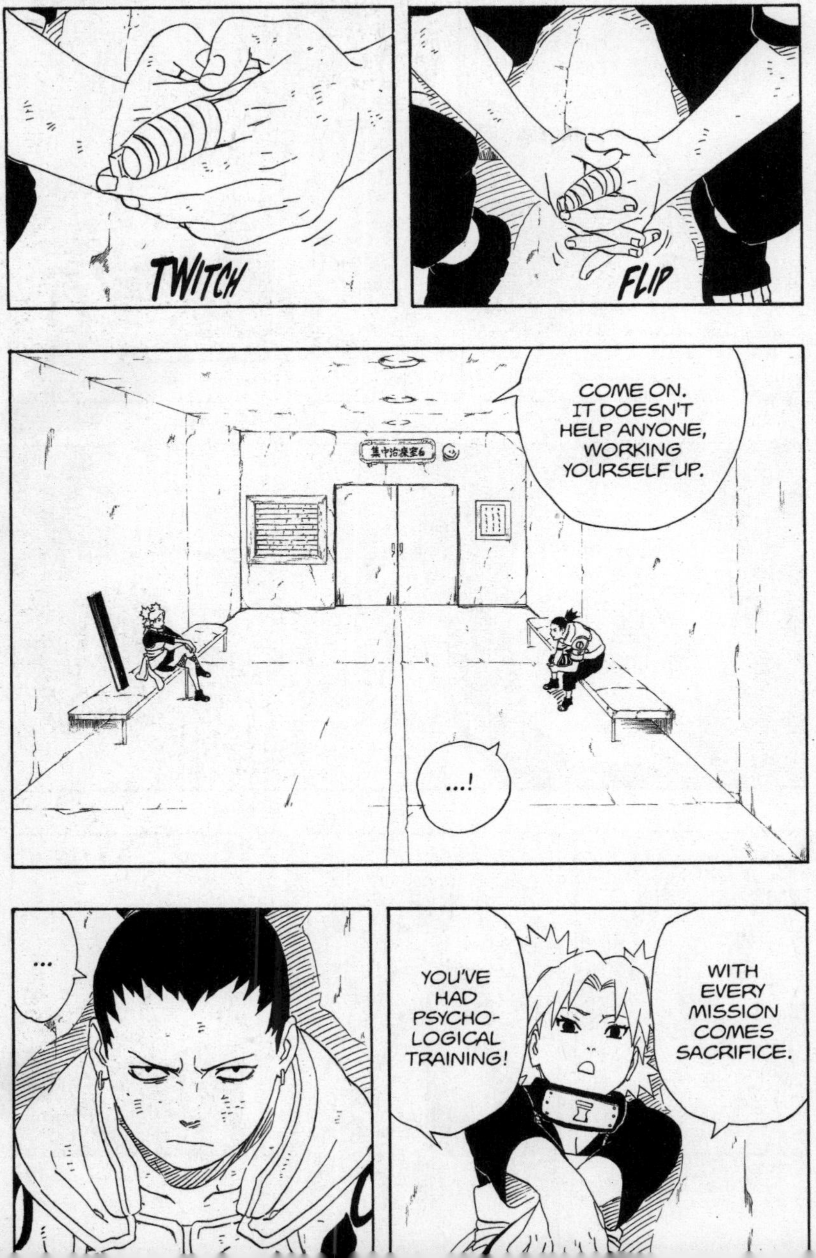

FLIP
TWITCH
COME ON. IT DOESN'T HELP ANYONE, WORKING YOURSELF UP.
...!
WITH EVERY MISSION COMES SACRIFICE.
YOU'VE HAD PSYCHO-LOGICAL TRAINING!
...

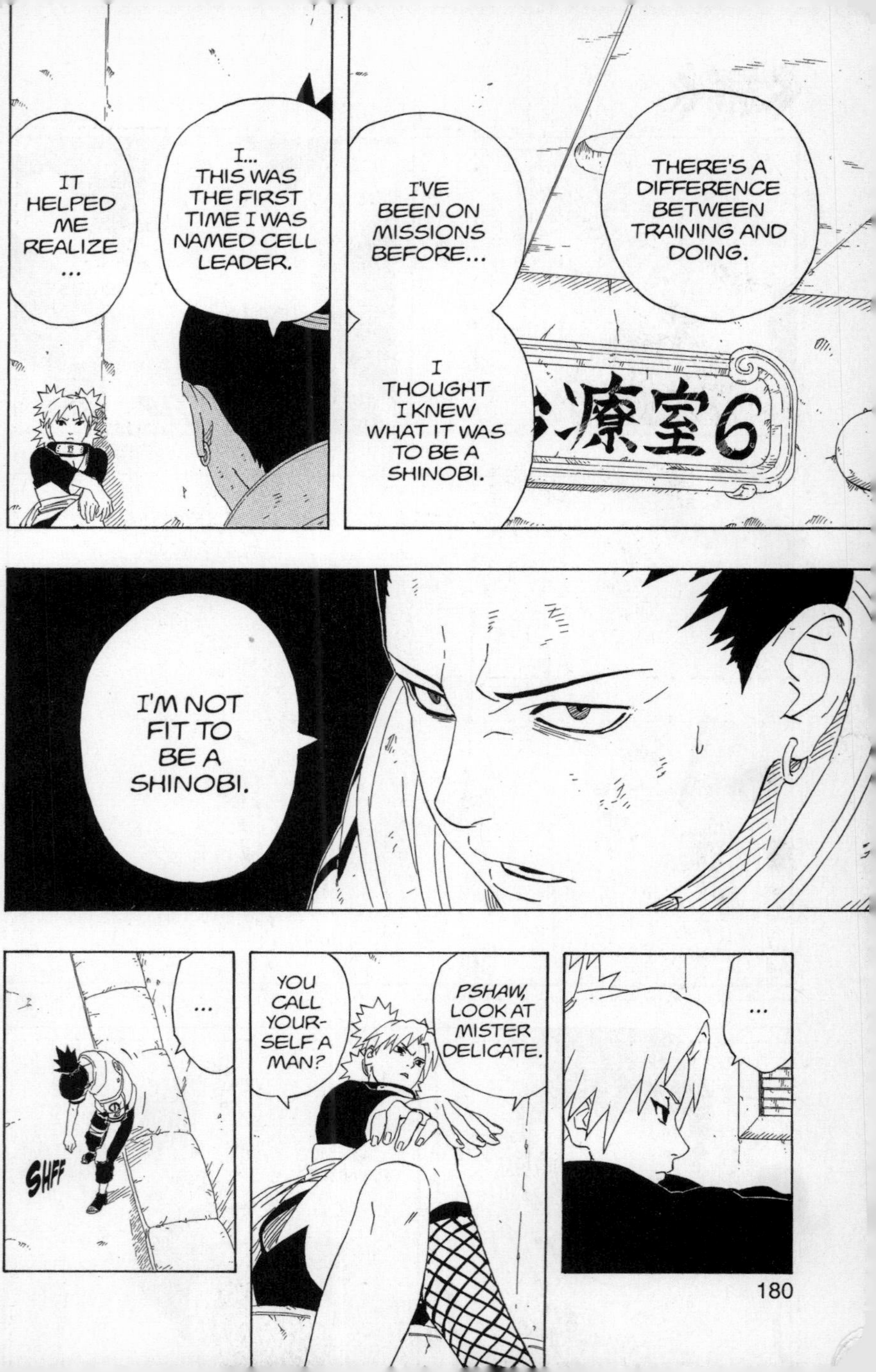
THERE'S A DIFFERENCE BETWEEN TRAINING AND DOING.
I'VE BEEN ON MISSIONS BEFORE...
I THOUGHT I KNEW WHAT IT WAS TO BE A SHINOBI.
I... THIS WAS THE FIRST TIME I WAS NAMED CELL LEADER.
IT HELPED ME REALIZE...
I'M NOT FIT TO BE A SHINOBI.
...
PSHAW, LOOK AT MISTER DELICATE.
YOU CALL YOURSELF A MAN?
...
SHFF

READ THIS WAY

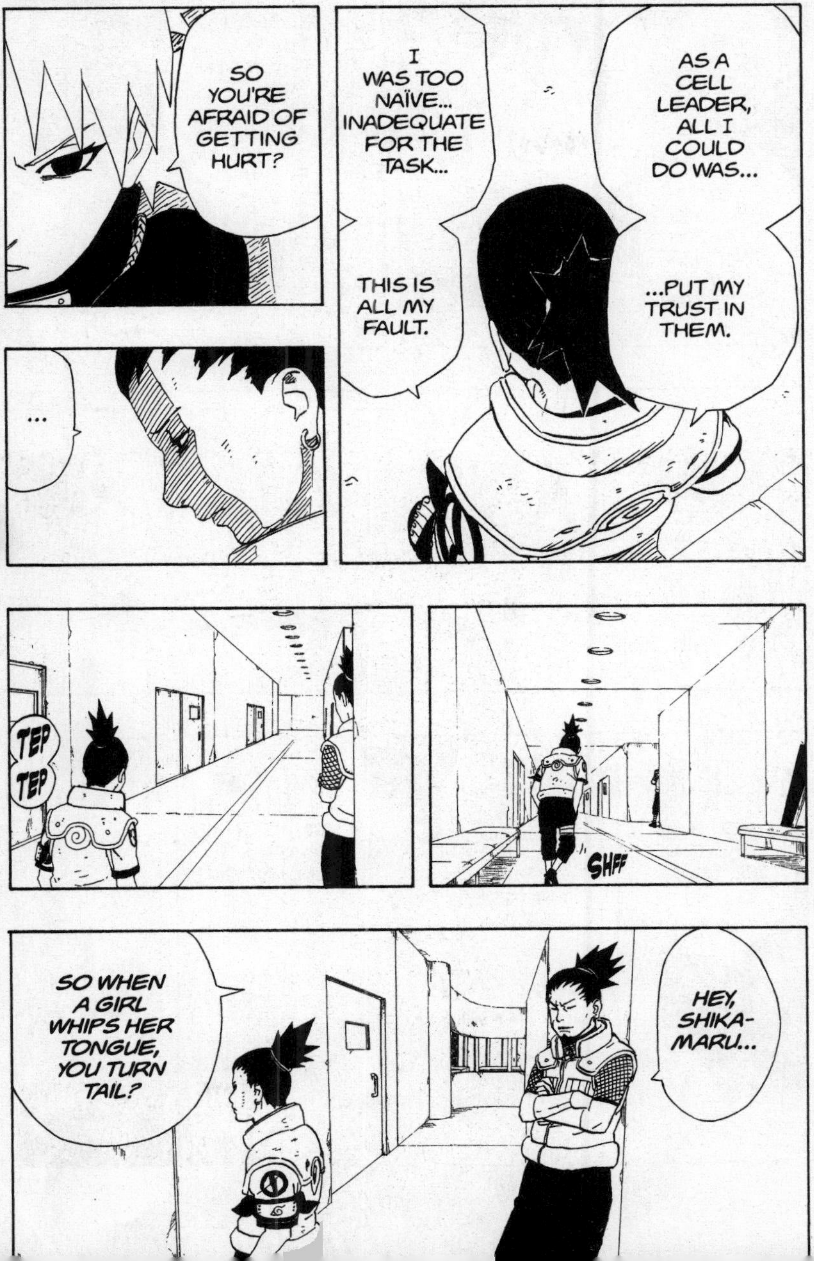
AS A CELL LEADER, ALL I COULD DO WAS...
...PUT MY TRUST IN THEM.
I WAS TOO NAÏVE... INADEQUATE FOR THE TASK...
THIS IS ALL MY FAULT.
SO YOU'RE AFRAID OF GETTING HURT?
...
SHFF
TEP TEP
HEY, SHIKA-MARU...
SO WHEN A GIRL WHIPS HER TONGUE, YOU TURN TAIL?

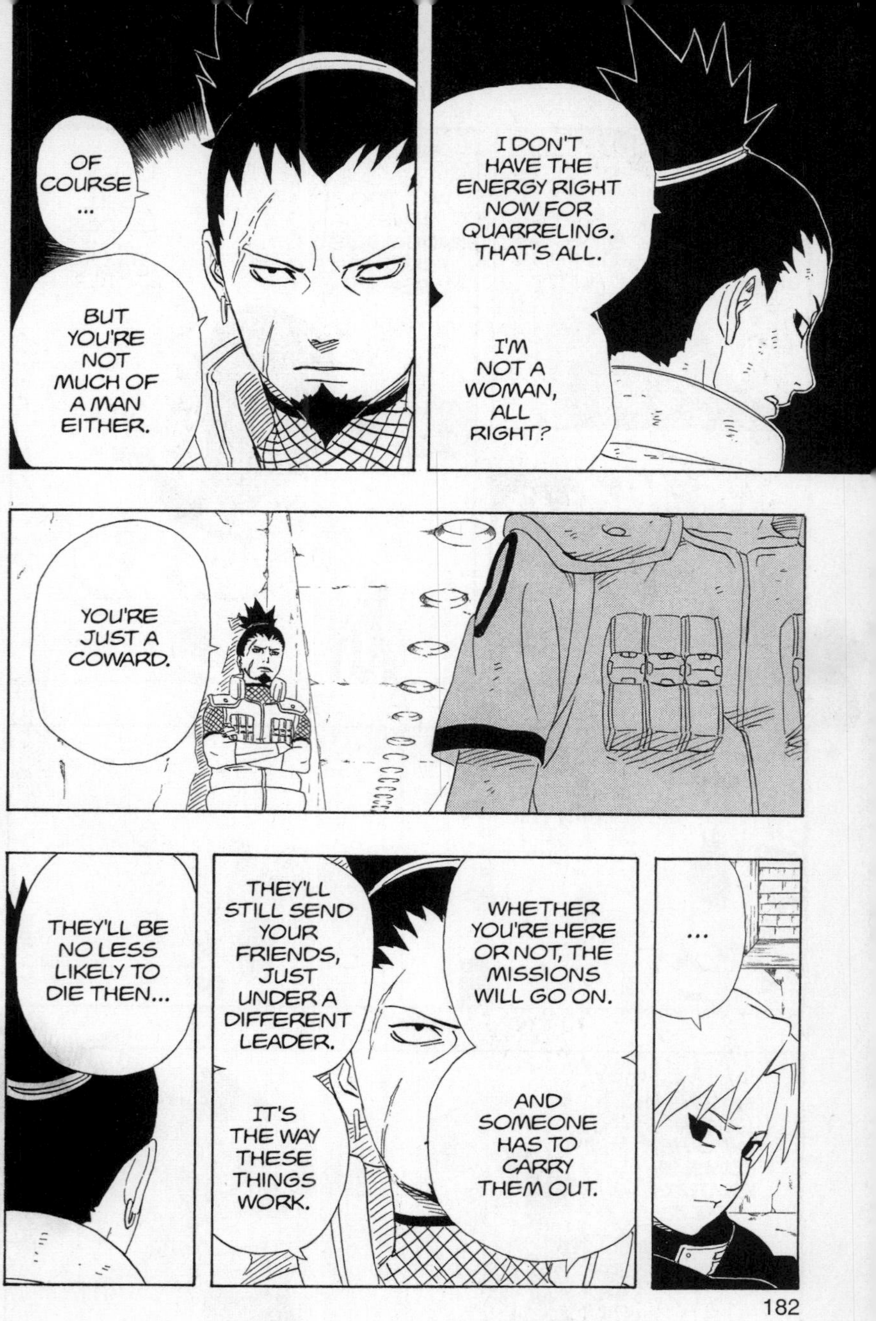
I DON'T HAVE THE ENERGY RIGHT NOW FOR QUARRELING. THAT'S ALL.
I'M NOT A WOMAN, ALL RIGHT?
OF COURSE ...
BUT YOU'RE NOT MUCH OF A MAN EITHER.
YOU'RE JUST A COWARD.
...
WHETHER YOU'RE HERE OR NOT, THE MISSIONS WILL GO ON.
AND SOMEONE HAS TO CARRY THEM OUT.
THEY'LL STILL SEND YOUR FRIENDS, JUST UNDER A DIFFERENT LEADER.
IT'S THE WAY THESE THINGS WORK.
THEY'LL BE NO LESS LIKELY TO DIE THEN...

READ THIS WAY

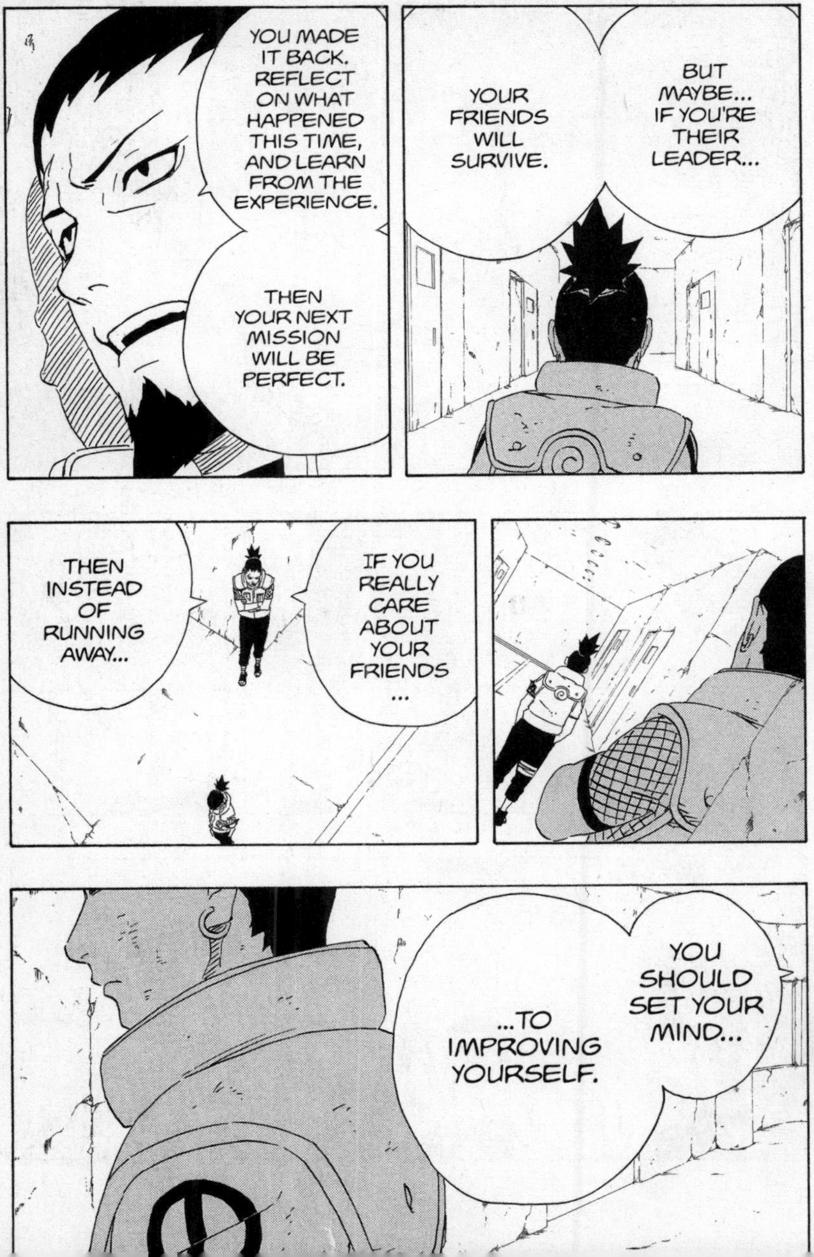
BUT MAYBE... IF YOU'RE THEIR LEADER...
YOUR FRIENDS WILL SURVIVE.
YOU MADE IT BACK. REFLECT ON WHAT HAPPENED THIS TIME, AND LEARN FROM THE EXPERIENCE.
THEN YOUR NEXT MISSION WILL BE PERFECT.
IF YOU REALLY CARE ABOUT YOUR FRIENDS ...
THEN INSTEAD OF RUNNING AWAY...
YOU SHOULD SET YOUR MIND...
...TO IMPROVING YOURSELF.

ISN'T THAT THE WAY FRIENDS BEHAVE?!

MILKSOP?

...

...

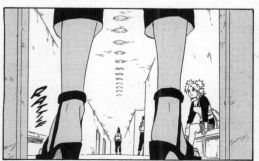

SHK

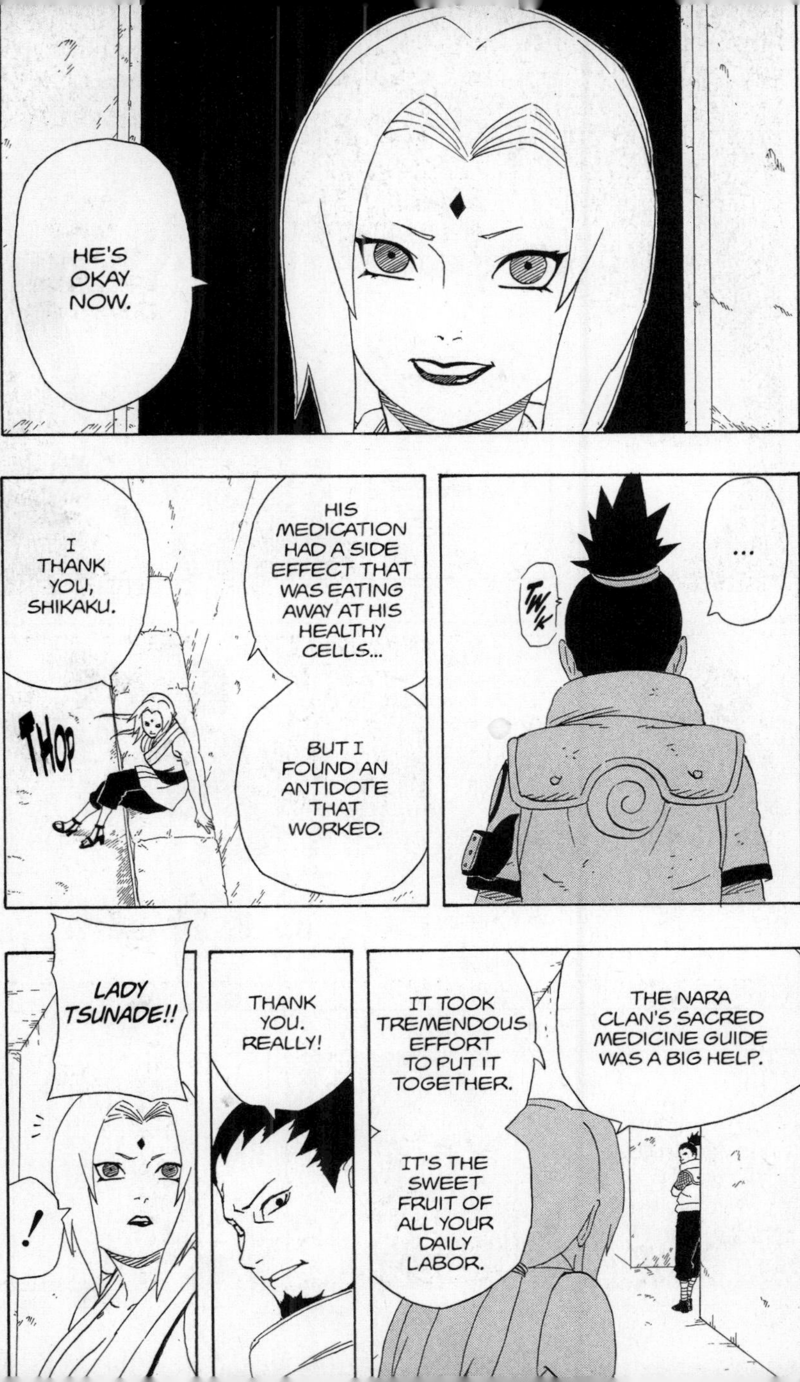
HE'S OKAY NOW.
...
TWIK
HIS MEDICATION HAD A SIDE EFFECT THAT WAS EATING AWAY AT HIS HEALTHY CELLS...
BUT I FOUND AN ANTIDOTE THAT WORKED.
I THANK YOU, SHIKAKU.
THOP
THE NARA CLAN'S SACRED MEDICINE GUIDE WAS A BIG HELP.
IT TOOK TREMENDOUS EFFORT TO PUT IT TOGETHER.
IT'S THE SWEET FRUIT OF ALL YOUR DAILY LABOR.
THANK YOU. REALLY!
LADY TSUNADE!!
!

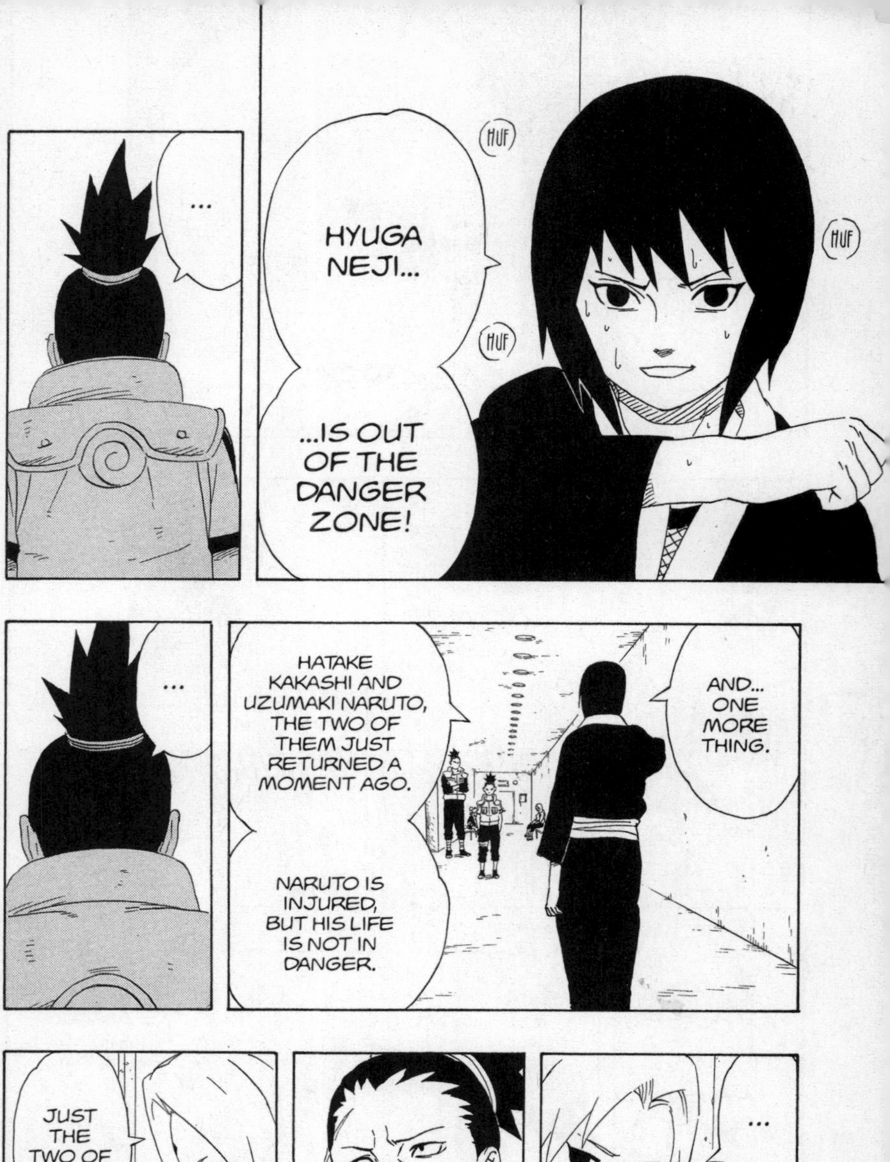
HUF
HUF
HYUGA NEJI...
...IS OUT OF THE DANGER ZONE!
HUF
...
AND... ONE MORE THING.
HATAKE KAKASHI AND UZUMAKI NARUTO, THE TWO OF THEM JUST RETURNED A MOMENT AGO.
NARUTO IS INJURED, BUT HIS LIFE IS NOT IN DANGER.
...
...
JUST THE TWO OF THEM?

READ THIS WAY

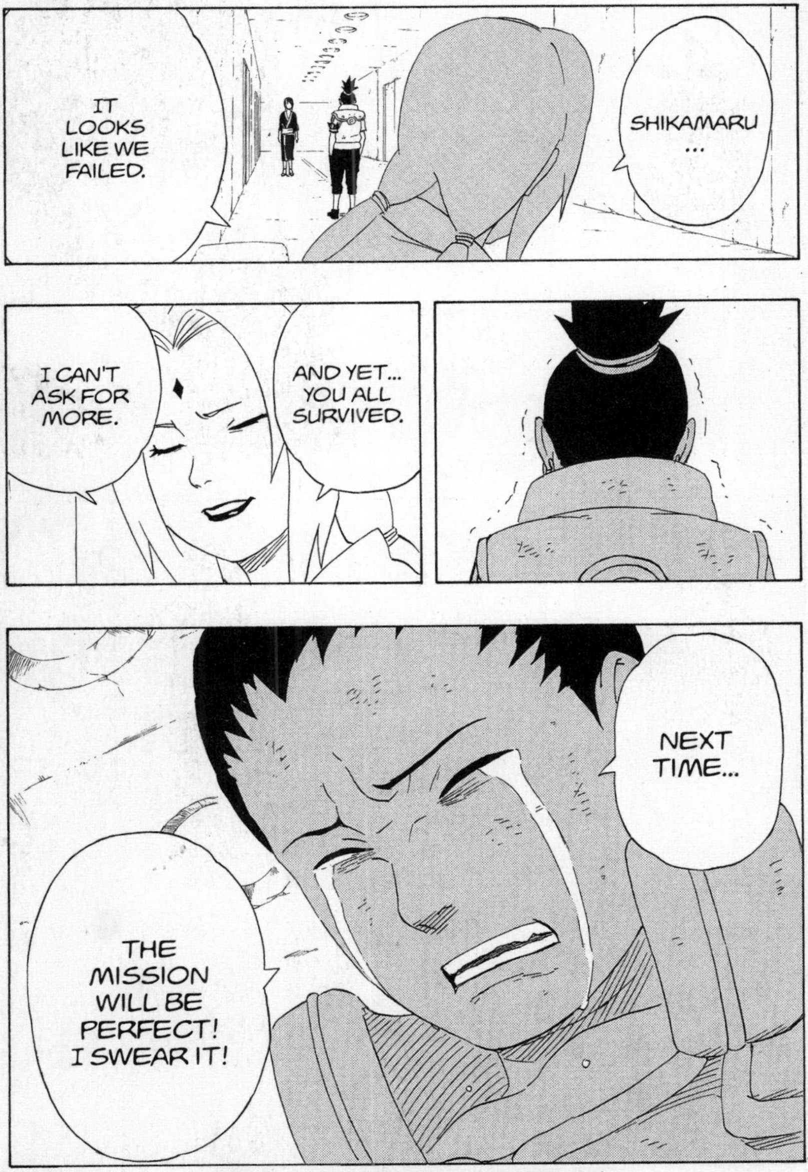
SHIKAMARU ...
IT LOOKS LIKE WE FAILED.
AND YET... YOU ALL SURVIVED.
I CAN'T ASK FOR MORE.
NEXT TIME...
THE MISSION WILL BE PERFECT! I SWEAR IT!

TO BE CONTINUED IN *NARUTO* VOL. 27!

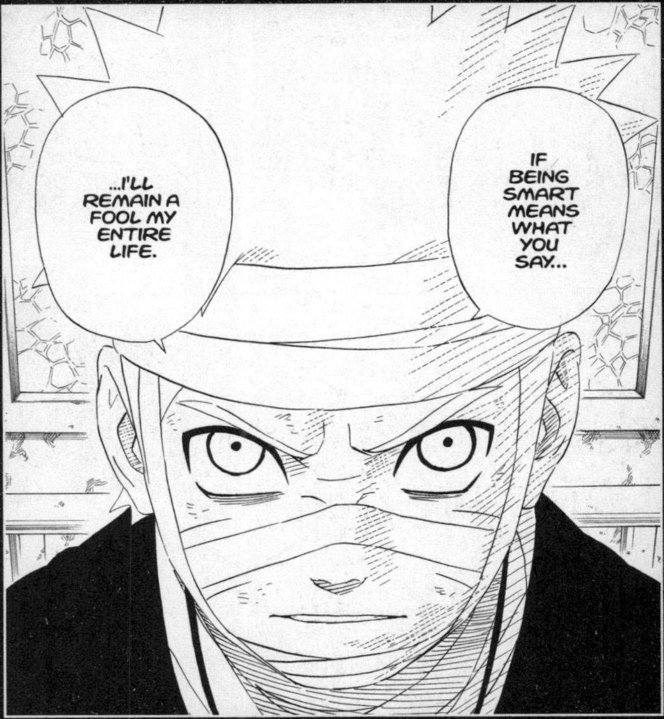
IF BEING SMART MEANS WHAT YOU SAY...
...I'LL REMAIN A FOOL MY ENTIRE LIFE.

IN THE NEXT VOLUME...

DEPARTURE

Sakura, Sasuke and Naruto part ways to begin new training, each with different mentors. You'll never believe whom they choose. Plus, take a trip back in time to finally learn the true story of Kakashi's greatest secret!

AVAILABLE NOW!

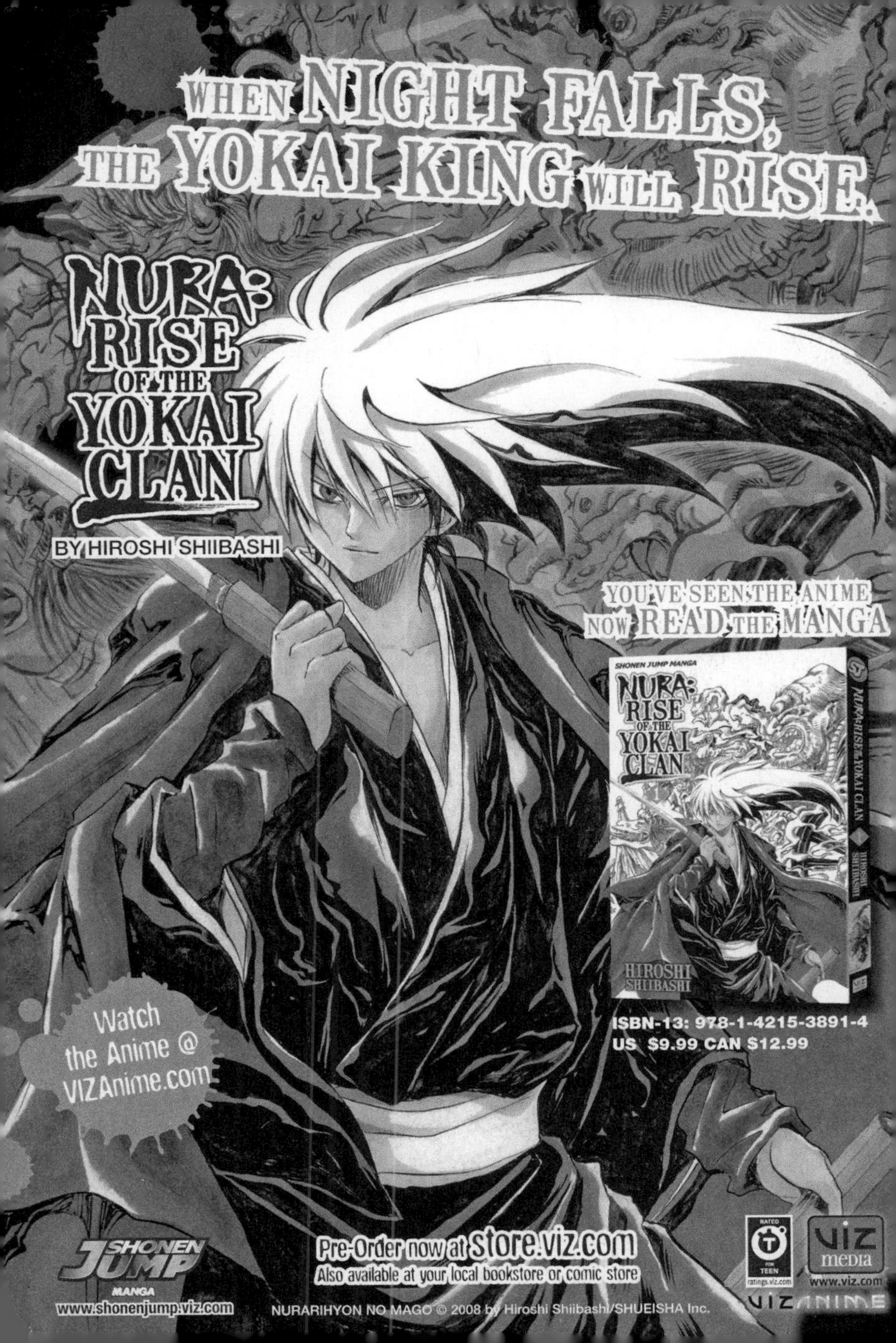
WHEN NIGHT FALLS, THE YOKAI KING WILL RISE.
NURA: RISE OF THE YOKAI CLAN
BY HIROSHI SHIIBASHI
YOU'VE SEEN THE ANIME NOW READ THE MANGA
SHONEN JUMP MANGA
NURA: RISE OF THE YOKAI CLAN
HIROSHI SHIIBASHI
ISBN-13: 978-1-4215-3891-4
US $9.99 CAN $12.99
Watch the Anime @ VIZAnime.com
SHONEN JUMP MANGA
www.shonenjump.viz.com
Pre-Order now at store.viz.com
Also available at your local bookstore or comic store
RATED T FOR TEEN
ratings.viz.com
VIZ media
www.viz.com
VIZ ANIME
NURARIHYON NO MAGO © 2008 by Hiroshi Shiibashi/SHUEISHA Inc.

⋃IZM∧NG∧

Read manga anytime, anywhere!

From our newest hit series to the classics you know and love, the best manga in the world is now available digitally. Buy a volume* of digital manga for your:

- iOS device (**iPad®**, **iPhone®**, **iPod®** touch) through the **VIZ Manga** app
- Android-powered device (**phone or tablet**) with a browser by visiting VIZManga.com
- **Mac or PC computer** by visiting VIZManga.com

VIZ Digital has loads to offer:

- 500+ ready-to-read volumes
- New volumes each week
- FREE previews
- Access on multiple devices! Create a log-in through the app so you buy a book once, and read it on your device of choice!*

To learn more, visit www.viz.com/apps

* Some series may not be available for multiple devices. Check the app on your device to find out what's available.

viz.com/apps

You're Reading in the Wrong Direction!!

Whoops! Guess what? You're starting at the wrong end of the comic!

...It's true! In keeping with the original Japanese format, **Naruto** is meant to be read from right to left, starting in the upper-right corner.

Unlike English, which is read from left to right, Japanese is read from right to left, meaning that action, sound effects and word-balloon order are completely reversed...something which can make readers unfamiliar with Japanese feel pretty backwards themselves. For this reason, manga or Japanese comics published in the U.S. in English have sometimes been published "flopped"—that is, printed in exact reverse order, as though seen from the other side of a mirror.

By flopping pages, U.S. publishers can avoid confusing readers, but the compromise is not without its downside. For one thing, a character in a flopped manga series who once wore in the original Japanese version a T-shirt emblazoned with "M A Y" (as in "the merry month of") now wears one which reads "Y A M"! Additionally, many manga creators in Japan are themselves unhappy with the process, as some feel the mirror-imaging of their art alters their original intentions.

We are proud to bring you Masashi Kishimoto's **Naruto** in the original unflopped format. For now, though, turn to the other side of the book and let the ninjutsu begin...!

—Editor

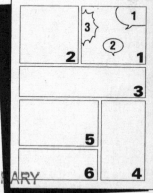